WHO CARED?
CHARITY IN VICTORIAN AND
EDWARDIAN BELFAST

David Scott, a blind boy and Sarah Armstrong, a dumb girl, pupils in the Ulster Institution, conversing together.
Drawn from life and presented to the Society for the benefit of its funds.
MAY, 1839

Silhouettes sold by the Ulster Institution for the Deaf, Dumb and Blind

Who cared?
Charity in Victorian and Edwardian Belfast

Alison Jordan

The Institute of Irish Studies,
The Queen's University of Belfast

For Fiona and Peter

For assistance towards cost of publication grateful thanks is expressed to the MacNeill Award Fund of the Royal Irish Academy and the Cultural Tradition Programme of the Community Relations Council.

ISBN 085389 406 X PB

ISBN 085389 407 8 HB

Printed by W.G. Baird Ltd, Antrim.

CONTENTS

ACKNOWLEDGEMENTS

I must thank the many people who have helped me in the preparation of this work.

Much of the information is held in the Public Record Office of Northern Ireland and I wish to acknowledge the permission to publish granted by the Deputy Director of the PRONI. Thanks is due to the following for use of their material in the PRONI: Ms P. Campbell Allen; L'Estrange and Brett; N.I. Chamber of Commerce and Industry; Mrs M. Paulin; Mrs I. Coey; Ulster Sheltered Employment Ltd, and G.A. Baker Esq.

I am indebted to the boards of management of the Ulster Society for Promoting the Education of the Deaf and Dumb and the Blind, the Ulster Institute for the Deaf (formerly the Mission Hall for the Adult Deaf and Dumb), and the Northern Ireland Institute for the Disabled (formerly the Cripples' Institute) for allowing me access to their records and giving me permission to publish extracts from them.

Thanks are also due to Mr James Anderson, the former vice-principal of the Jordanstown Schools and Mrs Maude Morton, daughter of W.E. Harris, the superintendent of the Mission Hall for the Adult Deaf and Dumb, for their personal recollections of these societies.

The book is based on my PhD thesis which was supervised by Professor L.A. Clarkson of the Economic and Social History Department of Q.U.B. I wish to thank him for his constructive help in producing the original work and for his encouragement to publish. Mr A.T. Sheehan's work as copy editor was most useful particularly in tidying up my syntax and footnotes. Mrs Valerie Fawcett typed and produced the manuscript with great efficiency and I am grateful for her work. I also owe deep thanks to Dr B.M. Walker of the Institute of Irish Studies, Q.U.B. who has guided the whole enterprise. He has found sources of monetary help and organised the editorial back-up and actual publication. Without him the book would never have appeared.

Essential financial assistance has come from the Royal Irish Academy through the Mary Alice MacNeill Award, and the Cultural Traditions Programme of the Community Relations Council.

I wish to express my appreciation to the staff of the Marie Curie Foundation, Beaconfield. During my stay there they provided facilities which made it possible for me to produce the outline of this work.

INTRODUCTION

This book is the result of a discovery that information on charitable endeavour as part of the social history of Belfast was sadly lacking. A small group of enthusiastic history teachers, who were entering students for the Northern Ireland G.C.E. 'A' level topic 'A social history of Victorian and Edwardian Belfast', found it very difficult to prepare their pupils for this aspect of the course. There is no definitive textbook on this subject so that individuals had to prepare their own database which took considerable time and effort. This inspired me to select the title 'Voluntary societies in Victorian and Edwardian Belfast' for my PhD thesis, of which this book is an abridged version. I investigated the history of those organizations which were devoted to the relief of distress in the city. All of them were purely local, private charities with no government involvement.

Often the people whose names are enshrined in the history of any city are the prosperous business and professional men who dominated society or were civic dignitaries. They are the men who are commemorated in statues, fountains and street names, but their activity in the life of the community was often limited to the economic field. Industrial cities in the nineteenth century were new phenomena where large numbers of unskilled workers crowded together, whose labour helped to produce the fortunes of great industrialists, but who are often forgotten. Today, however, social histories are being written which do highlight their importance in society and in the infrastructure of the town.

Because they have been neglected for so long it is very hard to develop an accurate knowledge of the lives of the poor. Generally they did not leave written documentation about their hopes, fears, relationships and financial situations but it is possible to piece together some information on these classes in Victorian cities. It is obvious that many of the unskilled men and women in urban environments must have lived on the brink of destitution, and the theme of this book is the effort made by caring members of the middle class in Belfast to alleviate the distress experienced by people in need.

The Victorian middle class has been regarded with some contempt for many years, looked upon as greedy exploiters of the poor. This was by no means true of all of them. This story is an attempt to redress the balance in some way and to show that there were indeed sincere devout Christians who really did try to follow their Lord's teaching. They were not always successful but it is only fair to give them credit for trying. Government confined its help to the provision of the dreaded workhouses and for generations private charity was the only barrier between the destitute and destruction.

Significant numbers of societies were founded during the Victorian era which devoted their attention to a specific area of need. In the nineteenth century there was considerable public interest in this work with detailed reports published in all the local papers which described the activities undertaken. By now most of the men and women who directed the work are forgotten but at the time they played an important part in the life of the city. Superficially it would appear from printed reports that the poor were deserving and grateful but the few minute books and letters which remain show that they were often the opposite. Existing histories of Belfast have concentrated on the industrial and political aspects of the community and certainly in recent years on the sectarian divide and its social consequences. The divisions run very deep and they affected the charitable life of the town. Inevitably the two communities had their own caring structures.

There is a striking similarity between the growth of Belfast and other industrial cities in the United Kingdom: no other Irish cities had the same form of commercial base or urban class structure. Belfast was more akin to Glasgow or Liverpool than anywhere else in Ireland. Many British towns have had their social history documented, though not in as much detail as their political or commercial past. Then, as now, local or national politicians had a better chance of publicity than the 'do-gooder' whose efforts are often derided. Too often benefactors were regarded as gullible targets who were easy victims of the allegedly needy who exploited their goodwill. It is easy to mock them but although few in number their endeavours were of great value to the underclass. After all, before the welfare state was created only the charitably minded could provide aid.

Several of the original societies still exist today. Credit was due to their founding fathers and it is still due now. The motivation of the members in the nineteenth century is hard to assess. They got no material benefit from their work for they were already prosperous and locally prominent and they failed to exercise any social control over the needy. It is hard to escape the conclusion that it was intrinsically goodness and a desire to share their benefits which inspired them. The same sort of people are still interested in improving the lives of the poor both at home and abroad, and our society is enriched by their efforts. It is to be hoped that such men and women will continue to give their time to those in need.

Not all the philanthropic societies in Belfast are covered in this book. Some have already been written about such as the Belfast Charitable Society and the Belfast Central Mission. The orphan societies run by three main religious denominations are not covered here; the presbyterians have a history already written and material from the Church of Ireland and the catholic religious orders waits to be analysed.

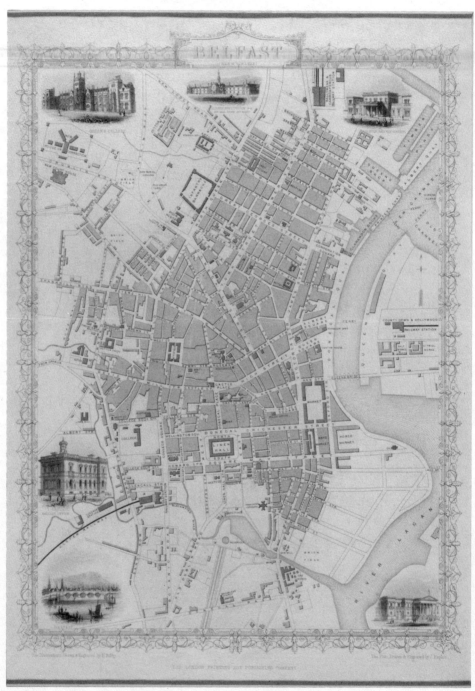

Map of Belfast by Tallis/Rapkin, c. 1855

xii

1

'The industrial beehive of Ireland':

THE GROWTH OF BELFAST
IN THE NINETEENTH CENTURY.

There is much in Irish history which is controversial but there is one fact which has not been disputed. This is the phenomenal growth of Belfast as a great industrial city in the nineteenth century. Belfast was a plantation town granted to the Devon Chichester family in the early seventeenth century. The Chichesters became the earls and then the marquises of Donegall but their settlement remained for many years just an unimportant ford over the Farset. It was, however, big enough to warrant the granting of a charter in 1613 which established the form of local government which operated until 1842. The Donegalls dominated the political and commercial life of the town for many years. They were lords of the castle, effectively choosing the sovereign, the twelve free burgesses, the constable of the castle and the two M.P.s of the borough, and granting the market licences. Until the end of the eighteenth century Belfast was untroubled by unrest but it was in this town that Irish Volunteers were formed in 1778 to resist a French invasion and here too the United Irishmen were founded in 1791. Perhaps surprisingly the 1798 rebellion passed the town by and it continued as a provincial backwater.

An assessment of the town at the beginning of the nineteenth century can be made through a study of the newspapers. The *Belfast News Letter* of 1801 gives a picture of a small town. On 2 January 1801 the main local news was of the implementation of the Act of Union. The *News Letter* gave an account:

Yesterday morning the Union flag was hoisted at the Market House at one o'clock and a Royal salute was fired by the Royal Artillery in the garrison in consequence of the Legislative Union between the Kingdoms of Great Britain and Ireland taking place.

The *News Letter* made it clear where its loyalties lay even though some people in Ireland opposed Union.

It is now our duty to bury, if possible for EVER all Political Differences – all Religious Animosities – all Local Prejudices; to consider the Empire, not as composed of distinct Political Bodies . . . but as containing only one PEOPLE united in *interests* as in *dominion* – whose Services ought to be reciprocal – and whose Objects are undoubtedly the same VIZ. TRANQUILLITY, PROSPERITY, and SECURITY.[1]

The advertisement of the police committee for tenders to clean central Belfast referred to the need to 'carry the manure to a place to be appointed for that purpose', a clear indication of the presence of livestock. However, there were signs of what became the important issues of later years. First there was the insistence of the local authorities on the fitting of ball-cocks and cisterns to control the waste of piped water which foreshadowed the involvement of the corporation in regulating public utilities. Secondly, the plan by the sovereign to provide a soup kitchen for the poor was an early example of corporate responsibility.[2] For the rest the paper carried advertisements for seeds, ashes for bleaching, wines and spirits as well as the letting of houses and land.

By 1900, however, the rural emphasis had gone, for the town had experienced the urbanisation and industrialisation characteristic of the north of Britain in the nineteenth century. The growth of Belfast can be measured in several ways, most obviously by a study of demography.

Table 1.1 Population of Belfast Borough 1801-1901

Year	Number	Percentage Increase
1801	19,000	-
1811	27,832	46.47
1821	37,277	33.93
1831	53,287	42.95
1841	70,447	32.20
1851	87,062	23.58
1861	121,602	39.67
1871	174,412	43.43
1881	208,122	19.33
1891	255,950	22.98
1901	349,180	36.43

Source: Ian Budge and Cornelius O'Leary, *Belfast: approach to crisis* (London 1973) p. 28.

The growth of Belfast was the most obvious example of urban development in nineteenth century Ulster. Most of the people who flocked into the town in the 1830s and 1840s were looking for work in the textile mills. The cotton mills which had begun Belfast's industrial revolution were replaced after 1828 by flax spinning mills. These mills were built in green field sites away from Smithfield where the cotton mills centred, along the lower Falls and Shankill roads. The new inhabitants found a marked lack of housing available in Belfast. The town centre was both residential and commercial and by now already over-crowded so it did not provide the low-cost housing which the factory workers needed. At this stage the mill-owners stepped in.

The result of this was the building of terraces of the archetypal red-brick, two up-two down kitchen house which was once seen everywhere in the city. A kitchen house could be built for between £40-£50 and let at between 2s.-3s. per week, within the range of the lowest class of labourer in Belfast.[3] Few of these houses were back-to-back even though they lacked amenities – in some cases they had no yard or privy. The densely populated streets radiated from the Falls and Shankill roads creating the nucleus of west Belfast. The houses were in the shadow of the great mills and in them the extended families and close-knit communities which were characteristic of Belfast took root. The 'rural migrants spun an intricate web of kinship, binding together town and country. In one direction girls obtained jobs in the spinning mills by being "spoken for" by relatives already in employment; city relatives, too, were useful staging posts for new-comers.'[4]

During the later part of the century local authorities took action to mitigate the worst aspects of workers' housing. After 1847 the corporation imposed bye-laws which restricted the freedom of builders and insisted on the provision of yards with ash-pits. Every room had to have windows, the ceiling height had to be 8ft and piped water was brought in. From 1878 new houses had to have a back access at least 9ft wide, no building could be higher than the width of the street and all new streets had to have kerbed paving.[5] In 1889 it was ordered that houses had to be built with damp-courses[6] – though it must be said that these bye-laws were seldom fully enforced because of the shortage of municipal staff.

One effect of the new laws was to end building by the mill owners. This would probably have happened anyway because there was a reduced demand for the very basic kitchen house and it would have been difficult to recoup such an investment at higher rents. As well, the demand for houses was no longer in west Belfast but in east Belfast where the Queen's Island was entering a period of great expansion and prosperity. Shipyard workers earned more than textile workers and they wanted better houses. Engineering workers earning 30s. per week compared with 11s. in the mills looked for the parlour house, and new agencies in the construction trade provided them. A parlour house could be built for £80-£90 and let for 4s.-5s. per week.[7] Finance came from building societies, investment companies, small builders and craftsmen and most developments were on a small scale, often six houses or less. Some of the middle class bought streets of houses for letting to skilled workers who, notwithstanding their high earnings, could not afford to buy their homes.[8] Houses with parlours, attics, bays and polychrome bricks, even small gardens, appeared in increasing numbers. The peak of building for the mass market was in the 1890s but thereafter because of over-building the numbers decreased.

Meanwhile the middle-class moved away from the dirt and congestion of inner city life. Belfast spread southwards as commerce concentrated in Donegall Place and the Linen Hall area. Streets such as Joy St and Eliza St were laid out and the merchants from High St moved in. Others moved first to College Square and Wellington Place and then, avoiding the slums of Durham St, Sandy Row and above all the notorious 'Blackstaff nuisance', to the Malone Ridge. Large mansions like Bertha, Derryvolgie and Drumglass were followed by parks – Wellington, Windsor and Adelaide. On the new Lisburn and Stranmillis roads substantial two and three storey houses were built for skilled artisans and clerks.

In north Belfast the Antrim Rd built in 1827 from Carlisle Circus was also almost completely residential as was the Crumlin Rd, up as far as Ewart's mill at Brookfield. Both of these roads had streets of parlour houses. On the Cliftonville Rd R.J. McConnell, who was one of the leading estate agents of the last decade of the nineteenth century, planned a garden suburb of detached houses all of different designs at a density of ten per acre compared with twenty per acre at Willowfield. These houses cost £350 with a deposit of £80 and weekly repayments of 8s to 10s. per week.[9] They were of course for middle class buyers. In west Belfast there was little middle class housing even on the periphery but in the east the rows of ship-yard workers' streets were bounded by the prosperous districts of Knock and Belmont. These areas were well served by the Belfast and County Down Railway Co. and the Knock station was the most successful of all the suburban halts. The B.C.D.R. and the Belfast Northern Counties Railway companies gave concessionary fares to builders of houses with a PLV of over £25. At the junction of Ormeau and Ravenhill roads at Rosetta, parks of substantial detached houses were laid out.[10] The Cregagh Rd began at the Woodstock Rd with small parlour houses but became more middle class as it left the city. This enormous expansion of housing led to two boundary extensions in the nineteenth century.

Table 1.2

Number of males in town	34,858
Number of females in town	40,450
Number of families in town	15,172

Distribution of inhabitants in occupations

		Percentage
Families employed chiefly in:		
agriculture	2,532	17
manufactures & trade	9,897	65
other pursuits	2,743	18
Families supported chiefly by:		
vested means or professions	643	4
the directing of labour	6,765	44
their own manual labour	7,202	47
means not specified	562	3
Males at and above 15 years of age who minister to:		
food	2,420	7
clothing	5,030	14
lodging, etc.	4,919	14
health	112	.3
justice	292	.8
education	133	.4
religion	71	.2

Males at and above 15 years of age unclassified	5,905	17
Males at and above 15 years of age without specified occpn	2,614	7
Females at and above 15 years age who minister to:		
food	246	.6
clothing	6,884	17
lodging, etc.	123	.3
health	24	.06
charity	14	.03
justice	1	-
education	122	.3
religion	1	-
Females at and above 15 years of age unclassified	3,435	8
Females at and above 15 years of age without specified occpns	16,417	40

Source: J.A. Pilson, *History of the rise & progress of Belfast and annals of the county of Antrim* (Belfast, 1846), pp 81–82.

Even in 1850 Belfast 'was still predominantly a port, market and agricultural centre', and its most important branch of commerce was cross-channel trade.[11] But this was about to change. Cotton manufacture was the first factory industry, in the Smithfield district of the town in Francis St, Winetavern St and Union St. In 1820 there were fifteen mills employing 2,000 people but by 1830 cotton had gone into decline.[12] A more efficient method of wet spinning flax which produced fine yarn had been invented by James Kay of Preston, and after this had been patented the Mulholland brothers tried the process on 1,000 spindles in their Francis St mill.[13] The success of this venture encouraged them to install 8,000 flax spinning spindles when they rebuilt their York St mill after a fire in 1828.[14] By 1850 Belfast had only four cotton factories but twenty-nine flax spinning mills. Linen had now changed from the domestic system operating in the Lagan Valley and beyond, to a steam-powered urban industry which was a major employer of labour in Ireland.

Table 1.3

Employment in the linen industry in Ireland 1850-1904

Number employed in linen mills and factories in Ireland

1850	21,000
1856	29,000
1862	34,000
1868	57,000
1871	55,000
1875	60,000
1879	56,000
1885	62,000
1890	65,000
1895	68,000
1896	69,000
1897	69,000
1899	68,000
1901	65,000
1904	65,000

Source: D.A. Armstrong, 'Social conditions in the Belfast linen industry' in *I.H.S.* vii (1951), p. 240.

Almost all of these workers were employed in Belfast, and the statistics of this manufacture for all Ireland are almost identical with those of the Belfast district. The figures of spindles and power looms refer to the whole country.

In the last quarter of the century there were some big business failures when respected and apparently solid firms went bankrupt. In the 1870s Wm Spotten & Co., Malcolmson & Co. and the Bedford Street Weaving Co. went down; in the 1880s John Hind went into liquidation, followed in 1898 by the Belfast Flax Spinning Co., Ligoniel Spinning Co. and the Co. Down Flax Spinning and Weaving Co. The linen industry never fully recovered its dominant position. However, in spite of the decline of linen it remained the largest single source of employment in Belfast. The majority of its employees were women and children and this meant that it was a low wage industry but the men who did work in textiles could earn more: mechanics in the mills expected as much as engineers working in foundries. For the industry as a whole real wages rose by around 200 per cent between 1850 and 1900.[15]

Linen alone could not have supported the population growth in the city, and between 1870 and 1914 (coincidentally at the beginning of linen's comparative decline) shipbuilding and marine engineering stimulated employment and immigration. Iron shipbuilding settled on the Queen's Island in 1853 when Robert Hickson, proprietor of the Eliza St iron works, took over the shipyard laid out by the harbour commissioners.[16] In 1854 the most important figure in late nineteenth century industry, E.J. Harland, came to Hickson's yard as manager. Harland had been an apprentice at Robt Stephenson & Co. in Newcastle-on-Tyne where he formed a friendship with Gustav Schwabe which was to be of incalculable importance in the future.[17]

In 1855 Hickson's failed but Harland remained. Two years later Gustav Wolff, nephew of Gustav Schwabe, came to Belfast as assistant to Harland. He was welcomed to the city by another German Jew, Daniel Joseph Jaffe, who had set up a linen business in Belfast. In 1858 Harland bought Hickson's interest and good-will in the shipyard plus a steam engine, boiler plant, tools and machinery for £5,000. Harland and Wolff became partners in 1861 and it was then that Wolff's uncle Gustav Schwabe became so important.[18] As a partner in J. Bibby & Co., a shipping firm in Liverpool, he was able to direct work to Belfast's shipyard. Of the first fourteen ships launched by Harland and Wolff eleven were for J. Bibby. From 1870 when Harland & Wolff signed a contract with the 'White Star Line' the shipyard was in the vanguard of steel shipbuilding. Tonnage produced by Harland and Wolff rose rapidly:

Table 1.4

1860	5,444 tons
1881	20,453 tons
1901	92,206 tons[19]

This industrial growth would have been impossible without the port and harbour. A lack of energy sources meant that imported coal was essential to power the steam engines of factories and foundries. Coal was the largest import into Belfast and by 1901 oil was also arriving in increasing quantities – 33,298 tons in 1901.[20] Already at the beginning of the nineteenth century the port and harbour were important to the town. The Irish Parliament in 1785 refused a request from Belfast for money to improve the harbour, but instead set up 'The Corporation for Preserving and Improving the Port of Belfast' otherwise known as the Ballast Board. Members were to be elected locally, and this meant that the interests of the port were in the hands of the men most vitally concerned with it. The story of the port in the nineteenth century is one of constant expansion both in acreage of docks and in shipping cleared.

Table 1.5

Tonnage and Vessels registered and cleared in Belfast 1840-1900

| | Tonnage Registered | | Vessels Cleared | |
Year	Vessels	Tonnage	Vessels	Tonnage
1840	355	45,632	3,323	361,473
1850	463	74,770	4,490	624,113
1860	508	74,049	6,658	885,413
1870	462	62,653	8,303	1,616,908
1880	399	76,386	7,965	1,225,566
1890	293	125,632	8,050	1,840,666
1900	210	147,575	8,318	2,325,936

Source: *Thom's Directory.*

This resulted from the entrepreneurial and innovative nature of the members of the board. Probably the most important decision which they took was the making of two 'cuts' to deepen the Garmoyle Channel and straighten the river so that ships could discharge directly on to the quays. Another vital decision was the laying-out of a shipyard on land reclaimed by William Dargan from the 'sleech' dredged from the new channels. This mud

created a new landscape . . . the opening of the Victoria Channel in 1849 was the beginning of a massive growth. During the next half century five major docks and basins were opened and tens of thousands of feet of quays were built, reaching a peak between 1870-1890.[21]

The Ballast Board was replaced in 1847 by the 'Belfast Harbour Commissioners' with the lord of the castle (the marquis of Donegall) as president and fifteen elected members. The new board acted vigorously, filling in the old Lime Kiln, Town and Ritchie's Docks, and extending the Donegall and Queen's Quays. Even with this the commissioners reported that the quay and dock accommodation would soon be inadequate. Already by 1852 Capt Gilbert in his survey of Belfast for the proposed boundary extension stated:

the natural advantages of the town as a seaport have been fully developed by the spirit and enterprise of the Harbour Commissioners in the construction of quays and docks, and extensive improvements, which enhance, in an eminent degree the favourable position Belfast enjoys for commercial purposes. The amount expended on harbour improvements has been upwards of half a million.[22]

In the last part of the century the opening of the Clarendon and York docks, the Abercorn Basin and the Hamilton and Alexandra Graving dock and the opening of the Musgrave Channel made Belfast Harbour the largest port in Ireland.[23] Harbour revenues also rose. Belfast had the third highest harbour revenue in the U.K. after London and Liverpool.[24] 'The local ownership of 200 ships totalling more than 300,000 tons, brought work for the ship repairers, chandlers and agents. Behind these was the essential support provided by local banks and commercial houses.'[25] These commercial houses were represented in the Belfast Chamber of Commerce founded in 1783. The trading history of Belfast is recorded in the annual reports of the chamber to which most leading businessmen belonged. Sometimes there were complaints that it represented only linen interests and in 1889 it was re-organised to widen its representation.[26] In 1890 among the members were:

Table 1.6

Membership of Chamber of Commerce

        27 flax spinners

        56 linen manufacturers and bleachers

        13 machine makers and iron merchants

        11 shipbuilders and engineers[27]

In most years the reports were optimistic, recording past achieve-
ments and future hopes though there were some bad years, notably
1878-9.

In 1899 Belfast industrially and commercially was complacent and
prosperous. It was described as

> truly the industrial beehive of Ireland, and its people must be proud of the fact that
> it is a self-made city, which testifies to their self-reliance ... The architectural
> concepts of many of the leading citizens have abnormally developed of late ...
> gigantic schemes have been taken up wholesale and put simultaneously into execu-
> tion; the erection of an elaborate electricity station for the lighting of the city is now
> an accomplished fact; the foundation of the new City Hall has been laid, and the
> work is proceeding; a new fire-station has been erected on a most extensive scale,
> and up-to-date in every detail; its work has been witnessed on several occasions by
> influential deputations ... Jubilee Day has been recognised in a most benevolent
> manner by the contribution of the city to the amount of £100,000 for the erection of
> the Queen Victoria Hospital.[28]

A tangible indication of the city's growth is seen in its three municipal buildings of the nineteenth century, and these show the pride of
the corporation. The first town hall consisted of one large room for
council meetings and six small offices and cells in Poultry (later
Police and later still Victoria) Square. This undistinguished building
no longer suited the image of the Belfast of the 1870s and it was
taken over by Cantrell & Cochrane as part of their warehouse.[29] A
new town hall, built in Victoria St by Thomas Jackson and his son, was
also regarded as too modest.

> The public offices in Belfast when first designed, were without a parapet; the
> townspeople protested that it was not a public building not having a parapet; and so
> great was the agitation that the plans had to be submitted for consideration.[30]

The new building, 'a sturdy brick essay in mixed historical styles', was
erected in 1872.[31] By 1879 the *Whig* was complaining about the
condition of the town hall buildings and courts. 'In the erection of
the existing building an inexcusable blunder was committed, and
they must ultimately give place to new ones.'[32] The smell in the courts
was intolerable though the sewers had been checked and found to be
perfect.

Having been raised to the dignity of a city the corporation wanted
suitably magnificent headquarters. So the old White Linen Hall was

demolished and an imposing stone edifice 'impressive and over-decorated . . . a remarkable building and one which in a number of respects, though not in all, is extremely successful' was built in its place.[33] The City Hall, which opened in 1906, used to be rather derided but is now regarded with some affection.

The other side of the great city was the existence of terrible poverty beside comfortable prosperity. Urbanisation had its bad side. What was the middle classes' response? They could not ignore the poor whose discontent might be translated into violence which would threaten the stability of society. As Lord Ashley said 'the middle classes know that the safety of their lives and property depends upon their having round them a peaceful, happy and moral population.'[34] The problems of the new cities have been identified by Eric Midwinter as arising from a changed social context:

. . . An industrialised society forced communities to face on the large scale what had hitherto often been the isolated problem for the individual and his family. And poverty, disease and crime were the most prominent of these social problems.[35]

It was in the nineteenth century that society in general had to face the changed needs of the poor and to decide its reactions to them. The solution for the Victorians was organised joint action carefully planned to help those truly in need. The growth of a large industrial urban population was accompanied by an increase in the foundation and prosperity of voluntary societies. In his *English philanthropy* David Owen writes:

the alarming and inescapable fact that large segments of the new industrial cities as well as the metropolis were inhabited by a population living the most marginal indeed sub-human kind of existence haunted contemporary observers, tough and tender alike.[36]

Private charity, it was assumed, would carry the burden of working class welfare. This was certainly true in Belfast.

The need for private charity in the town was all the greater because of the limitations of the government's plan to alleviate Irish poverty. The English Poor Law of 1601 had not applied to Ireland but the government decided to apply a revised form of the Poor Law Amendment Act of 1834 to Ireland. It did this in spite of the manifest unsuitability of the English system for Ireland – an unsuitability pointed out by the select committee on the state of Ireland in 1830.[37]

Although there were enormous differences in the two countries the Irish Poor Law of 1838 contained many of the same provisions as its English predecessor.

There were two crucial areas which were not the same. In Ireland relief was supposed to be administered through the workhouses with no outdoor help, and with no statutory right of the poor to claim assistance, while in England and Wales every person who was destitute had this right.[38] This meant that when Irish workhouses were full they could simply turn people away. As for outdoor relief which was never wholly excluded from English unions, it was considered likely to be abused in Ireland and so was only temporarily permitted in the worst days of the Famine, when the workhouses were full.[39] Belfast guardians were particularly opposed to outdoor relief. In 1906 the viceregal commission investigating the Poor Law found only 87 people getting outdoor relief in the city compared with 3,819 in the workhouse.[40]

Under the Poor Law, Ireland was divided into over 130 unions centred on market towns each of which had a grim stone workhouse built to a plan drawn by George Wilkinson, the Poor Law architect. The workhouses turned the Poor Law into 'the object of horror to the nineteenth century working class' who hated everything about them.[41] They hated having to give up their independence to live in the house, the separation and segregation of families, the discomfort of communal living, the dull tasteless food, the harsh discipline and the rough clothes which identified them as paupers. During the Famine a separate Poor Law Commission for Ireland was set up in 1847 which modified the rules on outdoor relief. In the face of this disaster a Temporary Relief Act allowed outdoor relief at the discretion of the guardians to infirm, sick and disabled persons and poor widows when aid could not be given at the workhouse because of lack of space or because of fever. Relieving officers could give relief in food, lodgings, medicine and medical attendance.

By the end of the century the Belfast workhouse (like most of the others) had become the refuge for 'the old, the sick and children, not for able-bodied men and women.'[42] It was an unpopular last resort for the destitute who were ashamed of having to go there. The intense fear of having to go to the workhouse helped to form working class attitudes to private charity. Acceptance of aid from voluntary societies could sometimes keep families off the union and was therefore welcome. Many people in nineteenth century Belfast were at risk of falling below subsistence level – men who were temporarily unemployed or sick, men and women who were blind or crippled and thus unable to support themselves, destitute children, abandoned or diseased women – all of these were the targets of voluntary societies. The Poor Law took responsibility for the aged, infirm and idiots while the Lunatic Asylum took in the deranged and dangerous, for these groups could never be trained or helped to earn their own living. The other needy sections of the working class could be helped to help themselves and this was the aim of the middle class men and women who worked for charities. The middle class was affected by the Poor Law for it was they who financed its operation through the payment of the poor rate. Obviously it was in their interest to keep the numbers receiving relief to a minimum to keep down costs, and this combined with genuine philanthropy encouraged them to become involved in charity.

Poverty was endemic in nineteenth century Ireland and most people who lived there were poorer than in comparative economies in Western Europe.[43] In reports on Irish poverty before the Famine almost all the evidence was concerned with the southern counties which were largely agricultural: Belfast and Ulster were effectively ignored. Was it because this area was different?

R.S. Tighe, a trustee of the Linen Board said

I attribute every superiority that characterises the North of Ireland over the Southern provinces to those improvements which have naturally followed the employment of the people; they have had sources and means of industry either furnished to them or acquired by themselves.[44]

Modern historians agree on this difference. S.J. Connolly believes:

Whatever refinements are added to our own picture of regional variations in economic and social developments, the basic distinction remains that between East Ulster, with its Protestant majority and its nineteenth century industrial revolution, and the remainder of the country.[45]

Indeed Belfast was much more like an English industrial city than the other parts of Ireland. When Mr and Mrs S.C. Hall visited the town in the 1840s they were impressed with what they saw –

As we drew near the only manufacturing town of Ireland – alas that it should be so! – its peculiar character became apparent. It was something new to perceive, rising

14

above the houses, numerous tall and thin chimneys indicative of industry, occupation, commerce, and prosperity, the volumes of smoke that issued from them giving
unquestionable tokens of full employment; while its vicinity to the ocean removed at
once all idea that the labour was unwholesome, or the labourers unhealthy . . . and
the contrast between this town and the towns of the south startled us, making us for
the moment believe we were in a clean Manchester.[46]

In the *Report on the state of the poor* in 1836 the section dealing with
Belfast gives a detailed and laudatory picture of the town and its
institutions; it said:

the condition of the poor in Belfast is, in some respects superior to that of other
towns; there are no inhabited cellars here, there is very seldom more than one family
living in a single room, and the houses are almost always sheltered against the
inclemency of the weather.[47]

And the citizens agreed. J.A. Pilson wrote in 1846:

The houses including even a large number of the public buildings consist of brick.
But they are, in general, so high, so neat and so regular, as to constitute a handsome,
urban-looking town. Entire streets are composed of houses of equal height and
nearly all on one plan; and even the poorest streets disclose the squalidness of
penury in their back courts rather than in the exterior front line . . . A cabin is now
almost unknown here; and houses so spacious and elegant as to be quite equal to the
majority of country mansions, are not only numerous but compose entire streets.[48]

In the 1850s even Rev. William O'Hanlon found some comfort in the
desert of despair which he usually saw, when he went to Victoria
Court off Durham St.

I marked a flower pot a sure sign of the taste and comparative refinement of the
inmates. Allowing for its narrowness, we found cottage neatness, cleanness and
comfort in Davison's-court – it did our hearts good going to look at these cottages –
the outside whitewashed, without a soil upon the pathway – and within, little palaces
for cleanliness and beauty. In this court there are twenty-eight houses, and fourteen
of them are furnished with neat clocks – a token of superiority of mind and habit. It
was like a vision of Dante's Paradise, after wandering through his Inferno . . . [49]

In Sandy Row

many of its people are doubtless very poor, and their domestic and sanitary conditions capable of improvement. But they are not shut up within walls which debar the

15

entrance of the pure air and light of heaven. The mountain breezes play upon their dwellings, and they have only to look around to catch some glimpse of the country.[50]

This did not mean that there was nothing to criticise. The assistant commissioners visited an unnamed lane which must surely have been among the poorest in the town.

The entry was very narrow and dirty, the houses dark and small, and in general without any furniture. One poor girl miserably infected with syphilis told them that she had rations from the House of Industry as often as she could go for them.

Another house visited may serve as a specimen of the poorest in Belfast.

It is situated near the quay, and called the Rookery; it is in so dilapidated a state that the House of Industry refuses relief to any persons living in it, being apprehensive of its falling . . . the circumstance calculated to add materially to the filth and unwhole-someness of the town is the total want of privies attached to the smaller houses. Whole rows of houses are built without any accommodation of this kind.[51]

Although improvement acts were passed between 1845 and 1850 laying down regulations on the building of new houses it took many years for these to be effective. In the meantime in the 1850s poverty still produced awful living conditions. The most vivid account of the horrendous back streets of Belfast in this decade is given by Rev. William O'Hanlon, minister of Donegall St Congregational Church. He was concerned at the moral dangers which he believed this poverty produced. He felt that it was largely because few of the middle-class considered what was happening off the main streets as important that reforms were not made; and in an attempt to stir the consciences of Belfast burghers he wrote a series of letters to the *Northern Whig*, graphically describing the surroundings of the poor:

How few of the church-going, orderly, affluent members of this community, have ever visited, or perhaps even heard of such places as Brady's Row, Green-court, Henry-square, Johnny's-entry, Poplar-court, Grattan-court, Morrow's-entry, Lynas-court, William's-lane, Patterson-place, Dickey's-entry, – mostly crowded with human beings in the lowest stage of social degradation. To attempt fully to gauge this immense mass of human wretchedness and vice, so as to give any adequate idea of its contents would demand weeks.[52]

He went on to give details of the conditions which he saw. Of Brady St he wrote;

Here my companion and myself fixed upon two houses as specimens of the whole. In one of these we found that seven persons live and sleep in the same room – their beds, if such they may be called, lying upon the floor. The desolation and wretchedness of this apartment – without windows, and open in all directions, – it is utterly impossible to describe. Four of the persons huddled thus together are females, the other three males. Among those females, two, a mother and her grown-up daughter, have no affinity with the other inmates. In the other house in the same row we discovered that a family of seven sleep not only in the same room but in the same bed. This information we had from the poor half-naked mother herself. Here the eldest daughter is nineteen years of age, and the eldest son twelve. The revolting and heart-rending spectacle presented by the interior of this hovel and by its inmates, it is impossible to forget. It haunts one like a loathsome and odious spectre, from which the eye and the thoughts cannot escape.[53]

If it might seem that Rev. O'Hanlon exaggerated, confirmation is found in the diary of Rev. A. McIntyre, a missionary with the Domestic Mission, a non-subscribing presbyterian organisation. He too worked among the poor of Belfast in the 1850s and describes distressing experiences:

1 September 1853: Spent the forenoon of to-day in getting two poor children into the Union workhouse. I met these two little boys on the Queen's Bridge. The first thing that arrested my attention was the circumstance of the elder abusing the younger. He was dashing his head on the crib stones. I interfered. A woman who was passing at the time stated that the elder was drowning and would have drowned the younger two days before but that some boys prevented him. I learned that the name of these children is Nixon, that the father was killed by some accident a few years ago in this town, that the mother and children had been in the workhouse some year or so ago but that she had come out and brought the children with her and that lately she has had to go to the hospital being taken ill of dropsy and that now the children have no-one to look after them or take care of them. They were both all but naked, and when I saw that the elder had to carry the younger on his back and beg whatever they got, I could not think it strange that he should sometimes be driven by hunger and fatigue to acts of cruelty and desperation.[54]

This illustrates very well the deep reluctance of the poor to go to the workhouse except as a very last resort.

He visited the same areas as Rev. W.M. O'Hanlon and found the same distress. In Johnston's Court off Gregg' Lane:

my attention was arrested by the abject poverty of a family of small children off the court. Mrs McDonnell said they were the poorest creatures that could be . . . I went across . . . there sat the mother Jane Mitchell almost naked, pale as death, seated on a stone, engaged in sewing, on her knee sat the skeleton of a child, fretted, emaciated, diseased, and death-like . . . she supported the children herself . . . but could not earn more than 4d per day by sewing.[55]

A particularly sad family was found in Meeting-house Lane:

The first sight that struck me on entering was a little child of about nine months laid out as a corpse upon a small stool . . . The mother was away trying to get a coffin to bury it in.[56]

McIntyre was so affected by her plight that he left 6d. with the local grocer for Mrs Hamill.

Given this picture of terrible poverty, how did its victims manage to survive? One way, perhaps the easiest way, was by begging, and inevitably Ireland had its share of beggars. Prior to the 1770s there was scanty provision in Belfast for the poor, or for beggars. The first systematic attempt to deal with the problem came in 1771, when an act was passed by the parliament in Dublin which gave rights to corporate bodies to collect funds to build and furnish houses of industry to take in

vagrants and sturdy beggars and vagabonds to be kept at hard labour . . . and to seize every strolling vagabond capable of labour who hath no place of abode.

It was this act which led to the establishment of the Belfast Charitable Society.[57] A later act of 1773-4 entitled:

An Act for badging such poor as shall be found unable to support themselves by labour and otherwise provide for themselves; and for restraining such as shall be found able to support themselves . . . by begging . . . [58]

drew a careful distinction between those unable and those simply unwilling to work. In 1792 the Charitable Society printed a notice warning that the sturdy beggars currently infesting the streets would be taken up by officers of the society known as 'Bang Beggars' who received a bounty of one shilling British (1s. 1d. Irish) for every beggar brought in. These officers were identified by the scarlet collars on their coats and continued to operate at least until 1817.[59]

The history of the Belfast Charitable Society is told in R.W.M. Strain's study, *Belfast and its Charitable Society*, which includes its attempts to remove the scourge of street-beggars from the streets. The *Belfast News Letter* applauded its efforts.

The public are much indebted to the Rev. Mr. Bristow and the other gentlemen of the committee of the Belfast Charitable Society for their exertions to free them from the host of beggars who daily besiege their doors. Several of these gentlemen perambulated the streets on Saturday last, attended by the Black Cart, when a number of mendicants were seized and conveyed to the Poorhouse. The public have been told of the healing virtues of metallic tractors, but we hesitate not to say that the Black Cart of Belfast is a more powerful agent for the cure of distress than all the tractors ever invented. The very sight of it gave vigour to the infirm and the lame became so fleet that their most ardent pursuers were completely distanced. They seemed near to adopting the sentiments of the poet –

He that begs and runs away
May hope to beg another day,
But he that's by the Black Cart ta'en
Can never hope to beg again.[60]

Belfast also had its Strangers' Friend Society whose work is described in an advertisement for a charity sermon preached by Mr Mayne in the Methodist Chapel in 1809. There was a pressing need of money to carry on its work.

Since last November they have been enabled to rescue several hundred families from the greatest distress – to restore many destitute fugitives to their disconsolate families – and provided employment for a number of the industrious poor – It is hoped, notwithstanding the many similar applications that Institution will not fail of support.[61]

The Belfast branch was amalgamated with the Society for the Employment and Relief of the Poor in the town of Belfast because the societies had the same object. The new society:

intended to embrace all objects pursued by the Strangers' Friend Society, it has been agreed to unite and co-operate in carrying the general plan into effect.[62]

Neither the Belfast Charitable Society which provided residential accommodation (unpopular with most of the poor) nor the

Strangers' Friend Society was able to end the severe problem of street begging in the town. An alternative experiment was devised which led to the opening of a house of industry in Belfast under the 1771 act.

At a town meeting held on 29 June 1809 it was agreed to found a society for the abolition of mendicity. The rules and regulations of the new organisation and proposals for its operation were published in the *Belfast Monthly Magazine*. Unlike the Charitable Society the House of Industry did not intend to give shelter to the poor but to provide them with work and to inculcate moral habits, which would, it was hoped, lead to the independence of the poor. Paupers were to be supplied with implements and materials which would be manufactured into goods to be sold in a repository. Any pauper who, through old age or illness could not support himself, would be subsidised. The result of these proposals would be that the mendicant, the stranger in town, the room-keeper and the temporarily distressed workman could all obtain support from the House of Industry so that there would no longer be an excuse for street begging. This at least was the intention of the society's founders.

These proposals give a clear indication of the thinking of the charitable in early nineteenth century Belfast. The poor were not regarded as morally responsible for their poverty and the main object was to give aid and at the same time retain the self-respect of those aided. This of course was in marked contrast to the ethos of the Poor Law introduced in 1838, which operated on the 'less eligible' principle to emphasise the shame of poverty. By contrast, in the early nineteenth century it was recognised that there were people who were simply not capable of providing for themselves through age or infirmity, and responsibility for them was willingly assumed. The poor who were rejected were those who begged and would not make an effort to help themselves – and even they were not merely pushed off the streets and left to fend for themselves with no resources, but were given a chance to work. The difficulty of finding work was acknowledged, in fact there was no censoriousness shown. The editor of the *Monthly Magazine* wrote,

It is in fact a matter of necessity that the wealthy and better informed should exert themselves in favour of their weaker and more destitute brethren; for if they do not, one of two things may happen, either that the poor of this class must perish, or else be supported entirely by alms.[63]

At the town meeting in June 1809 a committee of thirty-one of the leading citizens of Belfast was elected. It was agreed that a house should be procured for a repository and sales room where work of all descriptions should be provided for all who applied for help, and if applicants through inability could not support themselves the deficiency would be supplied. Funds were to be raised through voluntary subscriptions and the sovereign led the way by pledging £300-400 from the corporation. The town was divided into districts for which collectors were to be appointed and visitors were to inspect persons who might be considered fit objects for charity.[64]

Large subscriptions were raised and a building was leased on the corner of Marquis St and Smithfield by the trustees. The House of Industry was opened in an area which was a 'poor, populous and manufacturing neighbourhood.'[65] The trustees drew up a most detailed list of rules and regulations and beggars were ordered off the streets. It was hoped that the result would be that the town would be freed from:

the most disgraceful and distressing sight – a multitude of human beings brought up in the habits of idleness and vice, daily fill the streets and extort by their importunity, far more than is now sufficient to make them live at home in more comfort, and as they are also compelled to do something to earn a livelihood, there are hopes that they may in time especially the younger generation become industrious and useful members of the community.[66]

If beggars were taken up by the two constables by the authority of the sovereign they were confined 'in a miserable vault' in the House of Industry, initially for twenty-four hours but incorrigble beggars were brought before a magistrate.[67] A study of the rules and regulations shows the care with which the committee supervised the running of the house. They cover the annual general meeting, the treasurers' fund, the duties of the steward, gate-keeper, cook, the organisation of food distribution and labour down to the allocation of flax and the garments produced and the picking of oakum.

The Belfast House of Industry was the first society in Ireland to attempt to suppress mendicity by offering the poor the comfort of a settled home with outdoor relief of food and employment instead of indoor relief. There never was any accommodation, for the committee in general preferred outdoor relief because of the difficulty of monitoring moral depravity within the house. Dr Robert Tennent said, 'we even find a difficulty in keeping the aged and infirm in any kind of regularity or order with regard to their moral conduct.'[68] Indeed the poor would rather pay 6d. to 20d. per week for fairly inferior houses and retain a degree of independence.

The regulations for admission were very strict. Application had to be made to the steward who had printed certificates upon which the applicant had to get the names of two subscribers of at least 10s. per year. This certificate was given to a visitor who went to the house and asked the prescribed questions and then made a recommendation about granting relief. If the committee passed it, it then went before the sub-committee of distribution, who in turn visited the applicant and made their decision.

Although these visits were laborious the second visit was necessary because attempts were made to deceive and get aid where none was warranted. The first visit was expected and known to take place soon after he (the Steward) is applied to; and then every appearance of comfort is withdrawn from their abodes and the symptoms of illness, distress and destitution studiously manifested.[69]

The most remarkable part of the whole proceedings is the amount of time that the committee of important citizens was prepared to devote to carrying out their duties.

Those women who passed the stringent tests got the wheels, reels and flax which the committee had invited tenders for. They were employed to spin yarn for the house at a higher rate than it was worth: the committee was prepared to stand the loss in the hope that it might promote 'industrious habits'.[70] Another encouragement to industry came in the rewards offered for high production, £1 to the person with one child under two for the greatest quantity of yarn returned to the house. Men got work breaking stones until their yard had to be closed because the committee could not get rid of the stones.[71]

In addition to giving work, rations were distributed daily. Soup was supplied on the premises every day as:

no article of support can be furnished at less expense better calculated to answer the purpose of a Charitable Institution. Five hundred persons at the rate of a quart for each adult, are every day supplied with that wholesome and nourishing article.[72]

In addition seven lbs of potatoes, one lb meal, seven cwt coals per week were given and bread was also distributed.

Table 1.7

Aid given by House of Industry

Year	Rations	Spinners	Persons rec. bread	Mend-icants taken	Men breaking stones
1831	439	930	-	-	-
1832	725	853	-	460	60
1833	645	864	126	262	22
1834	626	794	116	264	-

In fact the whole system was so attractive as to make it necessary to restrict aid to those who had been resident in Belfast for five years. Even by October 1809 it was clear that the establishment of a work-house had removed 'gangs of strolling beggars who daily besieged the doors of the inhabitants'[73] and many 'public mendicants' fled.

However, the passing of the Irish Poor Law made the House of Industry redundant. From 1839 it had become very difficult to collect subscriptions because people knew that a poor-rate would soon be levied.[74] Funds were so limited that relief had to be cut and one of the constables dismissed, this at a time one year before the poor-rate for the Belfast Union would be raised. In the meantime the 800 persons getting relief in the House of Industry would be cast on the streets. This would 'be dreadful to the poor, and annoying to the inhabitants of the town and its neighbourhood.'[75] An appeal for subscriptions was not successful. In 1841 Rev. Henry Cooke as chairman of the society had to call a meeting to consider 'the exhausted state of the funds of the House of Industry.'[76] At this meeting it was decided to collect subscriptions for the purpose of liquidating its debt. At a meeting on 1 June 1841 Mr McTier proposed and Mr Magouran seconded a proposal that,

as it appears that the funds of the House of Industry are nearly exhausted the place be closed and its property be transferred to the Surgical Hospital,[77]

and a deputation was empowered to call on R.J. Tennent as the heir of Dr Robert Tennent (one of the original trustees) to ask for his assistance in carrying out this scheme as the other surviving trustees were abroad. With his agreement the House of Industry closed in 1841.

Concern about begging and the relief of poverty was seen throughout Ireland. It was mainly in the larger towns that organised efforts to clear the streets and distribute alms efficiently were made. In Ireland there were eight Houses of Industry – in Belfast, Clonmel, Cork, Dublin, Ennis, Kilkenny, Limerick, Waterford and Wexford, all of which were, according to George Nicholls, totally inefficient for detecting and repelling wilful idleness.[78] Perhaps because of this he found that no resistance to the regime had ever been made to any of the governors.

Had the Houses of Industry made any material contribution to the solution of the problem of begging? To some extent and for a limited period they seemed to do so. In 1813 J. Trail Kennedy of the Belfast House of Industry said that the committee had generally stopped the practice. Rev. Henry Cooke said that the town owed a debt to the House of Industry for being 'freed from the inconvenience, annoyance and imposture of mendicants.'[79] But the real difference in the situation came by the end of the nineteenth century, particularly in Belfast. Industrialisation and the availability of jobs in textiles, ship-building and engineering made a much greater impact than anything else. Besides, in the proud prosperous city of 1900 the sight of beggars on the streets would not have been acceptable and the thrifty burghers would not pay poor-rates and at the same time give money to mendicants. And if they got no alms they would not stay.

What the House of Industry did was to set the pattern for future charitable work in Belfast. Almost all of the voluntary societies of the Victorian and Edwardian town had the same structure – the rules and regulations, the committees, the fund raising and the same objects of care. This was its great contribution.

'Destitution and disease went hand in hand together':

RELIEF IN TIMES OF EXCEPTIONAL DISTRESS.

After the opening of the workhouse in 1841 the problem of concentrated street begging disappeared except at times of exceptional distress. Above the class of beggars was a stratum of unskilled or semi-skilled men and women who usually had jobs but who were likely to be made redundant in trade depressions. The workhouse provided no solution to the temporarily destitute, it was private charity which gave them a safety net. There were periods of distress throughout the nineteenth century in all parts of Britain when the needy were relieved by 'special town funds usually collected by the mayor and corporation thinly disguised as a committee for t he relief of the poor.'[1] Belfast experienced three times of major economic decline – the 'hungry forties', 1857-8, and the winter of 1878-9.

One great difficulty for the temporarily homeless was shelter at night. This was a problem in Belfast years before the potato failure led to the Famine. In 1841 the town was faced with

many houseless and friendless strangers, and the destitute among our own inhabitants, who, unable to pay for the meanest lodging, are compelled to seek the wretched cover of any spot that affords them partial protection from the inclemency of the weather, or even to wander the streets, night after night.[2]

People were already coming to the town to look for work. The citizens were worried about the problem as letters to the papers show. One letter from 'An inhabitant of Smithfield' to the *Northern Whig*, highlighted the crisis.

The extensive manufactories in town induce thousands of poor persons to come annually to Belfast to seek employment; failing to procure this their condition becomes one of the utmost destitution . . . I have seen groups of these unfortunate wretches huddled together, on the most inclement nights in Smithfield Market-house – certainly as comfortless a resting-place as could be chosen. Persons in this destitute situation, are, now and then, tempted into the commission of trivial offences, to obtain a night's shelter in the Police Office. An instance of this kind came under my own observation, some months since. I happened to pass along William-st. South about 11 o'clock, when I was accosted by a ragged and travel-soiled man, who carried a stout cudgel, with the extraordinary request; "Will you permit me, Sir, to knock you down?" "For what reason?" enquired I. "I have just left the Police Office, after having been refused permission to sit at the fire till day-break. If however, you would be charitable enough to give me in charge to a watchman, for an assault, I would be sure of a night's lodging."

The writer suggested that as the House of Industry was closed and up for sale it would be an excellent House of Refuge as it is in "a poor, populous and manufacturing neighbourhood".[3]

Unfortunately the correspondent did not let the readers know if he agreed to the request.

The *Whig*'s editor, F.D. Finlay, urged the need for a night asylum for the houseless poor and on 12 January 1841 a public meeting was called. At this meeting a request for a town meeting to discuss the plan for a refuge was signed by all of those present, businessmen, merchants, solicitors, clergy and gentry.[4] The organisers went ahead with their plans and the Night Asylum was opened at the beginning of December 1841, in a rented building in Poultry Square.[5] It had accommodation for eighty persons in one dormitory for each sex, was clean and on the whole was as comfortable as could be expected. A master (ex-Constable Kelly of the police establishment) and a matron were appointed who would, it was hoped, act humanely towards the unfortunate beings who applied for admission. It may have been as comfortable as could be expected: expectations could not have been high. Admittedly there was a blazing fire in each room which 'seems out of place in such a cheerless repose and strives to do its best for the honour of the house and the comfort of its inmates.'

But there were no beds, bolsters, blankets or coverings. Inmates slept on the floor resting their heads on a little raised bench. There were some forms in each room and this was the only furniture. The fires could be used to roast the potatoes which were usually the only food which the poor had, for the asylum provided none.[6]

It is a measure of the destitution which drove people to the asylum that they welcomed the miserable shelter of its roof as a happy exchange for the pelting rain and the piercing cold – the darkness and dreariness of night. The people who went there were of the lowest class, the homeless, strangers to the town, the deserted women glad of the companionship. When a 'gentleman' visited the House of Refuge and went to the females' room he saw a rough deal box acting as a coffin for a young child whose mother took comfort from the other women's sympathy even though she knew none of them.[7]

Money to support the asylum came mostly from subscriptions but there were other fund-raising events. In February 1843 the committee arranged a panorama of local and foreign views showing men, horses, various birds and animals as well as a splendid marine grotto in the Theatre of Arts, the Exchange Rooms. Tickets were 1s. for the front and 6d. for the back and could be obtained from the committee. It was a very successful show. The star items were the storm scene and the shipwreck, both dramatic and with a perfect 'fidelity of this scene with at once surprise and a delightful spectacle.'[8]

The government's revision of the rules on outdoor relief had a major impact on support for the Night Asylum. This was acknowledged by John McNeile who took the chair at a public meeting called to discuss the future of the shelter in the light of its diminished resources. Belfast people would not give money twice for the same cause and they were already paying rates to support the workhouse. So in November 1847 the Night Asylum closed.[9] This was an occasion when the work of private charity was taken over by the state, something which may have pleased and relieved the property owners of some of their financial burden but did not please the men and women who had no alternative to the workhouse.

While the Night Asylum was operating in 1847 there was a problem every day of what to do with its 100-120 clients plus about 30 discharged prisoners and patients from hospital. These unfortunate men and women roamed the streets looking for help, and were a considerable irritation to passers-by. The need for action became really pressing in 1847 as people from famine-hit districts came into Belfast. The Night Asylum which usually had 60-70 per night now had up to 230 applicants.[10]

A sort of re-vitalised House of Industry was proposed where work of the simplest kind could be done, oakum-picking, shoe-making and needle-work for the women most of whom claimed to be able to sew or knit. At the end of the day they could be paid and go home or

The Poor-House of the Belfast Charitable Society, c. 1820.

House of Correction, c. 1820.

to the Night Asylum. Then people might be able to walk in the streets with impunity and shopkeepers could get rid of the crowds round their doors.[11] An advertisement appeared in the *Northern Whig* on 3 April for a superintendent to take charge of a day asylum and free industrial school in a converted weaving factory, formerly S. Turbitt's iron foundry, on the left bank of the Lagan at May's Dock, Poultry Square. The superintendent would be expected to direct the inmates, to be of active business habits, able to write a good hand and keep accounts correctly. The salary for the post was fairly reasonable, £52 p.a. with a residence in the premises.[12] So all was ready for the reception of the first inmates.

The object of the movement was simply to abolish street-begging by providing the means of relieving vagrants and rescuing children, who, if ignored would graduate into a nuisance at a later date. This was one charity which straightforwardly tried to remove an eyesore which annoyed both the middle class and the working class. Only in the case of the children was there an element of improvement and salvation; for the rest the aim was to get them out of the way. Having arrived at the shelter the inmates were given free food, shelter and employment if they were capable of work, and if not capable sent to the workhouse. Education for the young was provided.[13]

There was great enthusiasm for the Day Asylum. The *Belfast's People's Magazine* ran several articles on it during the paper's brief existence. One entitled 'An Hour in the Day Asylum' drew comparisons within the town. Admitting that Belfast had little in the way of buildings to attract public attention while having a 'river crowded with shipping and wharves piled with treasures of distant shores', one building should be shielded from gaze as a 'plague spot marking our moral leprosy'. This was the new House of Correction, 'a magnificent temple to crime', a reference to the imposing prison on the Crumlin Rd. Here criminals were rewarded for their iniquity by being boarded and lodged while mere paupers were punished for their poverty by hunger and houselessness.

Then to another building architecturally mean but morally beautiful – *the Day Asylum.*

Its help to the waifs and strays of Belfast drew most praise.

Crowds of pale, ragged little beings thronging towards it – brothers of 8 or 9 years hastening onwards with lesser brothers of 3 or 4 on their backs, and little sisters (the tender sympathy of the female heart already budded greenly) dry the tears and stifle the sobs of sisters still younger – comfort them with the assurance that now at last they shall have food.

This was a magnet to the young.

They are vile and corrupt, and ignorant – loathsome if you will. Let them enter – they are not *lost*; and if there be moral redemption for them, put them in its way.

Even in the evening crowds on the stairs wanted admission

They crowd in, their little hands, feet, and faces red from cold (we can see no shoes or mittens among them) . . . welcome them all, ragged dirty and impure though they may be.

A walk through the streets would be beset with pauper children pleading, 'just one half-penny Sir, for God's sake, to buy a bit of bread or a drop of soup – I'm very, very hungry.'

As for the other inmates they were in a low compound which was intended for a workshop or refectory. The upper floor was divided into apartments for male and female adults and children. There was much public interest in the working of the shelter and most days there were visitors to see what was happening. All of them agreed that the children were better off than on the streets.[14]

As with the Night Asylum it seems that large numbers of people used the Day Asylum. It was calculated that between April and July 1847 there were 46,000 attendances by persons who were fed and cleansed, including 11,500 girls and 11,000 boys, who were not only fed and washed but taught as well. Girls were taught the use of the needle and the boys 'to use their hands'.[15] Showing the popularity of the shelter, the committee helped 6,060 times, while in the work-house there were just 1,900.[16] A soiree was given to the inmates by 40 ladies and gentlemen at which 'the appearance of these poor creatures was highly creditable both to them and to their kind patrons and teachers.' All of those present received a bap and a 'tin' of tea.

Just as support had declined for the Night Asylum it did also for the Day Asylum. The closing of the night refuge and the death from fever of William Mulholland, the main founder and guiding spirit, in May 1847, meant the end and the building was taken over by the Poor Law Guardians.[17] By 1849 the only relic of the asylum was an industrial school in Ballymacarrett producing mats and rugs for sale in England and locally, giving food and a limited literary education to poor children.[18] The two enterprises were examples of the efforts of the citizens to cope with a new problem. In their time they were a boon.

Belfast was less affected by the Famine than many parts of Ireland but its citizens were deeply disturbed by the horrific stories printed daily in the local papers, telling of the tragedies in Mayo and Kerry. Three funds were set up in the town intended to alleviate the horrors of the Famine in Munster and Connacht – the Belfast General Relief Fund, the Ladies' Association for the Relief of Irish Distress and the Fund for the Temporal Relief of the Suffering Poor of Ireland through the Instrumentality of the Clergy of the Established Church. The raising of money for them not only eased the consciences of subscribers but once again showed the differences between Belfast and the rest of Ireland.

The first inspiration for relief came from what, on the face of it, was an unlikely source, the anti-Romanist presbyterian minister and professor of theology, Dr John Edgar. As secretary of the Home Mission of the General Assembly he had visited Connacht in 1843 to inspect the presbyterian schools there and although disturbed by the 'evils of Romanism', he was impressed with the kindness and hospitality of the Irish peasants.[19] In his report to the General Assembly in July 1846 he made no reference to distress in the west but when he visited Connacht again in the autumn of 1846 and saw the ravages of the Famine he was appalled and determined to do something to relieve the people.

Dr Edgar called a meeting in Dr Cooke's May St church on 29 September 1846 where he made an impassioned appeal for help. In the *Missionary Herald* of November 1846 he wrote an article called 'A Cry from Connaught – an appeal for a land that fainted by reason of a famine of bread.' Twenty-six thousand copies were printed and sold and in the end £16,000 was raised by the efforts of Dr Edgar. As a result of the publicity money was sent to Dr Edgar which he distributed as it came in. However, the first organised attempt at relief was made by Belfast ladies who, inspired by the minister, formed the Belfast Ladies' Relief Association for Connaught on 22 October 1846.

In fact there was a degree of confusion in the well-meant but rather disorganised activities of the different groups. The Ladies' Association was the most important and it managed the distribution of relief through the agency of the local episcopalian clergy or their congregations in Donegal and Mayo. The sums were not large – for example, £10 and £20 of clothing were sent to Mrs Griffith, Templecrone, Donegal, £15 of clothing to Rev. E. Batt, Killgar, Donegal.[20] On 1 January 1847 a meeting was held which called for subscriptions to a general fund to be expended solely on food in any district of Ireland – a stipulation which led to later disputes. A committee was chosen, a treasurer and secretary appointed and a subscription list opened headed by the linen merchant Andrew Mulholland with a donation of £200.[21] A roll-call of those present included all of the important men of Belfast and the meeting led to the calling of a town meeting by the mayor John Harrison at which all religious denominations were represented, including the catholic bishop Dr Cornelius Denvir.

Five resolutions were passed at the meeting, the first proposed by Dr Denvir and seconded by Rev. J. Scott Porter which stated the objectives of the new fund. These were to raise money and provide food for those parts of Ireland where there was evidence of destitution, seeing that the poor of Belfast were already being helped. As the winter proceeded so did the efforts to help. But the disinterested good-will did not continue for long. Some episcopalians saw the Famine not just as a disaster to be alleviated but as an opportunity to break down the mistrust with which they were faced by the catholic people. In January 1847 the Fund for the Temporal Relief of the Suffering Poor of Ireland through the Instrumentality of the Clergy of the Established Church was launched in response to the many heart-rending demands directed to the Belfast clergy from the south and west by local episcopalian clergy, which emphasised the opportunities 'for conveying the light of the gospel into the darkened minds of the Roman Catholic peasants thus severely suffering.'[22] The anglicans acted quickly and as usual a committee was formed, all episcopalians.

The emergence of this new fund worried the existing committee of the Belfast General Relief Fund and R.J. Tennent wrote to the Temporal Relief fund asking for united action to bring relief to Ireland without distinction of sect or party but the established clergy refused. They said that divine guidance had led them and while in the past they had borne the odium of charges of sectarianism in order not to mar the work of the Relief Committee, now they strongly refuted the allegations and determined to continue their own special efforts.[23] These three committees, the Ladies' Relief Association, the General Relief Fund and the Temporal Relief Fund, virtually excluded Belfast from their sphere of action, at first because of the prevailing feeling that there was less need there. The ladies' committee did give £100 to the Belfast poor, by far the largest single grant they made, but this was most unusual.[24]

Although Belfast was less affected than most parts of Ireland the community became concerned about its own poor. There were many in the town who bitterly resented the fact that money raised in Belfast was not used to help its citizens and they became increasingly vociferous. On 26 January 1847 the *Belfast News Letter* commented on the spreading distress in the town (though it noted that not a single public house had closed) and over the next weeks there was a growing demand that local destitution should be relieved as well as that in Connacht. Ballymacarrett was one district where distress was severe, not because of the potato failure but because of the recession now affecting handloom weavers. It was full of poor weavers who had fled outside the boundaries of the town to escape borough taxes. They were in as bad a state as the peasants of Skibbereen and the Ballymacarrett Relief committee amalgamated with the Belfast soup kitchen, so that at least there was food available.[25] From the beginning of February there was comment and correspondence in the papers on the rights of Belfast citizens to help from local subscriptions. This public correspondence stimulated interest and a desire to know the truth.

In response to a request for accurate information on the state of Belfast all the doctors attached to the dispensary districts (College, Dock, Shankill, Hospital, Smithfield and Cromac), published accounts of the distress. They reported appalling misery, wretchedness, pinching poverty, poor clothing and bad housing. Destitution had increased.[26] Although these conditions were undesirable they could not compare with Connacht but they were serious enough to cause comment in the town. A few ladies of all denominations who decided to tackle Belfast rather than Irish distress met at Mrs Blain's in the Royal College. They agreed to call on clergy and their congregations to ask for support. Having failed to attract much response from existing funds the ladies directed their efforts to the establishment of an industrial school which would prepare pupils to earn a living, and to giving needlework to poor women of the town. By mid-March 1847 the Ladies' Relief Association for Belfast was formed and a committee chosen.

Having decided that the best way of helping local women was to give them work (for this committee only dealt with the female poor), and that it was most important to tackle the problem of the 'ragged, reckless, untaught female children crowding the streets clamouring for relief' they set about organising institutions for them.[97] On 18 March the school for girls and the room for sempstresses to work in and receive work was opened in the House of Correction. As this was not a suitable venue, negotiations were opened with the committee of the Lancasterian school in Frederick St for the use of their premises. They published an advertisement listing the work which would be made up by the women and the prices for goods.

Table 2.1

Goods made in Lancasterian School 1847

Goods	Price
Fine linen shirts	1/6 – 2s.
Common linen shirts	6d. – 8d.
Boys' shirts	1s. – 1/6
Handkerchiefs, hemmed	1d. – 2d.
Veined cambric handkerchiefs	6d. – 1s.
Chemises	8d. – 1/6
Petticoats	10d. – 1/4
Collars	10d. – 1/4

Tablecloths and sheets etc. hemmed at 1d. per yard.

This part of the effort fizzled out like most of the other 1847 funds but the school proved much more enduring.

There was already by 1847 a wholly Belfast establishment, the soup kitchen, which catered for those citizens who were respectable artisans normally earning a precarious livelihood but from time to time were the victims of trade depressions. The terrible Famine year 1846-7 brought misery to men who did not want to go into the workhouse nor to stoop to begging and the soup kitchen was designed to provide enough food to keep a family going until trade improved. As soup had been served at the old House of Industry, there was already a tradition of its use in Belfast so it was natural that a soup kitchen committee was set up in November 1846. There was general interest shown in Ireland in this form of subsistence and the Irish Relief Association produced recipes and costings which were published in the papers. The celebrated chef Alexis Soyer gave six different recipes for such kitchens. Soup was cheap to provide and relatively easy to prepare, 100 gallons could be made for just over £1. The cost was made up as follows:

Table 2.2

Cost of 100 galls. soup

	£	s.	d.
40 lbs rough beef @ 23/6		8	6
1 ox head		1	4
28 lbs barley @ 20s.		5	0
14 lbs peas @ 14/6		1	10
14 lbs oatmeal @ 24s.		3	0
Vegetables		1	6
1 lb cayenne			6
	£1	1	8[28]

At the end of 1846 a soup kitchen committee was set up in Belfast with the intention of supplying the needy who used the asylums and the unemployed. In December 1846 soup kitchens opened in the old House of Correction and Gt George's St, from 6.30 a.m. until 7 p.m. The soup was sold at 1d per quart to those who could afford to pay and given free to those who passed a committee which met daily at the House of Correction and handed out free tickets entitling the holder to one ration consisting of 1 quart of soup and ½ lb of bread. On Sunday mornings ¾ lb of bread was distributed and coals sold to the poor 'under special recommendation.'[29] Between 9 and 23 December almost 3,000 people came in for food.

In the early part of 1847 confusion developed over the distribution of money collected for famine relief. The General Relief Fund had guaranteed to give aid to any part of Ireland, but this at first was interpreted as any part except Belfast. The editor of the *Northern Whig* wrote 'We beg to observe that the committee have, to all events so far, acted in a manner which totally exonerates them from any charge of undue sympathy for the poor of their own town.'[30] A few days later he expressed regret that the committee would not help destitution at home. The pressure of public opinion forced the

35

committee to re-assess its policy. £1,000 was handed over to the soup kitchen committee but it was not clear if this was an exceptional grant or the beginning of regular support. The committee of the Relief Fund called a meeting to discuss the allocation of funds to the Belfast poor, for there was a substantial sum in the treasurer's hands. Of the £6,285 subscribed Belfast had received £1,870 while the rest of the country got £2,805 in 124 separate grants leaving over £2,000 as a balance.[31] Considering the degree of distress in Belfast compared to the rest of Ireland, Belfast did quite well. It seems odd that all the money was not given out at this time of widespread destitution. After considerable discussion it was decided by 21 votes to 10 that no change in the committee's rules in order to direct aid to Belfast should be made.

At the beginning of April a second subscription was given for the support of the soup kitchen and £250 was given to the Day Asylum, £50 to the Belfast Society for the Relief of the Destitute Sick.[32] However, the appearance of fever in the town distracted attention from the wider distress. It appeared in April and soon the streets were crowded with victims – a girl was found lying helpless in the street, a poor famished boy of 9 or 10 years lay all day in Donegall St and the Night Asylum was like a hospital it had so many cases.[33]

The enthusiasm of many Belfast people for the welfare of other Irishmen was already beginning to decline and a combination of the fever, an apparently better harvest and, perhaps even more importantly, increasing accounts of outrages in the disturbed areas changed the attitude of the General Relief committee. They stopped sending aid to those districts 'of widespread terror and a seemingly unquenchable thirst for blood' altogether. Instead the remaining money was used to help paupers being sent back from England and Scotland to Ireland by giving them food from the soup kitchen and money to take them to their original homes.[34] In late 1847 and early 1848, 6,045 such paupers were removed from Belfast in this way. The justification for this use of funds was the helping of people from all parts of Ireland even if aid was distributed in Belfast. In later years the fund had a rare accolade from Rev. Dr Thomas Drew who described it as 'the only harmonious fund I was ever connected with in the town of Belfast.'[35]

This whole episode was unusual for Belfast in two ways. Belfast people normally tried to detach themselves from Irish affairs in general and to administer their own charitable relief. It was natural for any town in any country to be mainly concerned at the poverty seen around it, so in the days before the immediacy of television showing starvation in refugee camps, it was hard to inspire giving unless there was a massive disaster. Most Belfast people never went to Connacht, never saw an Irish peasant in his habitat; normally their only contact was with unwelcome beggars. They had responded generously if somewhat ambivalently to the stories of the Famine, though it must be said that only about half of the money subscribed was quickly sent off to the south. On the one hand Belfast citizens were affected by the obvious need of the victims and hurried to help them, on the other hand many were irritated by what they saw as Irish catholic incompetence and ineffectiveness. There certainly was destitution in the town but it was on a manageable scale unlike that in Connacht.

Prosperity returned to Belfast and the organisations founded to help the distress in the 1840s disappeared with the exception of the Ladies' Industrial School. However, in the winter of 1857-8 the difficulties of the hand-loom weavers and sewers in the town reached crisis point.[36] As in 1847 Ballymacarrett was particularly badly hit, so John Boyd, the secretary, re-constituted the old relief committee and wrote to the papers appealing for assistance. In response the mayor, S.G. Getty, called a town meeting. Speaker after speaker stressed the growing distress in Ballymacarrett, Brown Square, Durham St and Barrack St where many weavers lived. Rev. William Johnston (Townsend St Presbyterian Church) whose parish was in this area described how the weavers operated. The custom was to take a shop with 4-10 looms for which they paid a rent plus the cost of gas, but as few had any personal resources they suffered when there was a trade slump. They had to pawn their meagre possessions and things became so bad that some even joined the militia.

A subscription list was opened, a committee was elected from the most important men of business and the professions – and the relief mechanism swung into action. It was decided to give employment where possible and to provide for those in urgent need.[37] The first necessity was to raise funds. At the initial meeting £300 was subscribed and it was assumed that the balance of money remaining in the old General Relief Fund would be handed over. Although it was only about £100, Rev. Thomas Drew and Thomas McClure (secretaries) refused until a meeting of the old committee had discussed it. In the end the money was divided between the Society for the Relief of the Destitute Sick (£50) and the present relief fund (£80).[38] Subscriptions were hard to come by and appeals were made to the generosity for which Belfast was noted. £1,035 was all that was collected, largely in small sums, for the large firms who were expected to contribute did not give the donations hoped for.

Two forms of relief were given. One was in the form of food, specifically baker's bread which had the advantage of being easy to distribute and needed no cooking.[39] This was handed out on Monday, Tuesday, Thursday and Saturday, the days on which the committee met in the old House of Correction to vet applicants and to organise the work of the two paid inspectors who investigated claims, in a vain attempt to prevent imposture. To supplement this charity J. Trueman of the English Bakery gave 100 four lb loaves. The other aid was giving work to men at stone-breaking though this presented a problem of finding a market for the product. They did manage to get a contract from the town council to supply 1,000 tons of broken stone which gave employment to 50 men.[40]

As a result of these difficulties after only seven or eight weeks of operation in February 1858 the committee had had enough and decided to close down leaving 950 families on the books requiring help, for it was assumed that the crisis would soon be over. However even in the middle of April there was still great distress: there were demonstrations by crowds of labourers and some of them visited gentlemen on the committee asking them to act as collectors for a fund. This sort of pressure was unlikely to meet with much public support and 'the outdoor parade of hungry mobs was not to be encouraged.'[41] Crowds of men also called at the *Whig* offices stating their distressed condition and there was so much agitation that a new relief committee was constituted.

Its chairman was John Scott of May St Foundry and the committee included William Spackman of the Northern Clothing Emporium, High St, Mr Carolan of the *Ulsterman* and Mr McBean – all relatively unknown in philanthropic circles and not members of the town council.[42] This new committee was very critical of the mayor, council and clergy for their abandonment of the destitute and stated its willingness to assist the most extreme and deserving cases. They made the point that men *did* want to work, but if there was no work would they have to starve? Not if the new relief committee could help. They certainly believed that it was the duty of the affluent citizens to give money and to teach workers self-reliance and self-respect by giving them something to do.

This committee was no more successful than the previous one in solving the problem of unemployment and disappeared during the

summer. Why were they not effective? There are several explanations. There was already a fund being collected in the town, the
Indian Relief Fund which was to give assistance to the wives and
families of soldiers killed or wounded in the Indian Mutiny. There
was much interest in the crisis in Belfast and the citizens always gave
generously to funds like the Crimean War Fund and the Mutiny
Fund. Then not every trade in the town was affected. The muslin
trade was badly hit but the engineers were still in good employment.
The secretary of the Amalgamated Society of Engineers wrote to the
Whig claiming that as over 90 per cent of engineers were in the
society and as the funds were in good condition there was no distress
among them.[43] The weather that year was unseasonably mild pro-
tecting workers from the worst suffering and there were few signs of
real distress. Added to this was the apathy and lukewarmness displayed by the collectors and the banks' refusal to contribute though
this did not surprise Rev. William Johnston. He said 'there's not a
worse place in town for begging than the banks. They are the greatest
set of screws in the community.'[44] The usual donations from influential firms were not forthcoming. This is partly explained by a letter
from 'a manufacturer' complaining about the amount of aid being
given which reduced the speed of work done by 'veiners' because of
the relief they were getting.[45] Finally the great body of operatives who
were in work were not prepared to do much for the unemployed.

The next major crisis came in 1878-9. In that year there was distress
all throughout the United Kingdom. A comprehensive catalogue of
economic disaster was compounded by the fact that the weather was
unusually severe. Some enjoyed this greatly – ladies and gentlemen
skated on the lake in Ormeau Park which was surrounded with lamps
so that they could continue at night. People went to Mr Montgomery's
estate at Ballydrain in crowds by car and rail. But the continuing,
deep and long-lying snow was a disaster for the poor. The wealthy
were urged to contribute gifts of coal, blankets, etc, to the indigent
poor while the weather lasted but a more organised and concerted
effort was necessary to deal with such a scale of distress which 'no
ordinary demands of charity, and no usual organisation for relief
would be at all able to grapple with.'[46] The weather forced the
closure of some industries and out-door work was made impossible
by the inclement weather.

The mayor and charitable businessmen of the town responded as
usual. Three times during the 1870s the mayor had instituted a Coal
Fund where money subscribed went to the purchase and distribution

of fuel. For example, in 1877-8, 486 tons had been distributed and 3,888 persons relieved. Times were so hard that the incoming mayor John Browne inaugurated a fund even before he took office, with his brother T.H. Browne as secretary. One major difficulty in the process was the organisation of fuel distribution so that only the 'deserving' poor got help (presumably the undeserving could freeze) and this year Forster Green suggested doing it through the clergy of the main denominations.

Of course this immediately produced a problem. What about the irreligious poor and needy? Would they be neglected? Rev. Greene raised the issue but Rev. John McCredy had no such fears for he was sure the poor would all find a denomination when they heard that coals were available. Rev. Charles Seaver suggested that they might even find two or three – a sally greeted with laughter by the meeting.[47] In fact because of the severe winter there were even larger applications from all denominations than before and the committee asked for a list of non-denominational poor who had applied. It was decided simply to allocate them arbitrarily to any denomination just for the purposes of the fund, a solution accepted by ministers of all creeds. Distribution began and by 3 January 1879 1,600 bushels had been delivered. By 17 January 778 tons of coals and 4,400 bushels of coke had relieved 5,000 to 6,000 of the poor and needy.[48]

Even with clerical co-operation all applicants had to make considerable efforts to get coal. Each list of applications had to be signed by a clergyman before coal would be given out but some of them refused to endorse names not of their own denomination. This confusion resulted in some people getting as many as twelve bags, some got three bags and some none at all if they could not find a sympathetic pastor.[49]

Another method of giving relief was by the distribution of food tickets which could be exchanged for coffee, broth or bread at any of nine places mentioned on the ticket. These tickets were sold at 1s. per dozen at the Book Depository to the 'charitable and benevolent' who handed them to deserving cases. It was not long before the old favourite, the soup kitchen, made its re-appearance.

The soup kitchen was now in Gloucester St. It was described in February 1879 by Charles Elcock, Fitzroy Ave. At no. 36 were the ruins of a coach factory which had burned down some months before leaving only the bare walls. The windows were broken and the yard piled with rubbish but it had the great advantage of having two entrances to the yard, one in Gloucester St and one in Seymour Row so that there could be a continuous flow of people through the building. Its owner, Hugh Hyndman, handed it over rent-free to the soup kitchen committee who undertook the mammoth task of rehabilitation. They organised white-washers to work over the whole building, clear the sheds, pave and sewer the land, have gas and water laid on and a zig-zag floor laid right through. The shed was divided into two parts, one consisted of the soup kitchen itself and the other had a common room, a small kitchen and a boiler room to generate steam to make the soup. Upstairs there were two stores and a boiler room where the soup was actually made.[50]

Soup was also sold at the relief works in Ormeau Park and at the stone-field at 1d. per qt. The committee members most involved were Vere Foster, the educationalist, Rev. J.C. Street, minister of Donegall St Congregational Church, and Rev. Charles Seaver of St John's, Laganbank who stood on a cart selling the 'capital soup to hundreds of grateful men.'[51] By the end of the winter the charity branch of the town relief committee had issued 40,542 tickets for soup, meal, flour, tea and sugar showing 'the immense amount of help which was given to the poor of our town in the time of their dire need.'[52]

Only the able-bodied were eligible for relief, for the aged, infirm, idle or 'vicious' had all to go to the workhouse. Every applicant for work had to supply information on his character, number in the family, normal earnings, cause of idleness and destitution and then he was inspected by volunteer visitors.[53] There was a great demand for work from the crowds of men, women and children who daily besieged the offices at the town hall looking for help. It was not easy to provide work for the men for which low wages could be paid. Most of the men were labourers with a mixture of flax-dressers, roughers, slaters, gardeners etc., but any work found for them would be unskilled. The work given had to be park improvements which would not be competitive with private enterprise. The whole enterprise was fraught with difficulty. The relief committee had to co-operate with the parks committee of the town council and the municipal officials and this led to friction.

As well as work in the park a small hill was removed on the Falls Rd, streets were swept (though many employed at this disappeared when they found that they were actually expected to work), some private individuals including Mr Sinclair and Mr Boyd took on some men and the Water Commissioners gave some work.[54] The other main occupation was again stone-breaking. The work in general was fairly useless but large numbers turned up, hoping to earn some money: in February over 18 days 1,500 applied.[55] Perhaps more useful was the payment of passage money to men who had a chance of a job in England or Scotland plus a trifle put in their hands, the redemption of tradesmen's tools from the pawn and a few set up as dealers or pedlars.[56]

By contrast the work provided for women was very useful to families. In the severe weather the clothing societies were busy handing out garments made by local ladies, or cast-off clothes, bedding or carpeting. The chief agency was established by Rev. James Bristow who

enlisted a large body of ladies of all denominations, who collected monies and worked with their hands, employed hundreds of poor women, and supervised their work, relieved many articles of clothing from the pawnshop and clothed many of their starving sisters.[57]

As usual the enthusiasm began to flag and by the beginning of March the committee experienced difficulties. The work of the committee finally ceased on 19 April 1879 when the stone-breaking ended, though the 800 men in Ormeau Park had been dismissed on 22 March. Over the past three months the committee had met daily, had investigated 3,000 cases at one time, had found employment for 2,250 of them which, allowing for 5 dependents per man, meant that 11,250 people had been helped.[58] The amount subscribed and spent over the year was not large when the numbers relieved are counted: £2,726 was collected from subscriptions and payment for labour and spent on paying men for their work, giving money to the associated committees (charity and labour), postage and advertising etc. leaving a balance of £45.15.1.[59] The money was raised largely from Belfast's leading firms. The assets of the soup kitchen were sold off after outstanding commitments were paid, leaving a balance of £22.15.3.[60] Any money remaining was put into an account in the name of the mayor to be used in later cases of need.

It is tempting to attribute any distress in Ireland in the 1840s to the effects of the Famine but clearly this was not so in Belfast. In 1841 the potato crop had not yet failed and yet it was necessary to open a Night Asylum because of the numbers of unemployed and homeless workers. This sort of distress produced the Chartist movement and its occasional riots in the industrial cities in England but not in Belfast. The political demands of Chartism meant much less to

Ulstermen who were more interested in the Repeal movement and hoping for its failure than vague hopes of political advancement for the working classes. Indeed this was one way in which Belfast remained an Irish town, in its obsession with local politics rather than the class movements which influenced the English workers.

The Night Asylum actually closed in 1847 at the peak of the Famine and although the Day Asylum lingered for a short time it too disappeared. Obviously therefore the pressures of distress which had originally produced these two asylums had either abated or else different mechanisms of relief (for example the amended Relief Act which liberalised the Poor Law) could alleviate the destitution. Although there were still men and women arriving in Belfast to look for work, there were fewer people coming on the faint chance of getting jobs, and in any case it is not clear how many came from districts hit by Famine. The distress in the 1850s and the 1870s came from trade depression and met with responses similar to those in the 1840s. Although the individual street-beggars had mostly disappeared there was a greater danger of general unrest if large numbers of the temporarily unemployed could no longer support themselves. The expedients of the soup kitchen and relief work like stone-breaking used in all three periods of distress were very definitely Victorian remedies.

The Ulster Institution for the Deaf, Dumb and Blind, Lisburn Road, Belfast.

'The fettered tongue shall hence be free –
The Deaf shall hear, the Blind shall see!':

THE ULSTER SOCIETY FOR PROMOTING THE EDUCATION OF THE DEAF AND DUMB AND THE BLIND.

Belfast citizens who encouraged self-help to discourage begging were equally enthusiastic to give an education and training to deaf children so that they could support themselves and not be a burden on the rates. It was this enthusiasm which underlay the establishment of the Ulster Society. This society for educating deaf and dumb and blind children still exists, operating the Jordanstown Schools for the Auditorially and Visually Handicapped, a change of name indicative of changing public attitudes. The deaf and dumb, the blind and cripples were cloaked in no such euphemistic names in the nineteenth century. What was done for them might today be regarded as carrying the stigma of charity but in the absence of state aid private charities were essential.

People who lived in Belfast before the 1960s remember the mock Tudor red-brick building on the Lisburn Road which was the school for the deaf and dumb and the blind, and the road up to it called 'the dummies' hill'. The Ulster Society which built it was a very important charity in the town and detailed reports on it were published; its minute books, annual reports and local newspapers make it possible to build up a picture of life in the institution, fund-raising, education, problems and controversies. Leading figures appeared on the society's platforms and committees, aristocrats like the marquises of Donegall and of Downshire as well as the businessmen and clergy of Belfast, for the charity contained elements of all the different classes in town and province. It illustrated the good and the bad features of Belfast benevolence: the generosity of time and money given by its supporters and the exclusion of all who would not accept religious education in the doctrines of the Churches of England and Scotland.

The two areas of greatest concern were the inability of the handicapped to support themselves and the absence of religious instruction which particularly affected the deaf and dumb. Dr Orpen of Dublin was the first person in Ireland to concern himself about the condition of the deaf-mutes and in 1816 he set up the Claremont National Institution for the Education of the Deaf and Dumb at Glasnevin. In Belfast money was raised to send children there, for no such institution existed in Ulster. Fees were 20 guineas per annum for education, maintenance and clothes and four children were supported there in 1823, through the efforts of the auxiliary branch of the Claremont Institution established in Belfast in 1821.[1]

The cost of sending children to Dublin was high and very few could benefit, so in 1826, William McComb, a Belfast book-seller, set up a Sunday School in Brown St school where he tried to educate some deaf and dumb children. An advertisement appeared in the *Belfast Commercial Chronicle,* 27 April 1831, for a course of lectures in the Lancasterian School in Frederick Street by Mr Samuel Gordon of the Claremont Institution on the instruction of deaf-mutes, to be illustrated by a deaf and dumb pupil from the Dublin school. Gordon's object was to 'lay the foundation of an effective and economical system of instruction for the vast deaf and dumb population of Ulster'.[2]

A committee was elected and the school for the deaf and dumb was opened in the Independent Chapel in Donegall St.[3] It was on a very small scale at first, with only eight pupils taught by George Gordon, brother of Samuel.[4] In 1834 the school moved to King St but there was so little interest in the society that it seemed as if it would close. In 1835, however, Rev. John Edgar, having inserted an advertisement in the local papers, followed it by a meeting in his manse in Alfred St. This led to a public meeting in his church where two major decisions were taken. These were to admit blind children as well as deaf and dumb because there was no provision for them; and to raise funds to build a boarding school because otherwise only Belfast pupils could be catered for.

In 1836 the school was opened at 17 College St at the cost of £784.5.6 $\frac{1}{2}$, and consisted of school-rooms, workshops, a dwelling for the master and accommodation for fifty boarders.[5] In 1837, the objects of the society were stated as 'to afford children whose parents reside in the province of Ulster a religious and literary education and teach them some useful trade.' Already by 1840 it was becoming clear that the first premises were not big enough to cope with the demands made upon them so discussions began on how to expand. Negotiations were opened with the Belfast Charitable Society committee who owned the land beside the school, for more ground in Fountain St. However the deal fell through because a question arose about the legal implications apparent in the committee of the Belfast Charitable Society alienating any part of their land.

When these plans had to be changed a new green field site was suggested and a search for a suitable area began in 1842. The secretary put advertisements in the local newspapers and several applications were received.

The Committee of this Society are desirous to treat for three or four acres of land in an eligible site in the immediate vicinity of Belfast, for the purpose of erecting a new Institution. They intend to expend about £4,000 on the building and hope that some Proprietor of land may be found willing to treat with them on very reasonable terms for the sake of aiding a benevolent cause and at the same time, increase the value of his remaining ground.[6]

(Proposals to Jas Shaw, honorary secretary)

An agreement was made with Mr Clarke for ground on the Lisburn Rd. Originally it was of four acres but another three-quarter acre was added at a total rent of £60 per annum.[7] Advantages of the site, which was between the turnpike and the Botanic Gardens, were 'its healthy locality, its public and prominent situation' and the fact that it could accommodate not only a large building but any extension which might become necessary.[8]

Once this was settled an architect had to be found and Charles Lanyon offered his services. He was the county surveyor and had built the new Queen's Bridge, so his skills were well-known. As a further inducement he offered a donation of £100 to the building fund of the institution – but only if he got the contract. The costs of the building were estimated to be £4,000 on which he would get 5 per cent for professional charges. Lanyon gained the contract and the committee set about gathering the money. This was a good commission for an important public building and Lanyon went on from it to design the new courthouse on the Crumlin Rd, the prison and then Queen's College.[9] Over £2,000 were collected in Belfast including a munificent £500 from the banker Thomas Hughes of Fisherwick, Ballyclare, out of the estate of his son, Thomas Hughes jnr, £300 from Bishop Stearne's charities, £200 each from Andrew

Mulholland and the marquis of Hertford and eight other gifts of £100.[10] By now the estimated price given by the builder, Cranston Gregg of Elmwood, had risen to £6,100 and in the end it actually rose to £11,000.[11]

New efforts were made to cost the scheme and interest potential supporters. They were successful and on 31 August 1843, the foundation stone of the new building was laid by the marquis of Donegall before an assembly of over 1,000 people, including all the local figures of importance in commerce and in the churches. Pupils of the school were also there. Dr Edgar, as one of the most devoted and diligent of supporters, read an historical account of the society and then deposited in a cavity in the foundation stone prepared for the purpose, a bottle hermetically sealed containing 'a *Belfast Almanack* for the year, a copy of the latest report of the society, a *Belfast Commercial Chronicle*, the names of the contractor, architect, committee, etc. on parchment, and several coins.'[12] Lord Donegall laid the stone.

In two years the building was ready and it was officially opened on 24 September 1845 by Lord Massereene and Ferrard. The building itself was an impressive sight. The committee could have saved £400 to £500 by making the building perfectly plain but they believed that the 'very beautiful exterior' would increase the value of the ground which could be leased for building purposes. Its frontage was 222 ft long and the two wings extended 164 ft to the rear. The central block contained the museum, office, and the head-master's dwelling and separated the male and female sections. On the second floor were the spacious dormitories with room for 150 beds, clothes stores, infirmaries and assistants' bedrooms.[13]

The regime in the school was strict. Household regulations detailed the hours for work, meals and religious worship, the rules for pupils to obey and made clear the absolute power of the principal. Pupils all had to do domestic work, cleaning and tidying dormitories. Boys and girls had to make their beds and tidy the rooms, deaf boys had to wash the floors of the bathrooms and sweep the dormitories of their section. Blind boys had charge of ventilation and opened the windows. Girls had the same duties on their side. The building was dark and cold with a very institutional atmosphere and bars on the windows. It was lighted by gas until electricity was installed in 1924.[14]

The diet was stodgy and uninteresting but plentiful.

Table 3.1

Weekly menu in Ulster Institution

	MENU

Breakfast

Every day	5 oz oatmeal in stirabout $\frac{2}{3}$ pt buttermilk

Dinner

Sunday, Wednesday, Friday	5 oz beef and 2 lbs potatoes or 7oz bread
Monday, Saturday Tuesday, Thursday	5 oz rice and $\frac{1}{4}$ pt new milk Broth with bones and beef heads with vegetable; 2 lbs potatoes or 7 oz bread

Supper

Sunday, Tuesday, Thursday, Friday	5 oz rice and $\frac{1}{4}$ pt new milk
Monday, Saturday	5 oz oatmeal in stirabout, $\frac{2}{3}$ pt buttermilk[15]

Meals were taken at long tables with benches beside them, eaten from enamel plates and mugs. The blind children had to eat with spoons because knives and forks were considered too dangerous for them. This was one of the only times that boys and girls mixed outside school because they had separate amusements and pursuits.[16] Sanitary arrangements were very important because cleanliness was regarded as essential and the pupils were 'obliged' to take a warm bath once a week in winter and summer. Visitors to the school often commented on the clean state of the school and its facilities.

The laundry, drying rooms, bathrooms, etc. were admirably arranged and fitted with modern equipment. Corridors had tessellated paving and fancy work of the same, wainscot on doors and a covered promenade beautifully tiled afforded space for exercise.[17]

The wash-rooms had twenty four basins arranged in double rows of six with cold water piped to them. Warm water was obtained from a tap in the corner. There was also a drinking fountain and foot-bath where a half-dozen boys at a time sat on a bench and washed their feet – for some reason girls did not have foot-baths. Round the room were hooks for towels and sponge-bags with tooth brush and tooth paste. There was a certain shortage of lavatories: only three upstairs and five downstairs for seventy boys.

Every pupil had to supply a full set of clothes on entry to the school. It must have been hard for poor families to find money for clothes. One important aspect of life in the institution was the discipline imposed on the children. It was difficult to maintain a balance of severity with compassion and unfortunately in the autumn of 1848 a damaging charge was made against the 'undue severity' in the school and printed in the *Protestant Journal.* This claim was made by Professor J. R. Young of the Belfast College. He applied to the town magistrates for guidance because five pupils had come to his house allegedly fleeing from the institution in dread of punishment. However, as he did not take out a summons the magistrates could take no action.

The committee was understandably concerned at the bad publicity. Certainly to modern eyes the discipline maintained in the school is distasteful. Sometimes children suffered the 'privation of being taught a lesson –, of supper –, of swinging, etc.'[18] which was unexceptionable, but they could also be beaten publicly before teachers and fellow pupils after having been sentenced at a monthly court. Faults and misdemeanours were entered in a register and produced on court days. It was claimed by the Youngs as notorious that some of 'these deaf mutes are seized in their beds in the dormitory stripped,even of their shirts and beaten then and there.'[19] Charles Young stated that he was disturbed one night by the lashes of a cane mingled with the cries of the victim to whom it was being applied.

The next morning Mr C. Young was addressed as follows: 'I suppose you were disturbed last night by the cries of that boy Kirkwood?' 'Yes Mr – I was; but do you not know that that boy is an invalid – that he is but slowly recovering from the effects

of an abscess in his side, and that he has been brought to the brink of the grave?'
'Oh, yes! – but a little excoriation of the part will do him good – I wished when I
subdued him to carry out the usual formalities, and to punish him further, on
another boy's back; but when I made him get out of bed for that purpose, he seemed
about to faint, and of course, I did not prosecute my intention.'[20]

This charge comes from a biased source but the reference to the
'usual formalities' carries a chilling conviction. The committee began a detailed investigation into the charge, closely questioning John
Martin and visiting the school. Dr Charles Purdon issued a certificate, supported by Drs S.S. Thomson and Thomas Read. The certificate said,

. . . having examined nine of the boys selected from pupils of the Institution, by
Adam Turner, as beaten severely: I find that there were no marks of punishment
except on John Miller, who had the slight mark of a rattan on the left arm, and James
Smith, who had the slight mark of the taws on his back.[21]

The committee completely exonerated the principal, and published
his explanations of the discipline. He stated that there were fewer
incidents of corporal punishment than under the previous principal,
Charles Rhind, and that there had been only one case of a pupil
being punished in bed. This was when an eighteen year old boy had
'squared himself at the principal, and threatened to box him in the
presence of the other boys' – no wonder he got a beating.[22] Martin
had also forbidden the assistants to administer corporal punishment
and only operated the court system to help to 'convey many important ideas concerning guilt, crime, accountability and their consequences' – particularly to deaf children. The committee criticised
the attempts being made to injure the institution and its principal in
the school, on the roads, in the grounds and even in church, by the
Youngs.

The whole disagreeable incident led to insubordination towards
Martin by several boys who 'frequently dared him to inflict any
punishment threatening him with transportation, etc. in case of his
doing so'.[23] Was the discipline in the Ulster Institution more severe
than in other nineteenth century schools? It seems unlikely, for
sparing the rod and spoiling the child was not favoured by the
Victorians. The whole episode casts a good deal of light on Victorian
attitudes to punishment. In fact strict discipline and a rigid timetable
were necessary for the efficient running of an establishment which

educated and boarded deaf or blind children with a wide range of abilities.

Life was not all lessons. The pupils had to have some entertainment for they spent almost the whole year at school. Term time lasted from mid-August until June and there were no Christmas or Easter holidays. A Christmas party was organised each year by ladies of the province who supplied 'an immense number of beautiful and suitable articles to deck the boughs of the [Christmas] tree.'[24] Other breaks from routine came occasionally. The committee of the Horticultural Society which ran the Botanic Gardens admitted teachers and pupils gratuitously and the Belfast Natural History Society gave free admission to the museum.[25]

The *Northern Whig* published a description of a visit to the institution which gives a very good picture of life there. The *Whig* reporter visited the school on one of the open days for visitors.

In a spacious and handsome building of tasteful architectural design and proportions, are located 87 inmates of both sexes between the age of 6 and 16, 12 of whom are blind and the remainder deaf and dumb. Yet strange to say, the Deaf and Dumb boy can converse with his blind school fellow and vice versa through the agencies of the manual alphabet. Entering through a neat vestibule, the visitor is shown to the schoolroom where the deaf-mutes are receiving instruction. This is a fine apartment fitted up with desks, forms and the walls covered with maps, pictures and other educational appliances. The children were all scrupulously clean and comfortably dressed; the girls especially bore a look of intelligence . . . . The boys' class was receiving instruction from the Principal of the Institution, the Rev John Kinghan, a gentleman who seemed to enter into the arduous and onerous labours of his office with much of that kindly feeling towards the objects of their charges which is so essential a quality to those to whom is committed the instruction and management of persons of this class . . . . In the girls' class instructed by Miss White, very much intelligence was manifested . . . . After this inspection of the schools, we were shown through the dining rooms, work rooms, dormitories, bathrooms, kitchen, etc., all of which were patterns of neatness, cleanliness and comfort. The grounds and gardens about the establishment were kept in first-rate order; and several of the older boys of the deaf and dumb school assist the gardener in his operations when not engaged in school. Not the least interesting part of the establishment was the girls' room for sewing, knitting, and general household work, which was beautifully clean and orderly.[26]

The detail in the published descriptions of the life at the school is an indication of public interest in the society.

The whole *raison d'être* of the Ulster Institution was, of course, the education of the deaf and the blind children of the province. There was tremendous interest in the literary and religious teaching of the pupils and considerable effort was directed towards this by teachers and subscribers to the society. From the beginning there was a very professional attitude to the teaching methods used in the school and Ulster teachers followed the changing patterns of instruction in the nineteenth century.

During the nineteenth century, there were many discussions about the education of the deaf and dumb and in Belfast they had five years at school compared with only three years for the blind.[27] Deaf children were not necessarily dumb but they often seemed so because they could not hear and reproduce speech. There were two forms of education which were proposed at different times – oralism and manualism. Oralism was the teaching of deaf children actually to speak by lip-reading and by touching the throats of teachers to feel the movements of their vocal chords. Manualism was the use of sign language, which was the first natural and untrained method of communication that a deaf child could manage.

By the 1850s the system of signs developed by the French teacher, de l'Epee, was used in almost all asylums but it had begun to degenerate and children were adapting it to use their own signs.[28] It was very important but very difficult to teach them the alphabet for they needed an accurate manual and written language instead of their own arbitrary system. So a standard alphabet was published. The biggest drawback of manualism was that only people who knew the alphabet could communicate in detail with the deaf. This meant that the deaf and dumb were locked into an isolation from ordinary life. On the other hand oralism alone was not enough for a child to take his place in society on level terms with other children, and without a knowledge of sign language he could not communicate with the adult deaf and dumb who only knew this form of intercourse.[29]

However, from the 1860s moves began in Europe and America for a return of oralism. The training colleges for teachers of the deaf in Fitzroy Square, London (1872) and Ealing (1878) both favoured oralism, and by 1886 it was standard in French schools and was spreading to the United States.[30] Alexander Graham Bell set up the Alexander Graham Bell Institute in Washington to encourage oralism. In 1880 a conference of teachers held at Milan passed a resolution in favour of teaching the oral system and in 1888 the Royal Commission on the Education of the Deaf and Dumb said that all children where possible should be taught oralism.[31]

This was going too far for many teachers. A conference in Manchester held in October 1889 came out in favour of a combined system of oralism and manualism. A group of principals printed a leaflet which was distributed to people concerned in the education of the deaf and to *The Times*, which rejected the idea of complete oralism for they had found that children taught by this method were less accomplished in understanding English than the others. An oral class was begun in the Ulster Institution but James Beattie, the principal, and the committee believed that the oral method alone was too exclusive for general use.[32] Belfast preferred the combined system used there for many years.

Deaf and dumb children would come to the school without any knowledge of names by which objects could be identified so the teacher had first to give his pupil a knowledge of written alphabetic language. In an attempt to shorten this process the society published guides to show parents how to prepare their children. The alphabet in sign language was printed and was available to potential pupils. Education for the deaf mute was necessarily slow and the teachers were satisfied if they could communicate with their fellows by writing or signing and could understand the duties and relationships of life and above all to understand religious experience.

Blind children learned reading from books with raised letters of the system produced in the 1830s by Dr Gall and Mr Alston of Edinburgh. This system proved to be both expensive and tiring for the children's fingers and was superseded by Dr Thomas Moon's type produced in 1849 and adopted in Belfast in the 1860s. The Moon system has letters based on geometric shapes and being based on the alphabet was quick to pick up; it is still used today by people with limited movement, particularly the elderly. The blind Dr Thomas Armitage of London, a noted worker for the blind, investigated the Braille system as compared to the others and after 1868 when he founded the British and Foreign Blind Association, later the Royal National Institute for the Blind, Braille was produced by the association. It became the main system used by the blind and was used in Belfast from 1887.[33]

The children learned reading by

. . . passing their fingers over the spaces with a delicacy of touch and rapidity of motion of which no sufficient idea could be conveyed of description.

Arithmetic was learned

. . . at a metal table with certain indentations and movable figures and on this the children could do muliplication, practice, tret and tare, etc. In Geography, they had large wooden maps of the four quarters of the world with the surface identations to represent the shapes of countries which they could easily identify.[34]

As for the advances in teaching the blind to write 'regular and legible calligraphy' they came from the use of a Braille writing frame. This consisted of a grooved metal bed and over it was fitted a brass guide. This perforated guide was fixed into a light wood frame attached to a grooved bed by hinges. Paper was introduced between the frame and the grooved bed. The writing instrument was a blunt awl which produced a series of little marks on the paper.[35]

It was a mystery to most people how the children could communicate with their teachers and one another – particularly how blind children and deaf and dumb children could carry on a conversation. On open days this skill was displayed for the entertainment of the visitors.

One boy of each class was called up, and the Principal, holding in his hand an object, we asked the blind boy to ascertain from the other what it was. My silent telegraphed inquiry was instantly put by the fingers, as rapidly answered in the same way; and almost as readily as we might expect the answer from lads gifted with all their facilities, the reply from the blind boy was 'a snuff box'. In the same way, he could tell the hour by a watch.[36]

Every year there was a public examination held in June at the school to which the public were invited. This event was very important for it gave subscribers a chance to see how well their money had been spent and encouraged them to continue their contributions.

A synopsis of the examination for both the deaf and dumb and the blind was published annually. The following example was produced in 1859.

DEAF AND DUMB

1st CLASS: Average, about five years at school – may be examined in the following subjects:
1. Religion in general;
2. Sacred history;

3. Sacred geography – map of Palestine;
4. Geography in general;
5. History of England from the Plantagenets to the present time;
6. Science – astronomy, the Solar System;
7. Natural history – class mammalia, and eleven orders;
8. Arithmetic, to practice;
9. Composition on any common word.

7th CLASS: Average nine months – Know 1,000 nouns and several adjectives.

BLIND PUPILS

1st CLASS: May be examined on religion; any doctrinal or historical subject; epitome of English history; geography in general; English grammar to syntax; parsing; arithmetic, to involution and evolution of the square foot.

3rd CLASS: Scripture – Genesis, Exodus, and the four gospels. Geography – Natural divisions of land and water, countries in Europe and their chief towns. English grammar – parts of speech. Arithmetic – common rules, simple and compound. This gave the proficient pupils a good beginning. Vocal music taught to all.[37]

It seems very foreign to modern educational practice to exhibit children in this way, but James Anderson, a former blind pupil says that the children quite enjoyed appearing in front of the audience. Details of the examination were published every year. This account comes from 1859. The proceedings began with the blind children singing the rather inappropriate hymn 'The Lord doth give the blind their sight' and John Kinghan then said a few words repeating his view previously expressed on the problems of teaching the deaf mute. He encouraged the ladies and gentlemen present to suggest questions to be put to the children, only asking them to remember that the questions should be suited to their capacity.

The proficiency of the junior class of the deaf and dumb was tested first. Then the senior class was brought forward and examined by the chairman, H.H. McNeile of Parkmount, and other gentlemen. A few of these questions and answers were given.

By what names is the Son of Man called in the Bible? He is Jesus Christ, the Mediator, the Redeemer, the Good Shepherd, etc.

Who is the Lord Lieutenant of Ireland? The Lord Carlisle.

Write something about Oliver Cromwell. He was born at Huntingdon on 25th April, 1599. He ruled England four and three-quarter years after the Commonwealth. Oliver Cromwell was the son of a private gentleman. His dead body was raised and hung up at Tyburn, by order of Charles II A.D. 1660. He had two sons, Richard and Henry; and four daughters, Bridget, Elizabeth, Mary, and Frances.

What is an eclipse? A darkening of the face of the sun.

Then the blind children were examined:

What is faith? An assent of the mind to the truth.

How does a sinner come to God for justification? Through Jesus Christ.

What was the first of the House of Stuart? James I.

At the end of the examination Rev. Thomas Hamilton expressed his admiration of the performance of the children, the doxology was sung and the meeting separated.[38] The public examination was a great publicity exercise. Undoubtedly the best children were chosen to appear and they certainly displayed a high standard of intelligence and learning: a child without any handicap could not have achieved much better. It reflects the different demands of educating deaf and blind children. Questions asked of the deaf attracted factual answers which could be learned by rote while questions to the blind had concepts and ideas at their roots.

Industrial education was also important in the school for the prevailing belief was that it was better to enable the pupils to support themselves – 'In our institution we give our pupils, before leaving us, what is better than even a large fortune, – the means of living comfortably by an honest trade.'[39] In former times the blind traditionally were employed as itinerant musicians either fiddlers or harpers, at markets, fairs, weddings or wakes. This could lead to drunkenness with unfortunate consequences as when 'two blind fiddlers returning from a whiskey dance perished in the same ditch'. Deaf and dumb people used to be fortune-tellers.[40]

Just as there was a belief that it was harder to educate the deaf and dumb, so there was one that they found it easier to get work because they could learn skills more quickly than the blind. Because 'of their excellent manual skills' the deaf and dumb were taught crafts like shoe-making, carpentry, weaving, embroidery, dress-making and domestic service which they could learn by observation and practice. The blind were in fact more difficult to prepare for work and this difficulty was compounded in the early days when there were no blind boarders. There was a work department but the attendance of the blind was very bad owing to the poverty of the pupils and a lack of inducement to attend. In 1839 a system of apprenticeship was introduced, thirteen pupils to be indentured to the society for four years receiving 5s. per week or weekly board and lodgings. The committee undertook to pay the 5s. from the beginning.

Then the question arose of which goods should be produced and as hemp mats appeared to be in much demand in Belfast they were to be made. Baskets were also made. However, the sale of mats was very disappointing in spite of advertising and even sending two boys round from door to door with the samples of their work and printed hand-bills.[41] Because of the lack of markets for mats and for baskets work was switched to the spinning of twine and rope-making which had already been undertaken successfully in Glasgow. It had the other advantage that being in the open air and requiring constant exercise it was healthy and, being in great demand the product could easily be sold. But the uncertainty of Ulster weather meant that production was often interrupted and the workers had to go inside out of the rain.

In the case of the deaf and dumb the society did not intend to teach them actual trades in the school but rather to have them apprenticed when they left school. Their years in the institution were in effect a preparation for later vocational training, with some practical experience to make the transition easier, and the committees faced with ruined materials and poorly trained boys preferred to apprentice pupils to outside masters.[42] In Belfast in 1853 it was decided to dispense with industrial training and apprentice pupils outside to trades.[43]

The problem of finding work to support themselves really began when they returned to their respective areas. The alternative was the workhouse. In some years a survey of former pupils was carried out to see if and how they were employed. In 1858 auxiliaries throughout the province sent in reports on the progress of their local deaf and dumb and blind. Almost all of the blind former pupils attended church. There are no records of blind girls being employed, and they had at that time either to stay at home supported by their family or else go to the workhouse.[44] These satisfactory reports were very important to the committee and the subscribers because they justified the efforts made and the money raised to educate and train the handicapped children.

Not only were these young people able to support themselves, they could in later years support their elderly parents. It also meant that when John Kinghan asked for the purchase of a printing-press and a set of types for the deaf and dumb and a harmonium for the blind, the committee was prepared to look sympathetically at his request. The printing-press would anyhow be a great boon to such an institution which produced so much literature on its operations and relied so much on the printed word for the education of the deaf and dumb. Information also had to be disseminated to the auxiliaries and to subscribers. If the school had a press pupils could be initiated into the trade thus giving them an advantage if they sought work as printers. Printing was a particularly suitable trade for a deaf and dumb boy, for it gave him continuous practice in the use of written language, which he needed most.[45]

The pattern of education established in the first years of the institution continued right into the twentieth century. Most of the children came from the working class and were fortunate to be able to earn a living in competition with ordinary workers. The crafts which they learned were carefully chosen and it seems that apprenticeships were available especially in country districts. The religious training which they got in the institution enabled some to work in the mission field and the Christian ideology encouraged them to continue to go to church. The choice of pupil was taken seriously by the society. Detailed questionnaires based on those used in the Claremont Institution had to be completed. Although in the early years a few Ulster children went to Dublin, after the Tandragee agreement of 1845 made between the Ulster institution and the Dublin school, it was specified that in future all Ulster children went to Belfast and those from the other three provinces to Dublin.

There were several types of pupil both in College St and on the Lisburn Rd. The superior class were the parlour boarders who lived *en famille* with the principal. All of the principals earned extra money from one or two children whose parents were prepared to pay for better facilities, and this was the custom through all of the British institutions. Sometimes terms were arranged with the parents which allowed the principal to collect a percentage of the fees, the rest going to the institution, or he took all the fees and the children boarded at his private table.[46] The pupils would 'enjoy the privilege of additional instruction, and every attention will be paid by Mrs. Rhind to their domestic happiness.'[47]

In College St, there were only deaf and dumb boarder pupils, twenty-five at first and then fifty. The others were indigent boarders paid for by the auxiliaries or nominated by those who gave £300 to the Society. The Belfast Juvenile Association was particularly important in this area – in 1842 fourteen pupils were supported by the association and eight by the parent society.[48] After the move to Lisburn Rd there were almost no day scholars and the blind were admitted as boarders. Until then the blind were boarded out in the town depending on charity, which was unsatisfactory.

As is clear from the application forms most of the pupils were from the poorer classes. Of the first ten applications for deaf and dumb boarder pupils, four fathers were labourers, one was a smith in Mr Boyd's foundry, one had a twisting mill, one was a carpenter, two were farmers and one had been 'a farmer but having squandered the proceeds of two lands' had emigrated. Another father was a Causeway guide at Portrush but much addicted to intemperance.[49] Some families had been deserted by the fathers, like Robert Gilliland's father who left his wife to support a family of whom three were deaf and dumb. In 1892, the same sort of families were seeking admission for their children; there were five labourers, four farmers and a variety of other occupations, including a few workers from the Queen's Island and a mill-worker, out of a total of twenty-four applicants.[50]

These people were above the lowest class of paupers. In 1843 the Poor Law Amendment (Ireland) Act gave boards of guardians the right to support deaf and dumb and blind children out of the rates. They were reluctant to spend this money but they did keep a few children in the Ulster institution and a few in the catholic St Joseph's, Cabra, in Dublin.[51] After 1862 the committee of the society decided to admit all the indigent deaf and dumb and blind children of Ulster, a decision which necessitated an extension to the building and a consequent appeal for funds.[52] Before this decision was taken not all of the children could be taken in. In 1844, for example, only ten were chosen. Sometimes as few as two out of twenty were successful so election meetings could be unhappy. Committee members hated having to reject candidates. Rev. James Morgan said,

Oh, to see the parents use their utmost exertions – canvassing the members of Committee – forwarding numberless letters entreating us to consider such a case – and when we look upon them, and try to gauge the dimensions of their misery – and when the day comes, and we are obliged to send eighteen out of twenty home to their disconsolate parents – that believe me, is a day of sadness – of such sadness, that I have sometimes purposely stayed away to avoid the painful scene. Enlarge therefore your Institution.[53]

The distress seems very understandable. Less explicable was the reluctance of some parents to send their children to the Belfast school. President Thomas Hamilton of Queen's College asked why it should be necessary to force parents to send children to be educated, for one might have thought that the light of nature would have made them see it as a duty.[54] Rev. John Kinghan annually sent out large numbers of circulars asking parents and clergy to recommend pupils. Rev. Walter Riddall, a governor, said that experience had shown that parents were slow to move and 'only the strong arm of legal compulsion will secure what is desired.'[55]

To be accepted into the institution certain criteria had to be observed. All pupils had to be given religious instruction in either the Church of Ireland or presbyterian doctrines and attend either St George's or Fisherwick Place churches. This meant that any catholics had to be brought up as protestants. This was an accepted fact and seldom caused any trouble. One of the few cases which did lead to acrimony was that of the Cassidy family of Clogher, Co. Tyrone. Their child who had measles had been transferred from the institution to the workhouse infirmary. Although the parents were catholic, for the purposes of the Deaf and Dumb Institution the child had been registered as a protestant, and its parents now regretted that they had 'sent it to the institution to be proselytised'. They wanted the guardians to keep the child in the workhouse where the catholic chaplain would register it as catholic. The board clearly wanted nothing to do with the dispute and as Mr Tierney said 'Let the parents go to the Deaf and Dumb Institution for it. We have nothing to do with its sickness.' They decided to hand it back to the institution and let the parents collect it from there.[56]

Another requirement related to health. Pupils were supposed to have had cow-pock, and small-pox and be 'not idiotic'. Health was a continuing concern for the deaf and dumb were considered to be 'in general constitutionally delicate, and will not bear with impunity much indoor confinement', and the close proximity in dormitories increased the chances of illness.[57] The children were also expected to be free from fits, 'the evil' (scrofula) and every symptom of chronic, acute contagious and cutaneous disease.[58] As for the blind the illness which led to their condition was investigated, and the condition of the children was closely monitored.

In the early days of the institution one or two pupils died each year but health improved in later years. One very distressing case, that of Michael Connelly, was described in great and upsetting detail. Michael was a deaf and dumb boy from Drumanat, Co. Monaghan and a special fund had been started to send him to Belfast for treatment in 1843. He had been born deaf and dumb and to add to his problems he lost an eye at the age of nine from a spark from the fire, and a cataract formed over the other one.

Dr Thomas Read and Dr Henry Purdon, the society's physician and surgeon, examined the boy as soon as he arrived and were of the opinion that an operation to remove the cataract had a hope of success. Michael settled down apparently fairly happily and the other pupils, feeling that he was even more unfortunate than they, were helpful and caring. Several other doctors came to examine him and it was agreed that Dr Purdon would operate at the first opportunity. This operation would thus be performed on the eyes of a fully conscious twelve year old boy and the thought of it is truly terrible. He had other visitors; General d'Aguilar, one of the committee, brought his sword which frightened and upset him. Parties came to view the interesting case.

At this time (1 March) he was quite happy and had at last been taught to keep quiet on his seat. Preparations for the operation began. Dr Charles Purdon applied ointment to his eyes over a period of several days. On 10 April, Dr Purdon and Dr Hunt came to perform the operation, but 'the moment the instruments touched his eye-lids, the poor fellow struggled so violently, and he so firmly closed his eyes that Dr Purdon considered it necessary to abandon the attempt for the present'. On 12 May Dr Henry Purdon had agreed to make another attempt, so the principal, Charles Rhind, began to train for this by placing him on a mattress in the operating room and examining his eyes which made Michael very uneasy. When made to lie down with his head on a pillow he struggled and moaned so distressfully that he was lifted off and given a few figs. However, after some 'resolution' was shown by the principal he lay quiet. Then he was wrapped in a quilt leaving only his head out and his eyes were examined with an instrument.

This happened on 8 May. Michael was bound and placed on a mattress where he laughed with delight. Rhind touched his eyes with water and then a silver instrument, opening the lids and keeping them open for two minutes. Some of the assistants and older boys were in the room and also touched his eyes. For the next twelve days this was repeated. On 21 May, Michael complained of a headache and medicine was prescribed which he was reluctant to take and six leeches were applied to his temples. From 1 June his condition gradually deteriorated and on 8 June the poor child died.

It may have been a merciful release from what would have been a frighful experience. The whole episode aroused the interest of the public, particularly of the medical profession and it is hard to avoid the suspicion that the boy was to be experimented upon. It was such a *cause célèbre* that a special appendix to the annual report was published based on the day to day records of Charles Rhind, from his admission to his death.[59]

As well as health problems there were also behavioural lapses to be dealt with. William Thompson, a new pupil, was very unwilling to go to the school at all and 'has shown such a dislike to restraint that he could not be prevented from occasionally returning home without leave.' So he was allowed to go.[60] In 1839 two boys were publicly expelled by Rev. John Edgar for dishonesty 'under peculiarly aggravated circumstances.' There were some successes. Richard Davison, speaking at the A.G.M. in 1849, cited the case of

. . . a deaf and dumb boy sent to the Institution from a neighbouring Workhouse. He stated that such were his vicious propensities and ungovernable character that he was frequently obliged to be chained to a post like a wild bear till his rage was subdued. He had not been three months in the Institution until his temper became thoroughly subdued, and in proportion as religious and moral education was imparted, his character from day to day became humanised, and he is now one of the gentlest and best conducted boys in the Institution.[61]

The most important position in the school was that of principal. Although the committee kept a close observation of the work in the institution, the day to day running of the school devolved upon the principal. It was he who set the standards and planned the curriculum and it was he who had to produce results to satisfy the subscribers. Thus this appointment was the most vital task of the committee. In the early years there were no facilities for training teachers of the deaf and dumb in Ulster, so all teachers came from Claremont or from Great Britain.

During the nineteenth century there were six principals, George Gordon, Collier, Rev. John Martin, Charles Rhind, Rev. John Kinghan and John Tillinghast. For the first twenty-three years of the twentieth century James Beattie was in charge. Little is known of the first two. George Gordon was the brother of Samuel Gordon of Claremont, whose visit to Belfast in 1831 led to the establishment of the school. He only stayed in Belfast until 1834, and his success may be measured by the fact that there were only seven or eight pupils in the school. Collier, his successor, is equally unknown. During his two years at the school, blind pupils were admitted for the first time in 1835 and the school moved to new premises in College Street.[62] He left in 1836 for a more lucrative employment in England.[63]

The next three principals made their mark on the school in a variety of ways and Rev. John Kinghan's fifty years' service meant that his imprint remained for many years. Rev. John Martin appointed in 1836, had been presbyterian minister of Newtownstewart, but left parish work because of illness through overwork. It was he who supervised the admission of boarders in 1837. For the next four years the committee was, in general, satisfied with his performance, though in 1837 he had planned to leave the institution because of his low salary. He carried out his duties diligently and he had a peculiar tact for engaging the affections of the young.[64] However, Martin successfully applied for the mastership of Claremont to which he removed at the beginning of the summer vacation. Letters of appreciation were written by committee members.

The new head was Charles Rhind who had been for the previous eleven years assistant in the Old Kent Rd, London Asylum for the Deaf and Dumb. He was appointed at a salary of £80 per annum. He began well and at his suggestion some minor changes in the arrangements of school hours were made, principally allowing an extra hour in bed in the morning from October to March and a slight alteration in the signs used was also made. Otherwise the plan of education which Rev. John Martin had initiated remained. In the next few years Rhind continued to give satisfaction and tributes were paid to him by the committee.

In 1842, it was reported that he 'fulfils his onerous duties with an ability, tact and kindliness which cannot be surpassed'.[65] He pleased the committee by getting married in 1842 for it saved money if the principal's wife could help with the female boarders. But in 1846, these good opinions began to change. At the public examination in 1846 the report was unsatisfactory as a result of inefficient preparation, and the committee decided not to hold another until the standard improved.[66] A sub-committee examined six boys on 30 July in Rhind's presence. The results of this test were so unsatisfactory that only one pupil was allowed to leave with his education completed and he only because his father wanted him to be apprenticed to a watchmaker.[67] The amount of time spent by Rhind away from the school was queried. These absences were calculated by him and confirmed by Mr Turner, another member of staff, as between 140 and 150 days over and above vacations and deputations.

Rhind did not take kindly to this and he handed in a letter of resignation giving three months' notice under certain conditions. These were unacceptable to the committee who in turn gave Rhind notice of dismissal.[68] At this point relations deteriorated further. Two pupils, John Devine and Jane McCormick made 'allegations' to the assistant, John Kinghan, about the conduct of the examination and in response to these Charles Rhind said that neither could be believed on oath. He went on to make insinuations against the morality and good conduct of the pupils in general, but unfortunately, he was unable to substantiate these and the committee was naturally annoyed. As a result they asked Rhind to leave before the end of the month and any compensation would depend on his agreement to this.[69] He duly left. What is really surprising is his request on 1 October –

He is most anxious to procure from them whatever favourable expression of his qualifications as teacher of the Deaf and Dumb as they may think proper to furnish him with.[70]

The committee refused to do this.

However, Charles Rhind's experience did him no long-term harm. He set up a new school for the deaf in Aberystwyth in 1847, and became principal of the Edinburgh Asylum in 1855.[71] In 1878, he took holy orders as chaplain to the Royal Association in aid of the Deaf and Dumb in London.[72]

In September 1846, an advertisement appeared in the local papers for a head master, qualified to instruct deaf mutes and competent to act as principal of the establishment; he would not have to teach the blind. In response to this advertisement Rev. John Martin reappeared. He had only stayed in the Claremont Institution until 1843, when he went back into parish work, with an excellent recommendation from its committee. Martin was unanimously chosen by the appointments committee. His second period in the Belfast school was far from happy. The charges against him of cruelty (examined earlier in this chapter), had to be investigated. Although the committee completely exonerated John Martin, he had to undergo unpleasant experiences and life in the school became more difficult for him. The secretary of the society proposed to submit the charges of cruelty to the magistrates and Martin immediately offered to resign – an offer refused by the committee.[73] The charges of cruelty were withdrawn but an examination had to be held to assess the principal's competence.

The examination completely vindicated Martin.

The result of the whole examination thus conducted has been a thorough conviction upon the minds of the Committee that the whole mode of instruction pursued in the Institution is eminently efficient and successful.[74]

In spite of his exoneration, Rev. John Martin found life at the institution disagreeable. The pupils' insubordination, described earlier in this chapter, meant that he could not remain in full control nor maintain discipline. In 1853, John Martin and his family left Belfast and moved to the United States. He was the victim of the malice and spite of Professor Young and his son.

Rev. John Kinghan, head assistant of the institution, was among nine candidates for the position of principal and his unanimous selection by the committee began forty years of commitment to the welfare of the deaf and dumb and the blind in this important post. He had originally been appointed to the school in 1845 as teacher of the blind but requested a transfer to teaching the deaf and dumb when Rev. John Martin returned from Claremont.[75] He regarded this as a promotion, partly because it was considered more difficult and thus attracted a higher salary and partly because the education of the deaf and dumb was the basis of the Ulster Society.

In 1849 he decided to leave teaching and devote himself to study for the presbyterian ministry – a decision greeted with regret by the committee. However, in 1849, Brown, the assistant secretary, left and Kinghan was appointed to this post with reduced hours and a reduced salary because he felt that he could combine this job with his attendance at his college course.[76] Rev. Kinghan duly became a minister though he was never ordained in a church. His opportunity came when John Martin left, and the good opinion of him held by committee members assured his choice as principal. The committee of twelve gentlemen under the chairmanship of the lord bishop of the diocese had no doubts about his suitability and the local press agreed.

Kinghan was regarded with admiration by his committee and supporters and indeed the institution made great progress during his term of office. His health began to break down in 1878 and from then until his death in 1895 he gradually relinquished active participation in the running of the school. Because of the esteem in which he was held by the governors they persuaded him to retain his connection with the society. In 1878 Rev. Kinghan gave up part of his salary as he would not be teaching full-time and his money could therefore be put towards paying a very good assistant. J. S. Hutton, principal for twenty-one years at the Institute for the Deaf and Dumb at Halifax, Nova Scotia, became vice-principal, while John Kinghan remained principal. Hutton did the actual work of teaching and administration while the principal held an honorary post.[77] In 1882, J. S. Hutton returned to Canada and was replaced by James Beattie, a former teacher at the school, 'an old and valued assistant'.

In 1880 Kinghan had had to give up teaching altogether, but he became manager and assistant secretary though by 1884 he was too ill even to attend the annual general meeting. He then had to give up the management of the institution though he still remained principal and superintendent, prepared to assist in carrying out the business of the society in correspondence and financial arrangements. In January 1885, John Bryden who had been five years assistant in Glasgow, three years in Belfast, two years head assistant in Liverpool, and for the last nine years the principal in the Edinburgh Institution, was elected out of a large number of well-qualified candidates, as head master.

Certainly John Kinghan was successful in business, for this presbyterian minister left £48,800, a fortune in those days. It would be very interesting to know just how he accumulated such a sum. When managing the financial affairs of the institution, he was told by the committee to invest money at 4 per cent but he actually invested it in Sinclair's bacon factory in Chicago – J. & T. Sinclair were the largest provision merchants in Belfast at that time, and strongly presbyterian too. These shares produced 10 per cent and John Kinghan invested his own money as well as the school's. He also kept pigs fed on the swill from the school meals, and parlour boarders added to his income.[78] Out of his fortune,[79] he only left £200 to the institution which he had served for so long: the interest on this was to go towards assistance to the blind when they left school.[80]

The governors were pleased with his stewardship and in tributes paid after his death to his ability in managing the affairs of the institution he was described as 'amply endowed with the business ability characteristic of his family, he administered its affairs with remarkable practical sagacity.'[81] Whatever the Ulster Institution was in 1895 it had been made by Rev. John Kinghan, and a bust of him was commissioned and placed in the entrance hall of the school.

Another blow came to the staff in June 1895, when Bryden, the head master was struck down with 'paralysis of the brain' and the governors had to dispense with his services with a pension of £72 per annum.[82] On the recommendation of Dr Thomas Gallaudet, president of the Deaf Mute College, Washington, an American, Joseph Tillinghast of Boulder, Montana was appointed. Tillinghast was born in North Carolina in 1871 and took the normal course at Gallaudet College for the Deaf, Washington. He taught in Boulder, Montana where he reorganised the school, and he was able to get the state legislature of Montana to pass a new law for schools for the deaf. He then raised funds for the building of a new school.[83] It was a tribute to his reputation and ability that he was able to get an important job such as that in Belfast at such a young age. His main value to the governors was that he could introduce the combined system of 'oralism' and 'manualism' which had come into use in 1878.[84] The governors were pleased with his innovations: 'their anticipation as to the wisdom of that appointment have been fully justified.'[85]

These changes were mainly in the field of industrial training – Slojd carpentry, woodworking for the boys and needlework and dressmaking for the girls. The large school room was divided into separate rooms by means of blackboard partitions and three additional classrooms were put on. Some of the staff attended courses in England to qualify them for this work. Four of the girls were trained as laundresses, the blind learned mat-weaving and clay-modelling and a new gym instructor with a certificate from the National Physical Recreation Society was appointed. Time spent in physical training was therefore much extended. The reading room was well supplied with newspapers, magazines, etc. Tillinghast continued to give satisfaction until 1900 when he resigned because he wanted to return to the United States. The new principal was James Beattie, who had been an assistant since 1872, leaving briefly to go as a missionary to the deaf and dumb adults in Manchester before returning as head assistant in 1882. During the interregnum on the death of Rev. Kinghan he managed the school very successfully and he won the Gold Medal of the National Association for Teaching the Deaf in 1900.[86] He met with the approval of the governors until his retirement in 1923.

The post of principal was no sinecure. Not only had he to live on the premises and supervise the education and welfare of the pupils, he also had to go on deputations to country auxiliaries and conduct the annual public examination. Certainly the Belfast principal would hardly have had the time to carry out the extra activities of the head of St Joseph's, Cabra, who had 'too many occupations; for besides teaching in the school, he keeps a grocer's shop and postoffice receiver, and is also a coal factor.'[87] The Ulster Institution was fortunate in its principals – between them Rev. John Kinghan and James Beattie gave over one hundred years of devoted service. Rhind and Rev. John Martin fell victim to internecine disputes but their work was mostly satisfactory. The ethos of the school was formed by these men.

The assistants are shadowy figures emerging only occasionally into the limelight as in the notorious Young case or when like Messrs. Kinghan and Beattie, they rose to be principal. W.E. Harris appointed assistant in 1874 became superintendent of the adult mission to the Adult Deaf and Dumb in 1914. In the early years the staff consisted of a master, matron and an assistant teacher and workmistress, but as the school grew, so did the numbers on the staff, so by the 1890s there was a principal, head master, five assistants for the deaf and dumb, and two for the blind.

Teachers of the handicapped in the nineteenth century got less pay than other teachers, in spite of their incomparably more difficult work – a sign of the lack of importance given to the disabled. It was neither an easy nor a well-paid job. Joseph Watson, headmaster of the Kent Rd, London school described the assistants as 'lion-hearted'. He asked,

If at times they were themselves cruel, who dare criticise them? In that unrelenting, unrelieved atmosphere of horrible habits and barbarous noises, of long toil for but slight satisfaction and reward, we may well wonder that any of them retain their sanity.[88]

They had to undergo a seven year apprenticeship. They were paid £15 for the first year, with an additional £5 for each successive year thus reaching £45 on completion of their apprenticeship. Then they were re-engaged at £50 per annum with free board and lodging. As time passed the education of the deaf mutes gradually became a science and teachers did receive special training.

The household staff were expected above all to be 'respectable' and preferably protestant as advertisements for employment made clear.

Wanted for a large Institution in Belfast, a Lady as Matron, Protestant, aged about forty, practical knowledge of nursing, superintendence of kitchen, laundry, etc. necessary; commencing salary 60 with board, apartments, laundry and medical attendance – application by letter only, stating qualifications and experience, with references addressed Honorary Secretary, Ulster Institution for the Deaf and Dumb and Blind, Belfast, to be received on 3rd August. Honorary Secretary, A. D. Lemon, W. H. H. Lyons.[89]

Generally employees gave satisfaction and there are no records of major disputes.

The staff were certainly important but without the support of the committee there would not have been a school at all. During the Victorian and Edwardian periods they took their responsibilities seriously. Money had to be raised, publicity organised, visits made both to the school and to auxiliaries and the annual examination attended, in addition to general supervision of the institution. In 1840, the committee passed a series of resolutions which laid down the duties which they were expected to carry out.

A member was expected to spend a considerable time on the affairs of the institution and as the committee consisted not of the leisured aristocracy, but the businessmen and clergy of Belfast, this was no small burden. These were men of integrity and high repute. Printed extracts from the minutes of the committee, 7 January 1840 listed their duties.

. . . resolved unanimously that, in order to secure such a regular supervision of the school and all other matters in connection with this Institution, as may promote its general prosperity, the Secretary be requested to notice the several members of the Committee in succession so that they may be prepared to visit the Institution, in weekly rotation throughout the year, and report thereon; and that for the better accomplishment of this object, the Secretary do furnish a printed form containing queries and space for remarks, which is to be filled up by each such visitor, and laid before the Committee at its monthly meeting.

The visitors were asked to report on the 'aspect' of the school, the state of the pupils, the cleanliness of the building, the children's food and to suggest any improvements needed. Often the public was not aware of the amount of work put in by committee members. But perhaps the most difficult task of all was to awaken the public mind to the importance of the work done by the society and indeed it was often a thankless job.

The most visible part of its work was seen at the annual general meeting and the public examination, the most important events in the society's year. At the annual general meeting the report was read, usually by the secretary. At these meetings the committee proposed and passed a series of prepared resolutions which gave the opportunity for prominent supporters to express their appreciation of the work of the society. From the beginning of the work, there were four trustees who were appointed by the committee. However in 1885, the Endowed Schools Commission requested the institution to lodge a scheme for the future conduct of the school. The committee duly drew up a plan which they submitted to the commission and Rev. Kinghan appeared before them in Belfast on 12 and 13 October, 1886. The scheme was accepted and the society legally became a corporation which did away with the necessity and expense of appointing trustees. From 1888 the committee was replaced by a board of governors of eleven presbyterians and eleven episcopalians, but the change in name made no difference to the composition of it.[90]

The society had most devoted secretaries. Alex Dickey and D. Clarke were joint secretaries of the original Deaf and Dumb school but they were replaced in 1837 by James Shaw of the linen firm of E. Shaw & Co., 72 Waring St, who lived at Ballyoran, Dundonald. He had become the head of his family at an early age and when he lived in Dublin had been involved in work for the deaf and dumb. He and his brothers were secretaries of the Juvenile Auxiliary to the Claremont Institution.[91] When they moved to Belfast they all joined the Ulster Society and James Shaw was secretary and trustee for twenty-two years – 'he found it in its infancy and left it in the maturity of manhood, he found it with £120 per annum and left it with between £2,000 and £3,000 per annum.'[92] On his death in 1869, his brother William of Marmion, Holywood took over with Charles Lanyon, as joint secretaries. On William's death in 1883, another brother C. W. Shaw, already a trustee became secretary – the third consecutive holder of the office from the Shaws. The committee was always anxious to emphasise the Ulster aspect of the society rather than looking on it as a Belfast operation. A vital part of the work was the network of auxiliaries which stretched over the province. The auxiliaries acted as collectors of funds and were hosts to the deputations which travelled round each year.

In 1842, there were forty-two auxiliaries in Ulster and they steadily increased in number over the years: in 1862 there were 129 and in 1897 there were 143. They collected a great deal of money – only £29.7.0 in 1837 but £887.10.0 in 1844 and £1,152.12.9 in 1884 though subscriptions fell to £1,090.0.4 in 1888. One of the main duties of principal, committee and pupils was to go on deputation round the towns which supported the society, to give the opportunity for sub-scribers actually to see where their money went. The deputations would be away for two or three days at a time and the pupils quite enjoyed the change in routine from lessons. It was no light task for there could be eleven deputations in a year with ninety-nine meet-ings in different venues. One consisted of Rev. T. B. Price, rector of Newtownards, Rev. Kinghan and two pupils and held meetings in the week beginning 30 July 1855. Their programme was punishing in the distances to be travelled –

Monday, 30 July	Faughanvale	1 p.m.
Monday, 30 July	Londonderry	7 p.m.
Tuesday, 31 July	Newtownlimavady	12 o'clock noon
Tuesday, 31 July	Coleraine	7 p.m.
Wednesday, 1 August	Portstewart	12 o'clock noon
Wednesday, 1 August	Portrush	7 p.m.
Thursday, 2 August	Bushmills	1 p.m.
Thursday, 2 August	Ballycastle	7 p.m.
Friday, 3 August	Cushendall	12 o'clock noon
Friday, 3 August	Glenarm	7 p.m.
Saturday, 4 August	Larne	12 o'clock noon[93]

At least the journeys were made in holiday time in the summer.

The deputations followed the same pattern in all the towns and the one to Enniskillen in 1844 can serve as a typical example. The Hon. and Rev. Henry Ward (son of Lord Bangor) and Charles Rhind attended with a blind boy, Adam McClelland (later a clergyman in New York) and a deaf and dumb boy, Charles Dogherty, both pupils of the institution. Rhind suggested that any of the friends present should ask the questions to remove any suspicion of a deliberate preparation for a public examination. The first test was put to Adam

McClelland on a gospel in raised type, where the boy opened the book at the page he was told, and read the page.

A lady near the platform was handed the book, she opened it at random and the boy identified the page and read from it even after a handkerchief was spread over the print. The boy then went over what he had read and answered a number of questions put by the examiner. Rhind explained that the deaf and dumb before education had no idea of God or reward or punishment, and the only natural disposition they had was a facility to imitate. It was through this that they were taught to write, by the teacher holding the boy's hand and causing him to make letters and words placed before them. He demonstrated the London method of teaching them to speak by feeling the vibrations on the teacher's throat. The boy answered questions by writing on a board. The principal then showed a variety of knitted work for sale which had been done by the deaf and dumb and the blind girls after school, and a book written by a deaf, dumb and blind pupil in America describing her progress of instruction whose sale proceeds would go to her support.

Henry Ward then addressed the meeting appealing for those present to support the Ulster Institution rather than Claremont. At the end of the meeting a total of £6.9.1 was handed in – £1.12.1 collected at the meeting and the rest coming from Captain Beaufoy's subscription and five collecting cards.[94] Deputations were held in town halls, market houses, court houses or school rooms, whichever would give most space so that as many friends as possible could attend. The principal or an assistant teacher always went while the other members varied but were always clergymen. Details of the deputations were published in the local papers. They continued until 1928 even after the 1923 Education Act for Northern Ireland integrated the school into the state system. Although the exhibition of these children is distasteful to modern educationalists it was regarded as being very important. Auxiliaries thus visited helped to provide for children who needed assistance with the burden of clothing themselves as the institution demanded, for no-one was admitted without the required uniform.

The raising of funds was a continuing necessity. In the first years of its existence the society had only a small income – for the twenty-one months ending in December 1832, before the blind children were taken in, it ran to £72.5.3.[95] This income increased quickly rising to £2,200 by 1844 and to £3,659.7.11 in 1903. At the beginning the largest amount of money came from the auxiliaries. Income comprised:

Table 3.2

1844 INCOME

	£	s.	d.
Balance	870	0	5
Subscriptions and donations	211	3	0
Contributions from auxiliaries	887	10	10
Congregational collections	115	3	6
One year's tuition, M. Leslie	2	2	0
Payments from Juvenile Association	114	7	6
TOTAL	£2,200	7	3

Over the rest of the century amounts collected rose steadily but by 1903, the sources had changed. Charity sermons had disappeared and the auxiliaries' contributions, while very important, were smaller than the money coming from fees paid by the guardians. Much of the income came from good investments. The committee had bought more land on the Lisburn Rd than was needed for the institution and they could charge substantial rents for this as the road became more developed. Rev. John Kinghan proved a wise investment manager and in collaboration with the committee bought and sold securities. £5,000 was invested in mortgages and landed property in Ulster and £6,000 in United States bonds and railways.[96]

Table 3.3

1903 INCOME	£	s.	d.
Donations	10	0	0
Bequests	390	10	9
Subscriptions	72	18	6
Contributions from auxiliaries	759	13	7
Dividends	570	0	5
Rents	724	11	7
Fees	901	0	1
Sales	11	13	2
Bank interest	4	19	6
Income tax refund	144	11	9
Balance	60	2	7
TOTAL	£3,659	7	11

Money was raised in other ways as well. It was very exclusive to be a life governor which could be achieved by a donation of £300 or £200 with an annual subscription of £5, giving the donor the right to nominate an indigent boarder pupil. Often the position came as a result of a legacy. In 1883 the life governors were:

LADY JOHNSON, Belfast by Donation of FIVE HUNDRED POUNDS per the late Thomas Hughes Esq., Executor of the late Thomas Hughes Jun., Esq.;
THE RIGHT HON LORD LURGAN, by Donation of THREE HUNDRED POUNDS, per the first Lord Lurgan;
HENRY HUGH McNEILE, Esq., J.P., Parkmount, Belfast, by a Donation of FOUR HUNDRED POUNDS, per the late John McNeile Esq.;
JOHN MULHOLLAND, Esq., J.P., D.L., M.P., Ballywalter Pk, by Donation of THREE HUNDRED AND FIFTY POUNDS, per the late Andrew Mulholland, Esq.;
THE TRUSTEES OF THE LATE BISHOP STEARNE'S CHARITIES, by Donation of THREE THOUSAND, ONE HUNDRED AND FIFTY POUNDS;
THOMAS GREER, Esq., J.P., Seapark, Belfast, by a Donation of THREE HUNDRED POUNDS, per the late John Owden, Esq.;
GEORGE ORR WILSON, Esq., Monkstown, by Donation of FIVE HUNDRED POUNDS, per the late Mrs Margaret Wilson, of Eaton Square, London.

These were the biggest contributors but in addition there were over two hundred life members who had given at least £10 – some gave more than £100. There were also life members as executors of some large estates.

Gentlemen on the committee were prominent in collecting money throughout the districts of Belfast, at least in the early years of the society's existence. Ladies were also active in the work of raising money, particularly in organising and taking stalls at the numerous bazaars held in Belfast. These sales were usually held after the annual general meeting in December and were described with enthusiasm in local papers.

Belfast citizens were generous in support of charity though Richard Davison, M.P., criticised the way in which the funds were distributed because almost as much went to foreign missions as to local needs –

. . . of these liberal and noble contributions of the people of Belfast, old and young, the Ulster Institution received the miserable sum of £330 while the same inhabitants give annually to the foreign missions £1,350, to the Society for Promoting Christianity among the Jews £439 and the Town Mission.[97]

What the committee really wanted to establish the finances of the society in a secure position, was for the boards of guardians of the province to carry out their statutory right to send destitute and afflicted children to the institution and support them out of the rates. Unlike idiot and imbecile children who had no state help in Ireland though they had in England,[98] an act of 1843 provided:

The Guardians of any Union may send any destitute poor deaf and dumb or blind child, under the age of eighteen years, to any institution for the maintenance of the deaf and dumb and blind, which may be approved of by the Commissioners, with the consent of the parents or guardians of any such child, and may pay the expense of its maintenance there out of the rates.[99]

This seems to have given the committee what they wanted but there were two problems associated with it. First, the burden of support fell on just the electoral divisions to which the child belonged and second, the definition of 'destitute' was not straightforward. In 1867 the committee wrote to the Poor Law Commissioners asking if some children of labourers, tradespeople and very small farmers who were unable to pay for them could be considered 'destitute' within the meaning of the Poor Law Amendment Act of 1843. The commissioners' reply gave no more information for they said that they left the definition to the boards of guardians themselves.[100] This therefore allowed considerable latitude to the guardians and as they had not been exercising their powers before they were unlikely to change.

Some unions did pay £12 per annum for the support of pauper children for three years, though they were allowed to pay up to £15 per annum. In 1868 the Ballymena, Dungannon, Magherafelt, Banbridge and Belfast unions agreed to pay for children.[101] Things improved after 1876 when the Poor Law Amendment (Ireland) Act allowed unions to charge the entire union not just the electoral divisions of the children's parents, which spread the burden. Some unions would only bear half of the cost so the institution had to subsidise these pupils. Pupils could be supported by the union even if they were not in the workhouse or their parents in receipt of relief, but of course some guardians refused to pay at all.[102]

In the 1890s the institutions throughout Ireland were still not full. Census figures confirm that there were many children uneducated by the institutions. In 1851, the census identified in Ulster 425 deaf and dumb and 295 blind of the right age to attend school but only 60 were in the institution.[103] In 1871 there were approximately 1,666 deaf and dumb children in Ireland of whom 478 were in Deaf and Dumb Institutions, 336 paid for by the poor rates. In Ulster there were 300 deaf and dumb, 57 deaf not dumb and 396 blind of whom 138 were on the books of the institution in 1891, showing an increase from 1871 of over one hundred in the blind and a decrease of 60 in the number of deaf and dumb.[104] The figures given in the censuses of pupils supposed to be in the school and those actually there, listed in the annual reports did not always tally and this can be explained by the removal of children in the middle of a year and absence through illness, or family needs for the children's labour at home.

However, the census figures did not distinguish the numbers of blind children of school age who were not being educated. Nor did they classify the religion of school age children so it was hard for the governors to find out how many eligible pupils they were missing. It was a small number of children who came to the school, but it was from choice that parents kept them away for all could have been taken in.

For many years after primary education was made compulsory and after acts were based for Scotland in 1890 and England and Wales in 1893 which made education compulsory for the deaf and dumb and the blind, there was no such provision for Ireland. This fact was greatly resented by the governors and the people of Ulster because it meant that parents could simply neglect to send their children, thus depriving the society of funds.[105] Every year there were demands that an act should be passed for Ireland even if it would cost money. H. J. Shepperd, assistant secretary of the society, wrote to the *Belfast News Letter* commenting that in response to a question by Charles Craig in the House of Commons, Walter Long, the Irish chief secretary, stated that £12,069 had been spent by the National Board of Education in teaching Irish as a special subject, while for half this sum 'which many people regard as public money wasted', education for the deaf could be undertaken.[106] In July 1905, the Irish Education (Afflicted Children) Bill was introduced in the commons with provisions similar to those applying to England and Scotland where local authorities had to provide for the education of deaf and dumb and the blind paid for out of the rates. Disgracefully the bill was dropped after its second reading leaving Ireland alone with no state provision for the education of the deaf.[107] The issue was still unresolved when the new state of Northern Ireland was set up in 1920.

Were the institutions successful? How did the children feel about them? What did the members of the societies feel that they achieved?

It is difficult to answer these questions – what does 'success' in the field of disability mean? The disability still remains but what the Ulster Society did was to ameliorate the condition of the children and help them to keep their self-respect by training them to earn their own living. The alternative was too often the hated workhouse. Even though not all of those eligible took advantage of the facilities, the institution was still important. Again it is hard to measure the reaction of the beneficiaries because of their difficulty in communication.

A letter written by one of the first boarders, Robert Gilliland, in 1839 was published by the society. He wrote to Charles Rhind of his ignorance before he went to the institution and went on –

I am happy that I was brought to this Institution . . . .. I am very grateful to the subscribers for placing me into this Institution; I wish I could speak to the Gentlemen and Ladies to thank them . . .. I hope that more Deaf and Dumb children will be brought to this Institution. I very pity them, because they are very ignorant . . .. I like to write letter to you, because I am very fond of you, you taught me many things, and you can teach the others many things.[108]

An uncorrected composition after three and a half years at school (age 13).

While it would be wrong to accept this at face value – would the society print an attack on itself? – it does appear that there was a general belief that the school was good. The pupils were certainly no worse off than if they had not gone to the Ulster Institution and many were much better. The visitors who went to the school on public occasions were pleased that

. . . the personal appearance of the pupils was highly satisfactory, whilst their deportment towards their teachers and each other leads them to conclude, that the treatment which they receive must have been a due combination of authority and kindness.[109]

James Anderson recalls that when pupils looked back on their education they felt that while life was often harsh they had gained greatly from it. Mr Beattie reported in 1902 that the conduct of the children was admirable: there were no flagrant breaches of discipline or delinquency. He said that no effort was spared to render their lives happy. Their material wants were well looked after, they had healthy exercise, every legitimate freedom was given to them, an interest was taken in their games and pastimes, sympathy and ready help was available 'for their childish grievances and trifling calamities.'[110] The dean of Connor (Rev. Charles Seaver) testified that 'pupils were instructed in an earnest and loving way with patience and kindness.' As for its effects, Miss Mary Hobson of the Workshops for the Blind, said 'undoubtedly morally, physically and intellectually those who had the advantage of being trained in early life turn out better in the other institutions.'[111]

Missions to the Adult Deaf and Dumb of Ireland.

President:
The LORD BISHOP OF CORK.

Vice-President:
W. P. BLUNDEN, Esq.

Patronesses:

The COUNTESS OF BANDON.
Mrs. BLUNDEN, Bonnetstown House, Kilkenny.

Lady MARY ALDWORTH.
Miss HUMPHREYS, Miltown House, Strabane.

Committee:

The Very Rev. the DEAN OF THE CHAPEL ROYAL.
Rev. Canon PEACOCKE, Monkstown.
Rev. W. E. BURROUGHS, Kingstown.
Rev. S. G. COCHRANE, Ballyshannon.
Rev. J. H. KENNEDY. Stillorgan.
Rev. J. POTTER, Londonderry.
HUGH GALBRAITH, Esq., Dublin.

M. F. G. HEWSON, Esq., Dublin.
DAVID STUART, Esq., Ballyshannon.
C. J. TREDENNICK, Esq., Bundoran.
Miss BINGER, Kingstown.
Miss HYNDMAN, Dublin.
Miss MAGEE. Monkstown.
Mrs. WEBB, Mallow.
Miss WAGGETT, Kingstown.

Central Executive:

Rev. Canon BRADSHAW, Roscommon.
Rev. THOMAS REILLY, Killashee, Longford.
Rev. WM. WELWOOD, Kilcommoch,   ,,

Mrs. ST. G. JOHNSTON, Rathcline.
Mrs. KINGSTONE, Mosstown, Longford (Hon. Sec. and Treas.)

Northern Executive:

The Very Rev. the DEAN OF DOWN.
Rev. W. RIDDALL. Belfast.
Lady EWART. Belfast.
Mrs. FOY, Belfast.

Miss HOBSON. Belfast.
MISS ANNIE HOBSON, Belfast (Hon. Sec.)
Miss MULHOLLAND, Hillsborough.
Miss W. TREDENNICK.

Miss GODFREY, Belfast (Hon. Treas.)

Southern Executive:

The Ven. the ARCHDEACON OF CORK.
Rev. Canon GALWAY, Cork.
Rev. Canon HARLEY, Cork.
Rev. Canon POWELL.

Miss AUSTEN, Blair Castle, Cork (Hon Tres.)
Miss SCOTT, Cork.
Miss WARREN, Cork.
Rev. GEORGE HERRICK, Kilroan (Hon. Sec.)

N.B.—Members of the Executive Committees are *ex-officio* Members of the General Committee.

Hon. Secretary and Treasurer:
Mrs. KINGSTONE, Mosstown, Longford.

Subscriptions payable to Bank of Ireland, Longford.

Missionary:
FRANCIS MAGINN.

Lady Superintendent of Mission Hall:
Miss W. TREDENNICK.

Committee of the Missions to the Adult Deaf and Dumb in Ireland 1889.

'Tell them of Jesus the Mighty to save':

MISSIONS TO THE ADULT DEAF AND DUMB

The Institution for the Education of the Deaf and Dumb and the Blind did its best to prepare the pupils for life after school in a difficult and often uncaring environment where their handicaps severely reduced their chances of being self-supporting. Their training and education were not yet completely finished and, in the case of deaf children, their communication skills were limited. It was hard for them to integrate into society and church life, a very important part of contact in rural Ulster communities. Children educated in Belfast scattered to their homes in all parts of the province at the age of thirteen or fourteen, which usually meant an end to industrial training for the blind and an end to language development for the deaf who left school with an ability in English equal to that of a normal eight or ten year old, so that the scope of their reading was very small.

The bible and most books were as if written in a foreign language and it was widely believed that if efforts were not made to keep them from temptation they would sink into a mere criminal existence, or at the very least experience a distressing isolation. Even in the towns there were few deaf people with whom the former pupils could continue to communicate so the skills they had learned in school soon atrophied. In fact it was reputed that they were a highly dangerous class, violent-tempered, drunken, immoral and criminal and one policeman went so far as to describe deaf mutes as amongst the most dangerous groups he had to deal with.[1] He exaggerated; but the story of the Workshops for the Blind shows that the handicapped were no better than the rest of society.

The people who had helped to educate deaf children were especially concerned about their spiritual life. Because of this, missions to the adult deaf and dumb were opened from the beginning of the nineteenth century. The first adult missions in Britain were founded in Glasgow (1822), Edinburgh (1835) and Manchester (1850).[2] The first Irish mission was conducted by Dr Thomas Overend in Dublin in 1826 but it took another thirty years before it was followed in Belfast. In America Dr Thomas Gallaudet of Washington, Messrs Morris and Hewson in Dublin and Rev. John Kinghan in Belfast gathered adult deaf and dumb men and women together for public worship.[3]

John Kinghan opened an adult Sunday school for former pupils of his school. He feared that they might lapse from church attendance because, unlike the blind, they could not take part in the service. At first there were only eleven in his class which held its opening meeting on 18 May 1857 in a school-room in King St.[4] It moved from there to another school-room in Gt Victoria St but these temporary expedients were far from satisfactory and Kinghan determined to build a hall for the deaf and dumb. A fund to make this possible was started in 1873, and by 1878 enough money had been subscribed to go ahead and find a site. The site which was chosen at the corner of the Donegall Rd and Sandy Row cost £250, the building of the hall and caretaker's house cost £410 and the total finally came to £722.5.4½. Donations of £482.5.0 came in from a variety of sources[5]: the deaf and dumb themselves collected £36.16.9.[6] The founder of the mission, John Kinghan was worried by his failure to raise all the money needed at one time but the building went ahead. It is quite sad to know that after all his work he was disappointed at the appearance of the hall, called 'the Bethel'.[7] Once established the Sunday school was run by Rev. Kinghan and other teachers from the school on strictly non-sectarian lines – protestant of course.

However, the Bethel provided a very limited service. It gave the deaf an opportunity to worship God but what they needed was more social contact with people who shared their problems and could understand them. The two services held on Sunday left 'the deaf mutes as sheep without a shepherd' for the rest of the week.[8] They were isolated from contact with the rest of the society yet they had nowhere to meet for 'recreation or secular improvement.'[9] Besides, the Bethel was in a bad neighbourhood and the deaf mutes, particularly the girls, were distressed by being harassed on their way to and from meetings. Services were disrupted by roughs bursting in the door, throwing stones, jeering and hooting so that several times the police had to be called. These difficulties were largely overcome by the Mission Hall for the Adult Deaf and Dumb (later known as the Ulster Institute for the Deaf) which opened in Belfast in 1888.

The founder of the hall was Miss Wilhelmina Tredennick, daughter of Col. T. Tredennick of Fortwilliam, Co. Donegal, and a cousin of Lavens M. Ewart.[10] The beginning of her work was near her home when she saw the deterioration of two deaf and dumb apprentices after they returned from the institution and lost interest in their trade. She wanted to help them so much that she went for six months to a school in Bristol to learn sign language in order to communicate with them. From this small beginning she founded in 1873 the Deaf and Dumb Christian Association with only thirty members and an income in its first year of just £10. Annual meetings and services were held at Ballyshannon to which delegates from England came and where the work began to expand. In Belfast in 1876 forty deaf and dumb people used to meet for worship, first at Wellwood Place school and later in the Magdalene church, but this was an unorganised effort.

Francis Maginn, later the first deaf missionary of the mission hall, went with his father to live and preach in Cork and set up a committee of the association there. In 1885 the association was reorganised to become the Mission to the Adult Deaf and Dumb of Ireland under the presidency of the bishop of Cork, run by a committee composed entirely of Church of Ireland members. This mission worked all over Ireland, with the exception of Dublin where Hewson had already set up his own structure. It was through this work that Maginn moved to Belfast where he was kindly received at the Ulster Institution, and even invited to preach at the Bethel by Rev. John Kinghan. In 1887 Miss Tredennick visited Belfast and when her father died in 1888 she made her home there. So the two most important figures in the Belfast Mission Hall came to the town at the same time.

The Mission to the Adult Deaf and Dumb of Ireland had a northern and a southern executive, the northern consisting mainly of Belfast people. The committee wanted to have a clear framework of operations and so the rules of the society were published together with its objectives and rules for the management of the hall.

Rules of the society:
The name of this society was 'The Mission to the Adult Deaf and Dumb of Ireland'.
Its object was to promote the welfare of the adult deaf mutes of Ireland.
A general committee of forty members from all of Ireland met once annually.
The mission was divided into two districts. The northern comprised the dioceses of Armagh, Clogher, Derry, Down, Kilmore, Meath and Tuam, the southern comprised the dioceses of Cashel, Cork, Killaloe, Limerick and Ossory.

The general committee chose three sub-committees, one for the business of the whole society and the other two for each district.

An A.G.M. was held annually, when the report was read.

The missionary was appointed by the committee and sanctioned by the episcopalian bishops of the dioceses where he worked.

The sanction of the incumbent was to be obtained before any class was opened in his parish.

The duties of the missionary included the holding of bible and secular classes, visiting deaf mutes at home, trying to find them employment, enquiring into cases of distress and making missionary tours.

All meetings were to be opened with prayer.

Within a short time the Belfast branch became independent. By 1892 it was holding its first public meeting and was stressing the non-sectarian nature of the society, for many deaf mutes in Belfast were presbyterian. However, it was anglican services which were held each Sunday in the hall. The objects of the society were also listed, of which the four most important were to provide religious instruction, to encourage continuing education, to help in getting employment and to enhance social contacts inside and outside the deaf community.

The mission hall was managed by elected committees, something which was customary in voluntary societies. What was very different was that the committee which managed the hall consisted of six deaf mutes. They supervised the reading room, coffee room and paid for gas and other expenses. This sub-committee was also expected to raise at least half of the rent and the cost of furniture and to pay half of the lady superintendent's salary and the caretaker's wages. A change in structure and the establishment of an independent Belfast mission in 1892 necessitated the election of a new committee and trustees who would represent local interests, for most of the people who would use the hall lived in Belfast. It was also agreed that the overwhelmingly episcopalian nature of the mission should be modified for the town which had a presbyterian majority, that the board of management should be widened and that the new trustees should be laymen. As part of the increasingly Belfast focus of the mission the first two trustees, Rev. A.C. Kingstone and Rev. W. Wellwood volunteered to resign in favour of four gentlemen from the town.[11]

As for the board of management a long list of gentlemen suitable for a mixed committee was drawn up which contained the names of men prominent in philanthropy, carefully identified as presbyterian or episcopalian. A board of fourteen gentlemen was eventually appointed, many of whom served for many years and who already had experience on the committees of other charities. There was an active ladies' committee which consisted mostly of women whose family had connections with the mission. Their support was useful because so much care was devoted to young deaf mute girls, and they were deeply involved in fund-raising. This organisation had a low social profile compared to the Ulster Institution. The Downshires, Rodens, Annesleys, Lurgans and Londonderrys made no appearances on the platforms at the annual general meetings. Lord Shaftesbury did preside at one A.G.M. in 1906 but this was in his capacity as lord mayor. He was always a welcome figure at Belfast occasions, particularly if they were charitable.

During its first 100 years the Ulster Institute for the Deaf has occupied three mission halls, the first at 7 Fisherwick Place, Miss Tredennick's home in Belfast. She rented it at £50 p.a. in the names of two trustees, her brother-in-law Rev. A.C. Kingstone and Rev. W. Wellwood. This rent and the furnishings of the house were to be supplied by the committee of the Mission to the Adult Deaf and Dumb.[12] The accommodation in the house was very suitable for the needs of the deaf in the town, particularly for the young deaf mute girls who came to Belfast looking for work whose plight greatly concerned Miss Tredennick. There were apartments for the missionary, a lady superintendent, a room for church services, a reading and coffee room and sleeping rooms for a few young girls.

When this house became too small for the demands made upon it as a result of the success of the enterprise, 11 Fisherwick Place which had more space was taken in 1892. In its turn this house became too small and the organisation looked for new premises in 1905. They were very fortunate in receiving a generous legacy from Miss Elizabeth Agnes Moore, Derryvolgie Avenue, of £2,000. This bequest, through careful investment, rose to £3,000 and with this money nos 5 and 6 College Square North (formerly the Metropole Hotel) were bought and converted to the needs of the deaf.

There was much more room here. The front portion had separate reading-rooms for men and girls, a bagatelle room, ample sleeping accommodation for the lady superintendent and for deaf mute girls coming from the country. At the back there was a lecture hall with a room for services built on, club rooms, a dining room for the girls, refreshment room and a dark-room for photography.[13] The present headquarters of the Ulster Institute for the Deaf, the successor of the mission hall, remain in 5 College Square North, still providing the same spiritual and social services as in Victorian and Edwardian times. The staff in the house were of the greatest importance. There were only two full-time employees, the missionary and the lady super-intendent. The first two were Mr, later Rev., Francis Maginn and Miss Tredennick whose salaries were paid by the committee.[14]

In 1891, after only three years in the post, Miss Tredennick died and she was sadly missed. It is impossible to over-estimate her impor-tance as founder and it was she who set the tone and the objects of the mission. Her death made the appointment of another lady superintendent an immediate necessity. Miss Tredennick had been a great benefactor to the deaf women and girls, about forty of whom lived around the town. They 'sadly needed a lady who understands them' and their isolation was compounded by their exclusion from the hall except for classes until the appointment of a lady superin-tendent. In the end the board asked Mrs Harris, a widow, to come as lady superintendent and live in the house. She began her duties by going with L.M. Ewart to inspect 11 Fisherwick Place and she was associated with the hall until her death in 1922.[15] Her care of the girls was acknowledged in the 1893 report and her 'energy and capacity of power' was praised at the opening of 5 College Square North in 1906.[16]

Francis Maginn was the missionary and superintendent of the men's section and his duties were multifarious. He was described as a favourite among his fellow deaf mutes, a young man of exceptional intelligence and attainment. The son of a 'respectable' Church of Ireland clergyman in the south of Ireland, he was educated at Dr Thomas Gallaudet's American College for Deaf Mutes, and this contact meant that Dr Gallaudet was a frequent visitor to the hall.17 The work attached to his post was demanding and meant long hours of commitment. He was there on the premises to see any deaf mute who needed his help in trying to find employment, he visited the sick and interpreted for them to doctors.

Employment was very important but it was not always easy to find. In spite of this Maginn found employment for forty deaf mutes and secured apprenticeships for seven boys and girls.[18] In 1908 two boys were apprenticed as painters, two as joiners and two as bakers. Girls often went into service and the lady mayoress in 1910, Mrs McMordie recommended ladies to employ them. She had had a deaf laundry maid for three years and was very satisfied with her.[19] The spiritual direction of the work was vital. Maginn, with the permission of Rev.

John Kinghan, preached at the Bethel in the evening on some Sundays and took services in the mission hall on Sunday morning at 11 a.m. for children and 12 o'clock for adults. In the afternoon bible classes for men were held by Francis Maginn and for girls and women by Mrs Harris.[20]

In addition to these two full-time members of staff, teachers from the Ulster Institution also helped. Foremost among them was W.E. Harris, son of the lady superintendent, appointed to the school in 1874 who played an important part in the contacts between the two organisations. He had become deaf as a result of contracting scarlatina when a child which meant that he was not mute and was much in demand for speaking tours to other U.K. cities and as an after-dinner speaker. When Rev. John Kinghan's health began to deteriorate in 1890 he asked W.E. Harris to take the Sunday morning class for presbyterians at the Bethel. In return the headmaster of the school exempted him from some of his duties as assistant teacher. He got board and lodgings in the institution and was paid for his work among deaf adults.[21] Harris became superintendent of the mission in 1914, a post which he held until 1932 and which he greatly enjoyed.

Church of Ireland services were held in College Square on Sunday morning, bible classes in the afternoon and then tea was served in the hall so that the deaf could go to the Bethel service in the evening without having to go home and then returning.[22] As well as these services two communion services were held each year in College Square Presbyterian Church and in Christ Church where Church of Ireland members were confirmed. This outside worship had come about in 1909 when seventy of the deaf mutes who were presbyterian petitioned the Belfast Presbytery to arrange for communion services and the Presbytery appointed Rev. R.T. Megaw of College Square to take charge of their spiritual welfare. In 1909 he carried out four baptisms for presbyterian deaf mutes either in the church or in the hall.[23]

The societies usually met in the mission hall. The Deaf Mute Literary Society had lectures on a variety of subjects including 'The life of General Garfield', 'Barometers', 'Education for the deaf in America' and 'Legislation for the deaf'. This last was given by E. Townsend, headmaster of the Institute for the Deaf and Dumb, Birmingham.[24] The deaf enjoyed lectures illustrated by limelight views and anyone who wanted to help the deaf and dumb was urged to give lantern lectures to them. The Temperance Society founded in 1887 was still flourishing in 1907 with fifty-two on the rolls, not surprising given the temperance enthusiasm in Belfast. Many took the pledge through it who 'formerly spent their evenings in the public house'. The Ephphatha Lodge of the Order of Ancient Free Gardeners was a branch of one of the friendly societies which were so much a feature of working class life in the nineteenth century. It was established in 1893 and by 1907 had £108 lodged in the Savings Bank to provide sickness and funeral benefits.

The Belfast Deaf and Dumb Foreign Missionary Society had as its main cause the maintenance of a small school for deaf children at Chefoo in South China, the only one in that vast empire.[25] Belfast was second only to the U.S.A. in support for this school, and Miss Sara Entrican B.A. organised a special effort in 1910 to raise money for the support of Boo Mei, a Chinese girl. This school was believed to be of great benefit to the deaf and dumb children of China 'who are treated little better than the beasts which perish', but the amount of money contributed by the society was so small that it is hard to see how it could have made much difference.[26]

For the women and girls there were work classes. The Dorcas Society made useful articles which were distributed among the poorer members of the Institute. In the dressmaking class a course of lessons in cutting out and making up blouses was given, while Mr Forth, principal of the Municipal Technical Institute, provided special cookery classes for thirteen deaf girls.

This was a remarkable series of groups giving valuable skills to the deaf but perhaps more importantly giving contact with people who could communicate with them. The reading room was open each week-day from 10 a.m. to 10 p.m. where there was a plentiful supply of papers and periodicals and a good library was gradually added.[27] The coffee room was open free to all where coffee and a bun could be had at a small charge. Educational classes were held as well. W.E. Harris began a language class which was carried on by Hugh Grant, a very useful class because the short school course which the deaf and dumb had, did not give them a proper chance to acquire a thorough knowledge of English.

As well as these regular meetings there were occasional entertainments: the annual tea given by Mrs Bruce with a handsome book for each child present, the annual excursion to a beauty spot such as Crawfordsburn where they went in four brakes to have a 'Pic Nic'[28] and one of the cinematograph entertainments given by A.R. Hogg which were all the rage in charitable societies in Edwardian Belfast. As in all the other benevolent institutions in the city there was a

Christmas party. The first in the new premises in College Square had decorations consisting of flags of all nations, wreaths of evergreen and fairy lights. In the entrance hall there was a 'lifelike' portrait of Father Christmas (done by Hugh Grant the deaf artist), in which his thumb was raised in the orthodox deaf mute sign. There was tea in the lecture hall, toys for the children and a cinematograph display by 'the clever young deaf scientist' W.J. Smyth. Guests came from all over the province and in the tradition of the hall deaf ladies were in charge of serving tea.

It had always been intended that there would be accommodation on the premises, particularly for young country girls of good charac-ter looking for work. At first there were few boarders, for there was only room for four girls, but the two rooms set aside in 7 Fisherwick Place were expanded after the move to College Square North. In 1908 there were still only four girls but there was also an aged woman and five boys, all apprentices. By 1910 the number of boarders had risen to twenty-three, most of whom were former pupils of the Ulster Institution and one or two from Dublin. Every room was full, so once again there was consideration of extension.[29] Until the 1970s there were rooms for girls, but terrorist violence in central Belfast ended this.

Like all voluntary societies the institute needed to raise money to support its efforts. The committee had discussions on the best method of fund-raising. There was a suggestion of following the American example of having an 'Ephphatha Sunday' when church collections would be devoted to deaf and dumb charities, either to the school in Dublin or Belfast, or to the two missions to the adult deaf and dumb, the Mission to the Adult Deaf and Dumb or the Dublin Protestant Association for the Deaf and Dumb. The difficulties of organising such a collection on an all-Ireland basis were too great, however, and it was never implemented. In fact, one feature of the mission was that, right from the beginning, collecting money had a very low priority compared with the fellowship of the hall. The deaf them-selves raised a large part of the funds by their own efforts. Rule 7 of the 'rules for management of the Mission Hall' stated that at least half of the cost of the rent, furniture and the lady superintendent's salary as well as the caretaker's wages and all the running costs should be met out of money collected by the users. It was a matter of pride for the deaf that they were so independent and the great fund-raiser, Hugh Young, a deaf mute who personally raised £57.2.4 from 1,909 subscribers, was held up as a worthy example.[30]

Like most of the rest of the funds it was collected in small amounts through the favoured penny collection cards which were used so much by Victorian charities. In 1888 £115.15.5 was collected from seventy-two penny cards showing 'the great exertions made by the deaf themselves, both because it shows their real desire for the work to go on, and also as a proof of the great results which can be accomplished by the diligent collection of small sums.'[31] In 1890 receipts from the hall were £250, expenses were £199 leaving a balance of about £100 of which £20 was ear-marked for a memorial to Miss Tredennick. By 1906 the annual income had reached £597 but this was a small amount compared with other societies.[32]

As well as the regular collections special events were held when there was a particular need. The ubiquitous bazaars or sales of work were the most popular and were held in 1889, 1893 and 1906 when the new premises were opened. The first was to help to defray the costs of setting-up and furnishing the original mission hall at 7 Fisherwick Place and the two ladies behind the effort were Miss Tredennick herself and Miss Annie Hobson, sister of the formidable Mary of the Workshops for the Blind. The amount needed was modest – £50 for present expenses and £300 to carry on the work of the mission.[33] The money was duly raised.

The move to 11 Fisherwick Place necessitated another bazaar held on 4 November 1893, though as James Henderson, later lord mayor, remarked as he opened it 'bazaars are rather numerous at present'.[34] This time there were no titled patrons present but the sale was well-attended and the stalls keenly supported. During the day ladies rendered musical items, Jerdan Nichols gave an exhibition of lime-light views and R. Ardle 'contributed an amusing ventriloquial enter-tainment', though the deaf cannot have got much enjoyment from this.[35] The sum of £260 was raised of which £100 was invested.

Again the move to larger premises in 1906 which gave Belfast what was described as the best mission hall of its kind in the United Kingdom, meant that more money was needed.[36] The generous legacy from Miss Moore had all to go to the purchase price of 5 and 6 College Square North so a sale was held to raise funds for furnishing and equipment and to extinguish the £300 debt. There were six teams of lady stall-holders who between them raised £295, though the amount was not very important. Today the Ulster Institute for the Deaf while continuing to raise money in familiar ways, e.g. by sales, gives much more to the deaf community by the fellowship it provides.

Given this enthusiasm it was a pity that the mission should have fallen victim to presbyterian/episcopalian rivalry. It was hoped that Rev. John Kinghan in the Bethel would be in harmony with the hall which was, significantly, mainly for recreational purposes for he was credited with the inauguration of an adult mission.[37] Precautions were taken to avoid interference with any denomination and the money for 5 and 6 College Square North came from a presbyterian lady.

Why, given these expressions of good-will, did controversy break out? In 1894 the missionary, Francis Maginn, wrote to the local papers commenting unfavourably on the proportion of Church of Ireland pupils to presbyterian in the school which were, he claimed, fifty presbyterian to twenty Church of Ireland.[38] He urged episcopalian parents and clergy to encourage their children to go to the Institution. Rev. John Kinghan reacted with hostility to this perceived criticism and challenged Maginn's assertion at the A.G.M. of the Mission to the Adult Deaf and Dumb.

Once again Maginn wrote a public letter attacking Rev. Kinghan's statement that only twelve eligible protestants were not in the school, and some of them imbeciles. Surely, he said, Mr Kinghan does not wish us to believe that a large proportion of the imbeciles are members of the Irish Church.[39] Rev. Walter Riddall tried to smooth things over but the correspondence continued.

It seemed that the death of Rev. John Kinghan would halt the deterioration in relations by removing one of the protagonists but in fact he was responsible for making them worse. In his will he expressed the hope that the Bethel would be sold and the proceeds added to his bequest of £2,000 to go to a new venture expanding the work of the Bethel.[40] His choice of the General Assembly as trustees led inevitably to a split from the mission hall and in the work for the adult deaf and dumb, particularly in Belfast. A minute book containing extracts from the originals of the mission traces the process from 1898. In that year the Bethel was sold without consultation with the mission hall whose committee began protests against this 'illegal' sale and the appropriation of the proceeds of the money thus raised, to a purely presbyterian mission.[41] They also resented steps which they alleged were taken to prohibit the holding of Sunday morning services in 11 Fisherwick Place.

The person in the most difficult position was W.E. Harris, the treasurer of the mission hall, who was also vice-principal of the Ulster Institution and a presbyterian. He wrote to Dr H.M. Williamson, minister of Fisherwick Place Presbyterian Church, about what he saw as an attempt to 'call out' the presbyterians from the Mission Hall for the Adult Deaf and Dumb, something which they themselves did not want. There was no disposition on the part of the presbyterians to acknowledge that there was even a problem, nor to make any attempt to seek a compromise. The committee of the mission hall reacted by passing a series of resolutions which were printed and distributed among supporters. These resolutions protested vigorously about the sale of the Bethel and the handing over of its purchase money to one denomination, the decision of the Kinghan Mission not to appoint a deaf mute as missionary, the introduction of sectarian strife among the deaf, the interference by Rev. H.M. Williamson with the Sunday morning service in the mission hall and the bringing to Belfast of a new English missionary. The committee recorded its gratitude to Maginn and Mrs Harris for their devoted work over ten years.

Despite this strong condemnation of the proposed Kinghan Mission the board of management did briefly consider a union with the presbyterians but by February 1899 they had abandoned the idea, for no scheme could be worked out.[42] Again they passed resolutions affirming their determination only to support a mixed board of management elected by a free vote of all the deaf who were subscribers to the hall and emphasising the need for accommodation for girls supervised by a resident lady superintendent.

In spite of the protests of the Mission Hall for the Adult Deaf and Dumb, the Kinghan Mission was established. The General Assembly of the Presbyterian Church took their duties as trustees seriously. A committee of clergy and elders was set up for the Kinghan Mission, with J.R. Kinghan (son) as convener.[43] This committee began to carry out the instructions of the Kinghan bequest. In 1898 a redundant Seceder church in Botanic Avenue was bought out of the £2,000 left by Kinghan and the proceeds of the sale of the Bethel.[44] The Kinghan Mission was officially opened on 15 May 1899 by the marquis of Dufferin and Ava in the presence of the lord mayor, Otto Jaffe. Therefore on the platform were a Jew and an episcopalian as well as many presbyterians, which Rev. Prof. Todd Martin cited as proof of the non-sectarianism of the mission.

The trustees were sensitive to the accusation that they had damaged the other mission by setting up a presbyterian church for the deaf. The Kinghan Mission committee regretted the spread of reports that it was 'purely sectarian and intended to take away the individual freedom of deaf mutes' and to create a spirit of hostility among the deaf.[45] They assured the General Assembly that they did not interfere with any other mission but they urged presbyterian ministers to send any deaf people in their parish to the Kinghan Mission. They alleged that the Fisherwick Place mission 'hindered' the deaf from the presbyterian body, and the General Assembly passed a resolution instructing its committee to 'take such steps as will secure the interests of the Presbyterian Church' in connection with the work.[46]

The work of the Kinghan Mission was mainly in holding religious services for the deaf though the missionary did visit people in their homes, and he preached in country churches. The first missionary was R.W. Dodds. He was experienced in the work, having taught in deaf and dumb institutions in Swansea, Manchester and Edinburgh before becoming a missionary to the adult deaf.[47] Dodds made the Kinghan Mission deeply presbyterian which made collaboration with the Fisherwick Place mission more difficult, for they were carrying on parallel and competitive work. In 1905 a home for 'aged and infirm deaf and dumb females' was opened. In 1909 two large houses were bought in Botanic Avenue opposite the Kinghan Mission, at a cost of £1,015. It was called the Jubilee Home because the money came from subscriptions given to mark the mission's golden jubilee in 1907.[48]

The General Assembly's hope that the episcopalians would come to see the benefit of two missions was not fulfilled. Relations between them were so acrimonious that in 1901 the governors of the school for educating the deaf instructed their teachers to avoid controversy by not taking part in the work of either. This meant that Harris had to leave the mission where his mother was lady superintendent. Eventually he resigned from the school in 1914 and became superintendent in succession to Maginn. Until 1904 the annual reports of the Mission to the Adult Deaf and Dumb ignored the split but in that year the board of management emphasised the unity seen in Fisherwick Place among all members and disclaimed any responsibility for bad feeling – 'if division now unfortunately exists among the deaf community, the responsibility rests on other shoulders than ours.'[49]

Of course the whole dispute was of concern to the supporters of both missions. A letter to the *Belfast News Letter* in 1905 commented on a meeting about extension of the premises which showed that workers for the deaf were worried about the need for a new house to provide a home for the aged deaf and young girls and a new hall.

They queried this need. The letter asked two questions: what use is being made of the hall in Botanic Avenue, is it not large enough for all the deaf in Belfast? and, why are two missionaries needed for the protestant deaf and dumb in the city who are less than 200? The writer said that there was an urgent need for the two missions to arrange this difference.[50]

The Mission to the Adult Deaf and Dumb continued to protest at the actions of the Kinghan Mission. In 1908 a leaflet printed by Hugh Grant, one of the deaf, criticised 'errors' which damaged a sister mission. The leaflet concluded that it was disgraceful that the small deaf mute community should be divided,

a state worthy of medieval times, and which has become among the other missions in the United Kingdom a bye-word, a reproach and a disgrace to Belfast.[51]

The Kinghan Mission mainly held church services, they visited homes but really could not compete with the mission hall in the services provided.

They never did come together. It was very unfortunate that this dispute developed. Rev. J. Kinghan does certainly deserve great credit for his initiation of the work in Belfast for the adult deaf, but he must have known that his choice of the General Assembly as trustees would lead inevitably to sectarian dispute. It is hard to know why he did this for it was generally believed that the deaf and dumb knew very little about the abstractions of sectarian differences.[52] At the meeting of the mission hall in 1907 the feelings of 90 per cent of the deaf and dumb of Belfast were that two missionaries and halls for the deaf were unnecessary.[53]

The mission hall does seem to have been shabbily treated by the sale of the Bethel and the use of its funds for a presbyterian church – and yet . . . although the non-denominational nature of the Fisherwick Place halls was so often stressed there was still a distinctly episcopalian flavour in its worship and involvement. The Church of Ireland Mission to the Adult Deaf and Dumb did not hold its meetings in College Square North, but the Church of Ireland bishop of Down and Dromore and Connor, who was on the board of the Mission Hall, was the main speaker at the A.G.M. and Francis Maginn was also its missionary, so the presbyterians did have some reason to have reservations about the religious bias of the hall.

But the main concern was social, and the institute differed from many of the societies in that the 'afflicted' were in control and that fund-raising played a comparatively minor role. The usual isolation of the deaf and dumb meant that recreation with people who had the same problems was very important for they enjoyed conversing with one another. The same sort of institution existed in England and Scotland, for their utility was well established. The most fundamental rule was that all denominations were welcome no matter what service they attended on Sunday and the missionary was warned to avoid denominational discussions. The emphasis on spiritual work was overwhelmingly protestant but it was claimed that catholics were seen in the hall night after night, though there is no evidence as to their numbers. Certainly there were no catholics on the board. The numbers of deaf and dumb round Belfast were small, about 140 to 150 in 1892, and of these approximately 58 went to the Sunday services and ten to twenty came in the evening. However, the small numbers should not minimise its value to those who came.

Workshops for the Blind,

28 Royal Avenue,

BELFAST.

Telephone No. 38.

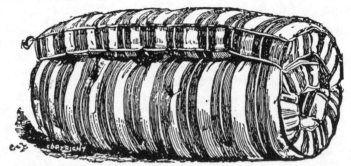

MANUFACTURERS OF

Hair, Wool, & Flock Mattresses.

HAIR MATTRESSES RE-MADE,

ALMOST EQUAL TO NEW.

Special Machinery for Teasing and Cleaning the Hair.

FEATHERS PURIFIED — Latest Machinery.

Cane Chairs Re-seated.

FURNITURE RE-UPHOLSTERED.

FEATHER BEDS,   PILLOWS,
BOLSTERS,   WIRE MATTRESSES,
BEDSTEADS.

Price List on application.

Advertisement for the Workshops for the Blind, Royal Avenue, Belfast, c. 1900

'He took the blind man by the hand':

THE WORKSHOPS FOR THE BLIND; THE HOME
TEACHING SOCIETY; THE HOMES FOR THE BLIND.

Blindness has always roused considerable sympathy, so traditionally societies for the blind have been popular charities.[1] Many of them were designed to help the blind to earn a living. Even if they had learned to read in any of the raised types (Gall, Moon or Braille), the range of occupations for which they could be trained was small.

It was in response to a perceived need and to clear the streets of blind beggars and the workhouse of blind inmates, that the Belfast Association for the Employment of the Industrious Blind was founded in 1871. The association was inspired by one woman who was to be the motive force behind its work until her death in 1891, Miss Mary Hobson. She was the daughter of the rector of Connor, one of whose parishioners, Thomas Cathcart of Broughshane, was blinded by a stone during blasting operations in the quarry where he worked. Miss Hobson became very interested in his case and with total determination decided to get him retrained to enable him to support his family and keep out of the workhouse. She tried asylums in Dublin, Dundalk, Edinburgh, Glasgow and Liverpool with no success.

Miss Hobson was left with no alternative but to establish a local workshop, and so with great enthusiasm she began her work. Lavens M. Ewart, of the great linen family, was equally interested in the idea of opening such a workshop in Belfast and both he and Miss Hobson carried on a frequent and detailed correspondence with John Martin of the Edinburgh Asylum, who was vitally important in planning the new institution. When they turned to him for guidance, he enthusiastically joined in their efforts, sending annual reports of his own concern to give an understanding of how such an enterprise was run and giving practical advice. He pointed out that it was essential to secure a large workshop with a back entrance in a good shopping area, to set up only three departments at first (mattress, basket and brush making), to raise £1,000 for stock and to appoint a good businessman as manager.[2]

In February 1871, L.M. Ewart and Miss Hobson decided to appeal for public support for the venture. A meeting was held in Clarence Place Hall, under the chairmanship of the merchant, David Taylor, at which three delegates from the Deaf and Dumb and the Blind Institution (Rev. John Kinghan, Rev. William Johnston and Alex Dickey) were present. Rev. William Johnston proposed and Rev. John Kinghan seconded the motion, 'That such an institution would be of benefit to give employment to the industrious and well-conducted blind.'[3] It would obviously be much in their interests to help the former blind pupils.

A further meeting was held at the beginning of May at which the basic objectives of the new society were stated. These were mainly to

... ameliorate the condition of the 'industrious' [i.e., able and willing to work] blind by affording employment in the trades at which they were already skilled and by giving them training in new trades.[4]

The committee moved to acquire suitable premises for the enterprise. Their first intention was to take the Fisherwick Place manse at 8 Howard St, but when this fell through 6 Howard St was rented instead. This was a substantial dwelling house with a garden at the rear which became Belfast's first workshop for the blind on 19 December 1871.[5]

Although similar in many respects to other local charities in its rules and operations, the workshops differed in two respects. It was always emphasised as one of the cardinal rules that people of all denominations should be admitted and as well as being a charity they were also expected to be a successful commercial concern. However, the objects of charity came from the same class and with the same sort of disabilities as were found generally in the other voluntary societies. The comments in the annual report of 1898 could have been transposed into most of the societies of Victorian Belfast which assisted the deprived people of the town, though their disabilities might have been different.

As Martin had warned, the appointment of a good, reliable manager would be crucial to the future of the workshops, for his duties were very extensive. Although the new workshops were operated as a charity collecting subscriptions, it was the commercial part of the business which was relied upon to furnish the greater part of its income. The manager's business acumen and enthusiasm would be vital. However, for the first few years, the workshops were exceedingly unfortunate in the managers, all of whom proved to be unreliable and unsuitable. When it became generally known that a manager was required for the new institution, over twenty-four applications were received over the summer of 1871, for the salary of over £80 was substantial and there was a possibility that accommodation would be provided. A wide variety of men applied, few of whom had any relevant experience. They included a retired R.I.C. head constable with a pension of £60 per annum, national school teachers, the superintendent of the Union Lunatic Asylum, a former sergeant with H.M. 95th Regiment and many others.[6]

In the end, Martin's favoured candidate was chosen. He was Alexander Youngson, a clerk aged twenty-eight who had done bookkeeping for the manager of Aberdeen Asylum who recommended 'his laborious, excellent, readily given and valuable services.'[7] He seemed highly qualified for the job, and the committee was hopeful of success when he began work in Belfast on 1 November 1871, at a salary of £100 per annum. By March 1872, however, problems had arisen. He caused a dispute with Martin over discounts on goods supplied and Youngson was taken to court by one of the blind workers who accused him of withholding wages. Although the case was dismissed it was bad publicity. L.M. Ewart wrote to Youngson on 14 November 1872 terminating his employment 'for the welfare of this institution', for he was not qualified to act as manager.[8] He was instructed to make up the books for which he was given a gratuity and the committee (somewhat surprisingly) gave him a testimonial. Youngson disappeared to no one's regret and Martin apologised for sending 'that base wretch' to the Belfast workshops.[9]

Once again there was a vacancy for a manager. The new manager appointed in December 1872 to begin work in January 1873, was Robert Erskine of Richmond Avenue, a partner in Erskine & Gilliland, brush and basket manufacturers of Castle St and Bank St, Belfast. Here was someone experienced in the basic industries carried on in the workshops. Erskine was appointed for an initial period of two years at a salary of £125 per annum. He began work in Howard St, where the workshops were located, running a Sunday school for the workers as well as his ordinary work.

At first all went well for he was described as zealous and indefatigable, but he did not stay long. In December 1874 he resigned to enter a partnership with Messrs Magill to manufacture brushes and bas-

kets. His departure was greeted with regret by the workers in the
workshops, both sighted and blind, six of whom signed an address to
him which was published in the local papers. In it they spoke of the

> ... ready and warm sympathy which you have extended to us in this our great
> afflication – the loss of our sight ... you have been our kind and true friend in our
> homes as well as in our work rooms.[10]

His connection with the workshops continued, though as a rival.
Relations quickly began to sour because the committee discovered
that there had been a huge loss of £228 in the last few months which
he had concealed from them.

This time the committee decided not to advertise for a manager
but to appoint George Bothwell, the basket-making foreman, as
manufacturing manager while Francis McBurney, the secretary, took
charge of the books, cash, etc. McBurney had been appointed in
1874 and his qualifications seemed most suitable for he had been
book-keeper and cashier at Linfield Foundry.

As usual everything seemed to be going well at first. Although he
took full charge as manager in July 1875, by March 1876 he was
clearly dissatisfied for he applied for a job in London without the
courtesy of informing the committee, who discovered this fact when
the secretary of the Institution of Associations of the Welfare of the
Blind informed them that McBurney was a candidate for the post of
manager of the institution. He had the misfortune to arouse the
hostility of the formidable Miss Hobson who mounted a short, vigor-
ous and wholly successful campaign against him, which brought
about his departure in September 1878. Her long and detailed letter
to the committee on 12 August 1878 was the result of surveillance
over several months during which she noted his absences from the
workshops, his destinations during these absences, his visitors, his
behaviour, his business acumen and did not scruple to question the
employees about him. The letter launched a savage attack on the
manager's competence, of which she claimed to be more aware than
most of the committee because of her frequent visits to the workshops.

The committee members were understandably dismayed by the
letter. Their first reaction was that Miss Hobson had been too strong
in her language about McBurney, but they could not ignore the
charges she made. Having discussed what to do they decided to call
him in to put the letter to him. It must have been a dreadful shock to

the manager. At the interview with McBurney the committee found his excuses unacceptable and so decided to ask for his resignation. At the beginning of September, he wrote asking his employers to 'overlook my previous faults' but to no avail.[11] On 4 September he resigned though he stayed on for some weeks to make up the books. McBurney found a 'desirable situation', so he asked to be released immediately for he needed to be available. He was subsequently employed in the Ormeau Brickworks and the committee surprisingly gave him a very respectable testimonial in spite of his dereliction of duty.

At this point in the history of the workshops their luck changed. It needed a man of impeccable character and honesty, a man who was devoted to the cause of helping the blind workers. The workshops got all of this in J.H. Hewitt (aged 28) who was appointed as manager, a position he held for forty-two years and in which he gave every satisfaction. He had been in the counting house at Liddell's (linen merchants) for thirteen years and had references from influential committee members, notably R. L. Hamilton of Richardson Brothers. He wrote of Hewitt 'I don't know a more highly principled fellow, steady as a rock – intelligent to a very high degree and one in whom the utmost confidence may be placed.'[12] A great deal was expected of him.

Hewitt's duties were exceedingly varied. He had to buy the raw material for the products, organise the production, send out samples and most importantly, sell them. It was he who went to London or Dublin to negotiate contracts with the G.P.O. and the War Office and urge them to support the workshops. He visited other blind asylums throughout the United Kingdom to observe their practices and products and see travellers' samples. In addition to these duties he had to select, supervise and discipline the workers, both sighted and blind, often a very difficult job. He produced a written report and prepared and presented the accounts monthly to the committee. He dealt with architects planning new premises and drew up contracts with owners of the old. He let the offices and other property of the institution and collected their rent. He even had to write to the police to get the embarrassment of a blind beggar removed from the doorway of the shop. For all of this Hewitt got a three year contract starting at £100 per annum, which had to be renewed at the end of each period. There were no automatic pay rises in the workshops so every year he had to ask for an increase.

His own description of his job certainly shows its demanding nature. Writing to the committee in 1880 and 1881, asking for an increase in salary he told them that after a year he had found that the job, far from being easy, required great care and attention. After two years he hoped that his work had been satisfactory. It should have been, for he had reduced the operating loss to less than half, subscriptions had gone up compared with Erskine's time, sales had gone up compared to McBurney's and the financial situation was much improved. To achieve this success he had had no holidays for a year, not even Good Friday, Easter Monday and the Twelfth and 'many evenings I have forfeited the comforts of home to spend them here in order to have more time during the day to look for orders.'[13] Sometimes he was so busy with travellers as not to get food from half past seven in the morning till close on six o'clock in the evening. He therefore hoped that the committee would not mind him asking for £100 per annum which was small compared to Erskine's £226.

It seems quite unreasonable that he should have had to go through this every year, even having to wait for his new engagement until the balance sheet was audited. Each year he had to ask for eight or ten days holiday to go to Newcastle or to Donaghadee. It was not surprising that his health broke down and he had to go to Rostrevor to recuperate. At least the committee recognised his value, giving him a bonus of 12 guineas which rose to £20, every year. His salary went up steadily reaching £330 per annum in 1893, a substantial income for that time and his term of engagement had risen to five years. The organisers also recognised that the success of the workshops was in great measure due to Hewitt who devoted so much of his time to the welfare of the blind.

What did he think of his employment? In 1898, he wrote

I have given my utmost attention to the work I have in hand, not with the aim to better myself but as a duty faithfully discharged; although I may have short-comings I trust my endeavour to faithfully carry out the work you have given to me, has been done to your satisfaction.[14]

Any business would have been fortunate to have Hewitt. Unfortunately his last years were saddened by the loss of his three sons in the First World War. His second son, like so many other Ulstermen, fell on the first day of the Somme and Hewitt only lived three years after his retirement in 1921.

The other members of staff were also crucial to success. There was a wholesale department which supplied country shops and most importantly, fulfilled government contracts, but the sales shop was where the public saw the products and where they had to be persuaded to buy. Subscriptions could depend on the impression given at the first contact, so the saleswomen had great responsibility. There were few respectable jobs for girls of a higher social class than the mill girls, but not sufficiently educated to be a companion or governess. The job of saleswoman in the Workshops for the Blind was therefore an attractive proposition so there were more than twenty applicants for the post in 1872.

The successful applicant was Miss Charlotte Quin who was also competent to assist Erskine when necessary. She got £25 per annum which did not include paid mandatory holidays for she always had to write to the committee when she wanted time off. She was not certain of getting it. If she was needed in the shop, she was refused leave, getting £1 in lieu of a holiday. Likewise if she wanted an increase in salary she had to write to the committee.

The Workshops for the Blind were a commercial concern and thus depended on efficient marketing and administration. In the early days the manager acted as commercial traveller but he was replaced by James Winnington who stayed with the firm for over thirty years. He was successful in his work: 'a very pushing salesman and a good traveller.'[15] The wholesale department supplied country districts with orders, operating with a charge hand and a boy around fifteen or sixteen, who 'could be trained to attend to customers, lay out orders, pack and make out an invoice if necessary and be generally useful.' One such boy, George Sherman, rose to be manager in succession to Hewitt. He held this post until his death in 1946 when his son Johnston Sherman took over.

Office staff dealt with everyday administration, correspondence and cash-handling. There were almost always plenty of applicants for office jobs, though some were not apparently suitable. Sometimes the easy access to cash proved too much of a temptation. In 1892 the young man in charge of the office pilfered £250. An attempt to improve the situation by appointing a man over thirty, in the hope that he would be more responsible, failed when money continued to disappear as did the book-keeper.[16] As the business increased so did the need for office staff, which gave good opportunities of employment for girls. The demand was more and more for modern skills like typewriting and shorthand though the pay was very low. One typist, Miss McConnell, was paid only 6 s. per week which was lower than the income of many of the blind workers. There were foremen for the main departments – brush, basket and mattress making, who played a very important part in the workshops. It was hard to find suitable men who could teach blind workers a trade for there were no such teachers in Ulster. The committee had to turn to employers like L. M. Ewart to find weavers who could be trained.

The relative importance of the staff is seen in their wage rate.

Table 5.1
Wages of staff in 1903

Mr Winnington	Traveller	£120 p.a. + commission
Mr Robinson	Book-keeper	£80 p.a.
Miss Gibson	Saleswoman	£20 p.a.
Mr Wilson	Charge of wholesale	27s. 6d. p.w.
S. Anderson	Mattress foreman	36s. p.w.
F. M'Gibbon	Blind traveller	13s. 6d. + 13s. commission p.w.
A. Gracey	Charge of firewood	28s. p.w.[17]

The workshops were established in Howard St in 1871 and for years a major preoccupation was the acquisition and maintenance of suitable premises. The manager in 1873, Erskine, advocated the acquisition of a more central site or, failing this, the opening of a branch shop in one of the main commercial streets of the town. By 1875 the committee was actively considering a plan to build new premises designed for the purpose of manufacturing and adapted for the blind, and a fund for this was set up.

The committee was stirred into action by a proposed increase in rent by the owners of 6 Howard St, in 1876. The rent was already too high so they were faced with the decision of either closing the whole enterprise or of raising enough money for new premises. A new decision was taken to leave the Howard St workshops and find a better, more central situation. At the annual general meeting of 1881, speakers referred to the excessively high rent they had to pay and urged that the time had come to find new premises for 'towns far inferior to Belfast in wealth and population – for instance Aberdeen – had such institutions properly equipped for carrying on the work.'[18]

This was all happening when the Belfast town council had decided to remove the shambles of Hercules St and replace it with a new, broad thoroughfare called Royal Avenue. The redoubtable Miss Hobson proposed that the organisation should tender for a site in the centre of the development, a suggestion greeted with horror by the committee, which was afraid to undertake such a momentous expansion at that time.[19] They decided not to proceed but they had not taken Miss Hobson into account. By the end of November 1881 she had undertaken surveys of the finances of the society and the possibilities of such a move. She appeared at a committee meeting and presented a letter to be read which said, 'the new street offers the most favourable opportunity for providing suitable workshops and a suitable saleroom without the expense of a second shop.' She pointed out that £1,300 was already in the new premises fund and the friends of the blind would hold a bazaar to raise more. Any deficiency could be met by borrowing and money would actually be saved in running the institution while more blind workers would be employed. Faced with her confidence the doubting men agreed to go ahead and William Ewart, M.P. (father of Lavens) was asked to attend the auction and bid for site 27 on behalf of the workshops. He was successful in getting site 25 at a yearly rent of £174.[20] It was a remarkable act of faith by the committee which had funds of several hundred pounds to go ahead with a project which would cost thousands, a tribute to the power of Miss Hobson's personality and determination.

So the work began. Negotiations were started with the Post Office, which had taken the adjoining site, to get more frontage. The progress of the building was not without some disagreements, particularly with Mr Robb who was building the Grand Central Hotel on the other side. In spite of all this the workshops were ready for the official inauguration at the annual general meeting in March 1883 after which the three hundred ladies and gentlemen invited saw Miss Hobson (as was only proper) lay the foundation stone.[21] A bottle containing newspapers and coins was put into the cavity. Miss Hobson was presented with a silver trowel, mallet and plumb line.

The new workshops consisted of two red brick, four storey buildings with attics, one fronting on to Royal Avenue, the other at the rear separated by a yard. On the ground floor was a shop for the sale of goods with a store behind it and a willow store in the other building at the back. On the first floor were the front rooms let out for offices, with an access door beside the General Post Office, a small basket room and a spacious room for large basket making. On the second floor the front part was used for mattress work and the back for brush work, which were also done on the third floor with mattress-making, chair-caning and teasing. Each floor had a store and foremen's room.[22] These new premises were formally declared open in March 1884 by the mayor, David Taylor.

A main use of a new building erected in 1899 was in recreational facilities for the blind. The ladies' committee set up a library and reading room with Moon type books presented by Sir Charles Lowther. Dr Moon donated a writing apparatus to enable the blind to write to their friends and Miss Hobson designed a machine to allow them to write to their sighted friends.[23] The manager was very anxious that the blind should have comfortable rooms where they could smoke, play dominoes or read and be read to. Often the blind had to leave their houses to get out of the way and consequently went to public houses for somewhere to sit. If they had rooms they could be used for bible classes, lectures, readings or addresses.

Another very valuable service would be the provision of cheap dinners 'as many get nothing but tea from one year's end to another which must be very weak and injurious.'[24] The workers could not easily go home at dinner time and if they went out they were exposed to mockery from the next door workers. As a result they had to hang round the work rooms. Besides they had no hot meal during the day. Other institutions in Leeds, London, Dundee, etc. provided dinners for their blind workers. In London women paid 4d. and men 5d. and the cooking was done by the caretaker. In Leeds two courses cost 3d. and some of the partially sighted assisted at the table. The dining rooms worked at a loss which was borne by the institutions. At first they were only operated in winter but the demand was so great that they began to open all year round.

One very big danger in the operation of the workshops was the ever present risk of fire, for there was so much inflammable material around. In 1881, in Howard St, their upper floor was gutted as the result of a fire. Fire broke out again in Howard St in July 1883, beginning at the rear of the workshops and spreading to the houses on either side. The new stores taken in Wellington St went on fire just a few days later to the great alarm of the inhabitants of Wellington Place. The concern of the committee was well founded. First a fire in the office rented by Mr Kennedy, travelling photographer, nearly burned the place down.[25] On 10 May 1908, the workshops were so badly damaged by a fire at the front of the building that the city surveyor issued a notice for it to be taken down.

Once again there had to be a new building. The foundation stone was again laid, this time by A.D. Lemon, the secretary. Unfortunately the bottle placed by Miss Hobson in 1883 was broken and its contents were thrown away by the workmen, who were not aware of its significance, before they could be placed in the foundation stone.[26] The new shop had additional windows and was in a completely different style. The manager wanted to retain the whole upper floor for a showroom with a customer lift which could easily be installed, indeed it provided an additional attraction. Basically he wanted to keep the whole building in the control of the association, with the offices upstairs, for this would make administration much easier.

By 1910 then the workshops had a substantial modern building fitted with the most advanced facilities. The best sanitary and ventilation systems were installed for the workers. A telephone was connected to the new telephone exchange in 1883 which was one of the early installations in the city. There were steam lifts by 1891. A gas engine which provided the power and light used in all areas was in operation from the beginning and was replaced by an up-to-date model in 1892. As the gas had to be kept on all year round in two of the offices, which was most unhealthy, the manager asked the committee to consider installing electric light and quotations were sought. Musgrave's put in a new heating system in 1893. As for shop fittings, a new glass display case was bought, a cash drawer replaced the old money box and, most modern of all, a cash railway and cash register were supplied.

The whole existence of the workshops depended on their ability to produce and sell their products, while the disabilities of the blind restricted the choice of manufacture. The main departments were basket, brush and mattress making. By 1873 the Belfast workshops were producing on their own account, and beginning to experience some problems. The manager complained that the other retailers 'were down on me' because the workshops were taking away customers. They accused the workshops of price-cutting, collecting subscriptions to cover their losses. Then there were objections that some goods sold by the shop were actually made elsewhere so that there had to be labels to distinguish them. The workshops' products had to be of very good quality to retain the support of customers and the public and compete in the market, though people expected prices to be lower than in other shops because of their charitable status. Frequently there were unfounded allegations that the workshops' goods were in fact dearer than elsewhere and the manager urged the committee members to point out the danger done to the cause by such rumours. He said of the 'friends' who complained – 'they might as well set fire to the premises as continue to talk that way – it is not done maliciously, but thoughtlessly', but it was still injurious.[27] He even sent Miss Bailie incognito to the Bank Buildings to compare prices. The biggest problem was that it was impossible to compete for wholesale trade with jails and reformatories which produced similar goods with no expense of labour at all, while the blind workers had to be paid.

The price list of 1874 sent to the principal families in Belfast shows what was made, some items quite obscure. What was a 'Jenny Lind' paper basket? or a 'Dundee Rod Work' reticule? or a 'Wool Bordered Van Dyked' mat? or a 'Super Skeleton' mat? The biggest section was the basket-making department with a huge range of products. Much business was done through the shop in Belfast where carriage, box, soiled linen and clothes baskets were most popular but a significant trade was carried on through the wholesale department which supplied shops throughout Ulster, and most importantly, with government agencies. It was always useful to have a regular contract with them so the manager spent a considerable time trying to negotiate the supply and repair of hampers for the Post Office. Government contracts were awarded in January when Hewitt would go over to London to canvass directly. He also used any Ulster local influence in England. For example, in 1905 he wrote to Lord Londonderry asking him to use his contacts to get orders for both the English and Irish Post Office operations.[28] In 1895 they got an order for 50,000 hampers to be used for the parcel post.

There were occasional differences with the Post Office over the hampers, for it had very exacting standards. As well as the Post Office, the War Office was a potential customer. Local orders came from Downpatrick Asylum, the Harbour Board and several railways. The workshops had to work hard to get and keep these contracts. Mill skips were another useful selling line. In a textile town like Belfast there was clearly a market and from the beginning of the workshops successive managers visited the mills looking for orders. Hewitt even called on fish companies and owners of boats for he believed that there would be a good trade in fish baskets. In 1911 the department won an order to supply baskets for used tickets to be installed in the tram cars. The most elaborate and impressive piece of basket work was a bath chair.

Over the years the amount of work varied considerably. Sometimes the men were on overtime to make up the orders, while at times there were fears of short time. Brushes were also an important line, and government contracts were sought for brushes too, particularly from the armed forces. Both the army and navy needed many blacking shoe brushes so tenders were submitted every year. The workshops won an order for 40,000 brushes in 1895 – but at below the cost price. However, it could not be refused if the workers were to be kept on, so the loss had to be accepted. The manager could never be sure of the numbers of brushes to be made nor of the price that the War Office would pay. 1903 was a good year for the army took 20,000 blacking brushes and then put in a second request for 10,000 scrubbing brushes and 1,000 clamp brushes. The navy took 6,000 scrubbing brushes in 1905.[29] The mills used machine brushes but as this depended on the state of trade there was not a steady market and private sources could not be relied on.

The success of the mattress department fluctuated, though it was one of the principal branches of work for the blind in institutions across the Irish sea. Lord O'Neill and the marchioness of Downshire encouraged the work by giving large bedding orders (something which helped to give publicity and increased support) but there was not enough work from private local individuals. The material used in mattress making, that is horse hair and feathers, required special preparation. In 1887 the manager asked for a ventilated place for teasing hair and he also wanted a new machine for extracting dust from feathers because the steaming machine they already had was not efficient. Mattresses were regularly supplied to most of the Ulster workhouses, lunatic asylums, the deaf and dumb and the blind school, the Belfast Charitable Society and the Ladies' Industrial school.

As well as making new mattresses there was a brisk trade in remaking old ones. In Victorian Belfast mattresses were not interior sprung and thus flattened quickly. The workshops were competing with private enterprise. This advertisement appeared in the *Northern Whig*:

Mrs McVeigh, 31 Church Lane
Clean your old beds and hair mattresses
Important discovery in practical chemistry in the art of
purifying feathers.
Surprising elasticity and freshness acquired by feathers thus
treated make them FAR SUPERIOR TO NEW ONES.
Out of three beds usually enough for four.

Certificate from the late Professor Stevelly, Queen's College. 'Feathers were rendered perfectly clean, free from all dandruff or other adhering dust or impurities.'[30]

Mattress making was never the large earner that baskets and brushes were, but it was a useful trade for a few blind workers.

These were the three main departments in the workshops but the manager was continually trying to find other employment to keep the workers from short time. Woollen and cotton rags were woven into mats and carpets with a strong, coloured warp, cane chairs were reseated (this work is still done in Lawnbrook Avenue), fancy cane blinds were made to order, pew cushions and matting for churches, offices and lobbies were supplied. When the new City Hall was being built he tendered for some of the furniture – 1,000 chairs at 14s. 6d. each, which would give a good profit.[31] The new Belfast cathedral needed 1,600 chairs for which the workshops tendered – first taking the precaution of putting the dean of Belfast on the committee.

Another possibility for the workers was massage, which was done by the blind in some parts of England. In 1898 the manager, while attending Dr William Whitla for rheumatism, enquired of him his opinion of the suitability of providing such a service in Belfast. Hewitt wrote to the British and Foreign Blind Association for details of the training, and discovered that it would cost about £20, including doctor's fees, rail fare, board, etc. which he thought would be a good investment if the local doctors would take an interest in it. Dr William Aickin, physician to the workshops, was not encouraging. He said that massage had not taken well in Belfast and he felt that the training would be too expensive, so the idea was dropped.

Firewood cutting seemed to be a better plan. It was one of the principal industries for the blind in some institutions in Great Britain and in the days when all houses had a fire there was always a need for wood to light them. Splitting wood by hand was unprofitable, but there was a patented wood-splitting machine produced by Glover & Co. of Leeds, which was simple to operate and could be used by the blind, which would cut 12,000 bundles per day.

Yet another sideline was piano tuning, for this fitted in with the traditional belief that the blind were good at music. In 1883 John Ross began training at the Norwood College for the Blind in London, through the good offices of Dr Armitage. He gave up before he got his certificate, returned to Belfast and asked to be taken on to work at basket-making. However the committee thought that this would be a waste of his talents so he was sent back to Norwood where he completed his studies.[32] Piano tuning proved to be successful service but the tuner became troublesome. He created a scandal in the workshops because of his immoral behaviour with one of the blind girls. The manager informed the committee:

I regret to have to report that something unfortunate has happened between J. Ross the piano tuner and Cassy Sullivan, one of the blind girls. It has been suggested by some that they should get married but as Rule 12 states that 'in no case shall permission be granted to marry where both parties are blind' it will be difficult to decide on how to act particularly as two blind persons were on a former occasion dismissed for marrying.[33]

Ross went off to Dublin, re-appearing in 1907 allegedly making a fresh start and asking help from the association in setting himself up in business as a tea-seller (something often done by the blind).[34] Willows were a vital material for the basket department, in fact the association assured any potential growers of willows in Ulster's suitably swampy ground that they would have a ready market.[35] In 1890 a new willow-peeling department giving employment to six hands was opened at the rear of the workshops. A flat roof was put on the new building in 1891 which would be most useful for willow-peeling, and the supply to basket makers was assured. Other trades were suggested. Cork-cutting needed more market research before it could be started, sieve-making by two workers lasted for a short time but was given up, file-making was investigated at Messrs Combe, Barbour & Combe but was rejected as unsuitable for the blind, as was a machine for making cardboard boxes. The association tried to exploit royal visits. When the prince and princess of Wales came to Belfast in 1885, the committee planned to rent out the windows facing Royal Avenue, the ground floor at 10s., the second floor at 50s. each. To their disappointment this proved impossible for the stands built along the route obscured the view. Instead they let customers in free to watch from the windows. The coronation visit of Edward VII and Queen Alexandra in 1903 brought orders for flags and bamboo poles, as well as for baskets for the rooms occupied by the royal visitors at Mountstewart. Lady Londonderry wanted these to be made by the blind.[36]

The delivery of the manufactures presented a problem to the committee. In 1891, Hewitt proposed that a horse and van should be hired to deliver firewood. The horses over the years brought some crises. One horse sprained his foot and, although put out to grass for a month in the hope that he would recover, he had to be sold at a loss of £10. More seriously, one horse bit a young man called Moore who claimed £10 for doctor's expenses. At first the committee refused but when he consulted a solicitor it was taken seriously. Members went to their own solicitor telling him to settle the claim as well as possible.[37] It was agreed at £6 compensation. The driver who had left the horse unmuzzled offered to pay £1 of the claim if he was forgiven, and the horse was exchanged for another plus £5.15.0 towards the cost.

As the premises in Royal Avenue were very extensive, too large for the direct needs of the workshops, the committee let out offices to a variety of tenants with mixed success. Few of them appear in the records of the institution (except Kennedy the travelling photographer who nearly burned the building down) and paid their rent without much trouble. However, between 1905 and 1908 there was great difficulty with Sargent who ran the Belfast Business College in the offices of the workshops, in getting his rent arrears.

Clearly the operation of the workshops was a complex and demanding task. Commercial success was most important to support the institution, customer relations and satisfaction were vital and the public perception of the association meant a great deal. Most years were busy and routine, but there were tragedies which received unwelcome publicity. In one case Lizzie Noble, a blind girl, fell down the hoist and was killed. Her sister and aunt claimed compensation from the workshops for the loss of her earnings but the committee, understandably, immediately denied liability, saying that they were a charitable institution with no funds for this.[38] In 1908 the local newspapers reported the death of a boy called Robert Laverty on the workshop premises. He had come to take one of the men home and without permission went to the boiler house, climbed on to one of the tanks and, in an attempt to get over the boiler one of his legs slipped, and he was so severely scalded that he died two days later. At the inquest the coroner exonerated the association from all blame but the Nationalist M.P. for West Belfast, Joseph Devlin, asked a question in the house of commons and was told that adequate precautions had been taken. The boy's parents asked for help with the funeral expenses which amounted to £11.13.11 and were given £3.[39]

Society's view of the handicapped tends to put them apart from ordinary life. They are expected to be quiet and decorous, conforming to the rules and behaving well to show their gratitude to those who pity and help them. This was the attitude to the blind as to other people with disabilities, perhaps even more so for the blind did have more public attention and support than most. A general survey of Victorian and Edwardian charities in Belfast tends to confirm the stereotype of the grateful and deserving poor, for few of their records survive, meaning that the information on their operations must be derived from annual reports and newspaper accounts of their proceedings. There is no implication that this information is incorrect but it would be strange if the organisers did not carefully select the most effective stories of gratitude and appreciation. After all they depended on public support which was less likely to be given to the failures.

In the case of the Belfast Association for the Employment of the Industrious Blind, the monthly manager's reports and the minute books survive from the earliest days giving a much more accurate account of life in the workshops than is derived from published material. These records show that the blind were far from the idealised picture many people had. In a report of the Mission to the Adult Deaf and Dumb, a policeman was quoted as claiming that the deaf and dumb were among the most disorderly customers he had and certainly the blind got drunk and created considerable trouble in the town. In contrast the committee spoke in praise of the behaviour of the blind workers 'who showed the greatest cheerfulness and contentment existing among them, the peculiarities connected with their sad affliction being taken into account.'[40]

Most of the blind workers came between the two extremes of drunkenness and saintly cheerfulness and the workshops were crucial to their lives. They were anxious to be admitted in the first instance and re-admitted when they misbehaved and were expelled, with the alternative of begging or going into the workhouse. Most of the blind in Ulster were in their local workhouses, for few families could support a handicapped member. Thus the ability to earn their own living was much prized and the opportunity of gaining a training was eagerly sought, not only by the men and women blind from birth but perhaps even more keenly by those who became blind in later life. Because of the very special nature of the enterprise, detailed rules were drawn up to regulate the operation of the workshops. The twenty-one rules produced give a clear picture of the ethos of the society and its close control of its workers.

The workshops were only for men and women from Ulster because the funds for its support were raised in the province. Applicants had to fill in a detailed form to be signed by a clergyman and two householders and be certified as suitable for admission by a doctor, though the committee sometimes took in people who were refused a certificate by Dr Browne. Often they had to wait for a long time until there was a vacancy for there was always a waiting list of around forty or fifty people 'pleading for admission' who could not be allowed in until the funds permitted. People who had been educated at the Lisburn Rd school were particularly keen to get in, for although they had been taught to read and count they could not possibly compete with sighted labour, especially the released prisoners who had learned the same trades in jail.

From the beginning the organisers were advised of the importance of only selecting young strong workers, capable of learning. They were not always successful in achieving this, and out of the thirty-eight admitted in the first year, thirteen left, because so many middle-aged and old people were admitted. By 1876 the age pattern of the workers had been established and most were under twenty years old.

Table 5.2

Table of ages of blind workers in workshops for the blind

Age	Numbers
15 – 20	13
20 – 30	9
30 – 40	5
40 – 50	2
50 – 60	1
60+	1

The sixty-one year old was Cathcart whose plight had inspired the opening of the workshops. It was recommended that no one over forty should be admitted 'unless very intelligent and of a particularly strong constitution.'[41]

The twenty-two men and women who were admitted in 1873 were grateful for their chance. Punctuality was important but, as the manager said bitterly, some employees came at 7.00 am 'while others thought 10.00 am a more suitable hour.'[42] Over the years working hours were reduced, beginning at 8.00 am and ending at 7.00 pm on week days and 2.00 pm instead of 3.00 pm on Saturdays. Any man late three mornings was fined 1d. per morning while women were fined

½d., with two mornings' grace for all. The manager thought that women should be treated the same as men for they just came and went at times suitable to them, often leaving at 6.00 pm.[43] New factory legislation of 1905 prohibited fines for lateness so punctual attendance fell off.

The manager was instructed to keep out latecomers until dinner time, something even more unpopular than fining, for it meant the loss of a half-day's pay. Workers had to be at the door exactly when the bell rang which was hard for them to arrange and this led to a loss of earnings, so they asked for it to be left open for longer. The manager in 1873 suggested that workers should have their breakfast before they came in, to avoid having to go out in the rush hour with consequent danger from traffic.[44]

The employees were paid on piece work so there was a wide variation in what they earned. The conditions on which they were admitted were:

Table 5.3

Payment of blind workers

First three months	No wages
Until end of first year	Half usual pay for all saleable work
Until end of second year	Three-quarters usual pay
Third year	Full wages at piece-work, they being considered as journeymen

Apprentices were paid on a sliding scale. They got no wages in the first year and by the end of their apprenticeship in the fifth year they got three-quarters of journeymen's wages or 9d. in the shilling.[45] In some cases the guardians supplemented the pay, perhaps by as much as the worker earned. Robert Callaghan earned 5s. per week while the guardians also gave him 5s. In a typical year men could earn between 10s. and 25s. per week but the women only got half of that – 5s. to 10s. per week.[46] In addition the manager could give bonuses as an encouragement or to make up enough pay to live on, though he risked being accused of partiality.

The problem for piece-workers was that their earnings depended very much on the supply of material provided by the foremen. This is why the workers were so hostile to George Bothwell when he failed to keep them at work, and why, when there was a proposal to cut the working week by an hour to 2.00 pm on Saturday, there were protests from the workers. Workers who had sickness certificates got half-pay during their illness. During the winter months the men who could not make enough to keep them asked for a supplement because of high prices of food and coals.

There were holidays at Christmas, Easter and the Twelfth, but, like the sighted employees, the blind had to ask for other holidays. Special events brought more holidays: a visit by the duke and duchess of York in 1897, Queen Victoria's sixtieth jubilee and the royal visit in 1903. As well as the blind workers some sighted men had to be employed to assist in setting up the work. Of these, deaf and dumb former pupils of the Ulster Institution got preference in apprenticeships. Other men with a good deal of sight could do the bamboo work and a girl was employed in the dining room when it was opened, though she wanted to go to the basket room where she could earn more. Another partially sighted man, Bolger, set up a partnership with a totally blind man, Morgan. These were two willow-peelers who bought an organ with money left to Morgan and set off to go round the towns begging.[47]

As far as possible the workers were treated like any other work force. Where they differed was in the trouble they caused the committee, trouble which would have led to instant dismissal in a purely commercial enterprise. But in the workshops they were tolerated, mainly because expulsion from the workshops was a sentence to the workhouse. Month after month the manager's report recorded misbehaviour and yet the culprits were kept on, or were re-admitted and given yet another chance. Men were caught smoking in the W.C. which was most dangerous, for once the paper caught fire and set the partition alight.[48] As a result smoking was strictly forbidden but some men still disobeyed.

Then there was the stealing of material. A deaf and dumb apprentice, William Morrow, was arrested for stealing three brushes out of the workshops. Then he was again arrested for stealing in the following year. This time he took Miss Quin's opera glass from the desk drawer where she had left it. Maggie Kernaghan tampered with and stole from the other girls' dinner baskets. She was caught because she was seen doing it, bad luck in the blind institution.

Miss Graydon, the home teacher, and Mrs Pim's nurse (from the Homes for the Blind) who visited the blind in their homes, reported in 1906 that Thomas Kerr was treating his wife very badly. He refused to let her go to hospital or the infirmary and was not feeding her properly. Mrs Kerr was partially blind and had been employed in the workshops until she got a severe cut on the head since when she had been getting 3s. per week from the workshops and 2s. from the guardians. The case was so bad that Mrs Pim thought it should be reported to the 'cruelty'. The manager wrote to the dispensary doctor asking him to examine her. The doctor said that she should go to hospital but while her husband still refused permission for her to go, no-one had power to compel him to send her. Kerr was warned that his allowance would be discontinued if he did not consent but it was not expected that this would make any difference.[49]

The workshops suffered an embarrassment in 1908. Each year the workers were taken on an excursion to a seaside town, with the totally blind able to bring a guide who got a free ticket. When John Mooney, a partially blind man asked for a free ticket for a friend he was told that he must wait to see if funds allowed. He then went about shouting that if he did not get a ticket he would make the committee show what they had done with the public's money. This, said the manager, 'was insolent and mischievous' and the foreman was told not to give him one. Mooney's next move was to write to the *Belfast Telegraph* asking contributors to the association to demand a statement of what had been done with the money, and to the horror of the committee the *Telegraph's* editor sent a reporter to investigate the case. The manager wanted Mooney to be suspended for at least two weeks and have his wages cut by 1s. for this misconduct.[50] But as usual he was forgiven and his wages restored.

A more bizarre issue surfaced in 1906. In June of that year an anonymous letter and one signed by John Flynn were sent to the principal of the Deaf and Dumb and the Blind School, making allegations of heresy against one of the other workers, W.J. Donnan. Flynn was not a savoury character, making mischief and continually grumbling about the cane and willows he had to work with in addition to making threats to tell Inglis's Bakery that their hampers were left out in the rain in the yard. It emerged that the charges had actually been made twenty-two years before, on the grounds that some sceptical views had been expressed by Donnan in a religious discussion one dinner time, for which he had been called before the committee.

These were irritations but were not regarded too seriously by the management. There were, however, two areas of real concern to the committee: one was the problem of drunkenness and the other was the intermarriage of blind workers. From the beginning of the operation the manager's reports contained incidents of alcohol related troubles. Although the committee was very slow to expel people, in the event of a drinking bout leading to absenteeism it had to be done, with the distressing consequence that wives and children suffered.

Sometimes drunkenness led to criminal behaviour. One boy, Hugh McRoberts, was arrested at Easter 1874, drunk and disorderly and cursing the pope. In his case the committee did take a firm line and dismissed him.[51] On another occasion, one man who had a record of drunkenness had his wages withheld from him and paid direct to his wife. Another was dismissed for drinking and going to work for other people during hours when he was supposed to be in the workshops, indeed he would only come in three days a week. Even then he would rise from his job and walk out without permission, sometimes to drink, sometimes to fill orders for other shops. The committee was worried about the reputation of the workshops, for the sight of eight blind men and women staggering about the streets with everyone looking as happened in 1898, was bad publicity. Four of the workers were in one house and when a fight broke out among them the police had to be called at 2.00 am on Saturday. Their punishment was just the loss of one day's pay.

It really is not the expulsions which are surprising but the failures to dismiss repeated offenders. One deaf and dumb apprentice, Wilson Curran, was regularly in trouble through drink from 1886. His father tried to keep him under control by having Wilson's wages paid to him, but the boy continued to drink. Then the committee gave him another chance because his father had died. In 1890 he was once again in trouble when he was dismissed for going on a 'begging tour' to England and Scotland. It was incredible that Messrs Ewart and Lemon agreed to this, for Curran was not only a drinker but untrustworthy and a bad worker. He was finally sent away in 1891.

The association was greatly concerned over the marriage of two blind people. The reasons for blindness were not known in the nineteenth century and it was feared that the intermarriage of the blind would inevitably mean that any children they had would also be blind. The annual reports contained guidance on the prevention of blindness which, it was believed, was due to infection from a contagious discharge getting in the eyes of babies during or soon after birth.

In spite of rule 12 which forbade intermarriage there were frequent cases of marriage between workers. After all this was the only

118

place where blind men and women met socially so inevitably some wished to marry. Usually the committee dismissed either or both of the workers with the consequence that their income was drastically reduced. The risk that they would have to go to the workhouse often made the committee more lenient, allowing one or other back in. So many of these weddings occurred that the manager consulted other institutions in Scotland to find their policy in these cases. Most of them simply accepted the fact and the Glasgow Asylum had long ago given up having anything to do with the marriage of the blind. Sometimes the Belfast committee took no action, particularly if one of the parties was partially sighted. In May 1895 a statement was issued which explained that in future the rule absolutely forbidding any blind workers to marry in any circumstances would be amended so that the committee reserved the right to dismiss them. In later years the marriage of blind workers was merely recorded, or the woman was also allowed back.[52] These weddings were still not popular with the management.

Over the years of the workshops some names recur again and again in the records, usually for causing trouble. John O'Neill was one of the first men employed in the Howard Street workshops, at the age of seventeen and he died in their service in 1905. During that period of association there were long stretches when he was in disgrace. At first his name appeared as one of the catholic workers who objected to the scripture reading, other times as asking for a wage rise which he sometimes got, but in 1886 his troubles began. In May the manager reported that 'J. O'Neill a catholic is going to marry a blind protestant girl in the house, only about sixteen years of age' – Lizzie Reynolds.[53] He was thus committing three misdemeanours: marrying a blind fellow worker, marrying a girl under sixteen years of age and marrying a protestant.

O'Neill was duly dismissed along with Mrs Rea, a woman who worked in the sewing room and had encouraged the liaison by allowing them to meet in her house. By November he had begun a determined campaign for re-admission. Month after month through 1887 and 1888 after the wedding had taken place he applied for re-admission and was refused. He wrote a letter from Granville St making a powerful appeal. The first crack in the committee's determination came in July 1888 when, although he was not allowed back into the workshops, the manager was permitted to give him outside work.[54] This was the thin end of the wedge as O'Neill well knew. More pressure was applied when two letters were received from the ladies' committee asking to have him and his wife re-admitted. In April, the committee continued to weaken, agreeing that he should be given a room fitted up in the new premises in Charlemont St. His persistence paid off for the committee agreed to take him back.[55] He started work in January 1890 and he must have worked well for he got an increase in wages within six months, and his death in 1905 was noted by the committee.

Margaret Campsie was an unconventional character. Like O'Neill she was one of the first employees in Howard St, the only worker on the sewing machine for making up ticking. Never prepared to accept management decisions without question she complained in June 1876 direct to the ladies' committee that the manager would not give her coals to cook with. She was really in trouble later in the year. She was accused of gross misconduct with George Pogue for which she was dismissed. This charge she completely and consistently denied. The case of Margaret Campsie continued. The matter was taken very seriously and a sub-committee was set up to review the case, but after hearing McBurney's evidence they decided that she could not be re-admitted.[56]

Undeterred she then approached several ladies who presented a petition on her behalf which was referred to Miss Hobson to bring it before the ladies' committee. When this failed she sent a letter again in March 1877 appealing for re-entry but the committee decided not to reconsider the matter. Margaret Campsie did the wisest thing by turning to Miss Mary Hobson who took up her case. The outcome was inevitable: Miss Hobson wrote asking for a copy of the letter sent by Margaret to the committee and by August 1877 the committee had agreed to accept her back on trial to do whatever work the manager set her. What was really unfair about the whole business was that Pogue was judged to be sufficiently sorry for his misconduct to be re-admitted after only two weeks while Margaret had to wait for almost a year.[57] However, this may have been because Campsie was thirty-six years old while Pogue was only twenty-one at this time.

Next year she was involved in a series of fights with Mary Henderson, one of the really disturbed workers and had to appear before the ladies' committee, her usual supporters. Margaret Campsie died in 1908 at the age of seventy-two, still connected with the association as she had been for thirty-eight years, for they were giving her a pension of 5s. per week. This was another example of a difficult, even rebellious worker who gave nothing but trouble but was still cared for by the workshops. Was she 'deserving'? Her need was the only criterion.

Mary first appears in the records in 1890 when the manager reported 'Mary J. Henderson a girl in the mattress room is getting very troublesome.'[58] This understatement gave no warning of the problems she was going to cause. Dr J.W. Browne was asked to examine her: he described her as 'not dangerous although a little bit queer.'[59] At this stage she was just very quarrelsome and disobedient and was brought before the committee and reprimanded. After a short improvement she was back for fighting with Margaret Campsie. In 1892 the committee decided that she must be dismissed but was to be looked after. This came as a result of extremely distraught behaviour. The manager said that she was very jealous of the woman beside her and always wanted the same work, which caused ill-feeling. But on the previous Saturday she became outrageous and ran at the foreman with a pair of scissors. He caught her wrist to stop her and when another foreman came to his assistance she kicked his shins and bit the hand of the charwoman. She then tumbled the furniture which was being done, and ran screaming down Royal Avenue. Apart from this outburst she was also stealing ticking.

Unbelievably she was allowed back though the manager disclaimed any responsibility for her actions. Mary became even more unrestrained in her behaviour. In 1893 a policeman had to be called to the workshops on two occasions. The first time she sat for several hours hammering on a table as hard as possible and refused to stop. The second time she took the whistle out of the speaking tube causing great inconvenience to the shop assistants and keeping the customers waiting.

In October she started using bad language and throwing brushes at the blind workers so she was sent home for ten days. In November 1894, she threw a bucket of water and tea leaves down the stairs which might have hit someone, and on the day before this incident she walked up and down loudly beating a tin can. Indeed during the previous ten days she had twice had hand-to-hand fights with two of the blind workers. It is not surprising that 'the blind believe she is out of her mind and are in terror of her.'[60] In spite of this awfulness she was treated leniently because the committee wished it, though she was now to be dismissed. This time she really did have to go and the committee stuck to its decision, refusing to re-admit her.

She got her revenge by turning to street begging where she did a great deal of mischief to the workshops by making false statements that she had left the workshops to nurse her mother who had subsequently died, and when Mary tried to get into the workshops again, her place had been taken by a sighted person. She then had to wander round on her own at risk of injury, for she was sometimes knocked down by vans. The manager was in despair at this bad publicity. Mary used to call into the building when she happened to be passing and he remonstrated with her over these lies but she explained that she just told people what suited her. Hewitt suggested that the damage might be limited by writing to important people giving the facts.[61]

Of course, life in the workshops was not dominated by immoral drunkards: it was not all toil and trouble. The workers were given Christmas dinners at which ladies and gentlemen entertained them. Baskets containing food, fruit and sweets with socks for the men and stockings for the women were distributed at a Christmas tea party given for the blind and their guides and attended annually by Lord and Lady O'Neill who provided tea and music.

In 1887 there was a jubilee excursion to Shane's Castle which the O'Neills paid for, receiving the blind with great kindness and, at the end, giving each person a bouquet and a short sketch of the queen's life. The workers got a day's holiday for this, indeed some pushed their luck by asking for a day off after the excursion as well – presumably to recover from the excitement.

Music played a major part in the entertainment of the workforce. The committee was keen to encourage the blind to perform (though not like the two blind persons dismissed in 1898 who went off by the Great Northern Railway to sing and beg together). It agreed to support Cassie Marshall, one of the blind girls at the Royal Normal College for the Blind to be educated in music. Cassie did not show much gratitude. In 1909 she had been staying off work reputedly sick, but when Miss Graydon the home teacher was sent to visit her because of the manager's suspicions, she found her playing the piano and an advertisement in the window for lessons. Her sick pay was stopped and in consequence she became very insolent to Miss Graydon and would not let her in when she called.[62] In spite of all the difficulties, the discouragements and the problems, the workshops took blind men and women off the streets and out of the workhouse. They may have been unruly but they were grateful for their chance.

The census of 1871 listed 1,612 blind people in Ulster. These included men and women who were too old, or too young, or not capable of learning or who had no accommodation in Belfast or who simply did not want to work. They were thus not candidates for admission to the workshops. The numbers employed over the years showed the greatest increase after the opening of the new building in Royal Avenue, and as more work rooms were put up larger numbers were employed.

Table 5.4

Numbers employed

Year	Number
1876	31
1883	43
1890	75
1897	100
1907	125

There were on average forty people waiting for admission to the workshops because once into the establishment most workers wanted to stay. When John O'Neill stayed for almost thirty years and Michael Magennis for a similar period there were not many openings. Indeed between 1871 and 1888 only one hundred and six people had been employed.

The Workshops for the Blind which started off in 1871 with no capital became a substantial business enterprise in Belfast. In 1876 their capital was assessed at £1,558 but by 1910 the capital had risen to £25,500. The turnover of the operation was comparable to some of the industries in town. The financial structure of the workshops differed fundamentally from most of the other local charities which (apart from the female refuges) relied on subscriptions from the public. While money was always a matter of concern, it was not a problem. With the subscriptions and the income from sales the committee was able to buy machinery or replace it when necessary, to keep a horse and even to build whenever there was a need for expansion. Any shortfall in funds was made up by special efforts.

Once the first few precarious years had passed the workshops were prosperous enough to enable the work to go on. While the workshops were a charity and did collect subscriptions the most important source of their income was the sale of their manufactured goods. Money could be given to the blind 'not as charity doles but their legitimate earnings', allowing them to support themselves.[63] The institution aimed as far as possible to be self-supporting but this was considered less important than keeping the workers employed all year full-time. From the beginning an annual loss of at least £150 per annum was expected, though sometimes profits were made. The committee produced a list of reasons why the work could never be self-supporting.

Reasons why the workshops were not self-supporting:

No blind worker has ever been *dismissed in consequence of bad times or dull trade,* since the opening of the workshops twenty-two years ago. The blind in all departments are taught their trade, involving *considerable loss of material in learning* and the constant attendance and *time of experienced foremen* to teach them.

The articles made by these learners likewise, not being of the best appearance, have to be sold at reduced prices.

Further there are many of the workers who, having become *blind in mature years* have not the same facility as other young persons who, though likewise blind, have the advantage of youth wherein to acquire the necessary proficiency.

Such as these are never able to earn sufficient to support themselves, and in consequence they receive a *small gratuity to supplement their earnings.*

In time of sickness also, an allowance is given to those unable to work.

These surely are *sufficient reasons* that the subscription list should not be allowed to fall to the small amount acknowledged in this year's report.[64]

The turnover rose enormously over the years.

Table 5.5

Income of workshops

Year	Sales £	Wages £
1873	2,184	350
1881	4,250	1,172
1897	13,1O7	3,866
1910	18,235	4,704*

* Though there was a serious loss of £1,167 in 1909 as the result of the fire.[65]

The Workshops for the Blind; the Home Teaching Society; the Homes for the Blind.

The statement of accounts for 1897 shows the source of income and the expenditure in a typical year:

Table 5.6

1897 statement of accounts for workshops

Receipts	£	s.	d.	Expenditure	£	s.	d.
Sales	13,077	4	5	Material	7,795	11	2
Rents	13	1O	4	Wages	3,866	6	8
				Salaries	385	0	0
				Interest	59	9	9
				Coal, gas, insurance	100	8	0
				Alterations, painting	43	6	6
				Printing, stationery, advertising	114	10	9
				Postage	42	13	6
				Expenses	76	2	7
				Horse expenses	72	2	7
				Saleswomen, travellers and commission	181	8	4
				Telephone	10	0	0
				TOTAL	**£12,456**	**19**	**5**

As well as sales, more funding came from the workhouse, not in the form of a direct grant but by contributing to subsidise workers, who could not earn enough to support themselves and their families. An early applicant was John McIlroy who was in the workhouse, and had written to the committee asking about admission to the workshops as he would like to support himself, his wife and two children, but he could not leave the workhouse without bringing them out. His wife was willing to work if she could get some. Unfortunately he could not afford to live outside without help. The secretary to the union, Mr Taylor, replied that they saw a difficulty in making a grant to McIlroy as it would raise the whole question of outdoor relief, though they promised to investigate the case. In fact McIlroy proved impossible to retrain for he was too old though he was given a trial. Some women lived in the workhouse and worked in the workshops but they preferred to live outside if they could. Other unions wrote to the association asking them to take in workers from their districts so that they could earn their living and they gave some help. Gradually the guardians relaxed their rules and Antrim, Banbridge and Monaghan unions sent local people to Belfast and supported them there.[66]

The payment of this outdoor relief was not wholly popular with the guardians. At a meeting of the Belfast Poor Law Guardians in 1907 the chairman pointed out that 37s. 6d. per week was paid in this way to the blind and that ratepayers who provided the money and had businesses had to compete with the workshops which thus had an unfair advantage. It was mandatory for the guardians to support disabled apprentices while they were learning a trade. The master of the workhouse offered to give 10s. per week for two lessons of two hours each to four blind inmates. It was a form of investment for the union expected that the apprentices they had paid for would be admitted to the workshops after they had been trained, thus keeping them off the rates. In 1910 Mrs Payne and Miss Clarke, poor law guardians, came to the workshops asking for two blind children to be admitted, promising to try to get more orders for the workshops from the union. There was no guarantee that they would get in because there was such a long waiting list of deserving hopefuls.

For several years the workshops had given training to ten or twelve blind children from the Deaf and Dumb and Blind school, for which the school paid a nominal sum.

Table 5.7

Payment to workshops for the blind for training children

Year	Per pupil £
First year	15
Second year	10
Third year	10
Fourth year	5
Fifth year	5

Subscriptions were never more than a few hundred pounds per year – £232 in 1873, £300 in 1881 and £255 in 1903.

Of course the ladies' committee played an important part in the collection of funds, something which had been planned from the beginning. As they did in other societies they divided the town into districts where they collected. There were regular donations to the society both for ordinary expenses and for the new buildings: these were small sums ranging from £10 to 10s. amounting in 1879 to a total of £152. Money was donated from church collections from all over the province, again in small amounts. Three names dominate the list of donors – Lady Johnson, daughter and heiress of the agent of the Donegalls, a 'lady whose name is proverbial for her benevolence', Dr Armitage of London and Forster Green. Lady Johnson was a most generous benefactor to many local charities and she was particularly generous to the workshops. She gave £200 to the original workshops in Howard St, £500 in 1881: she promised another £500 in 1885 if the remaining £2,000 needed to liquidate the debt on the new buildings was raised and in 1890 yet another £500 if the rest of the money needed was collected by May 1891. Dr Thomas Armitage gave similar sums on similar conditions. The third donor, Forster Green, gave over £1,250 during his years of connection with the workshops, including £500 for the dining rooms and the Misses Rose and Catherine Hamill of Coleraine anonymously gave £300 to the cause of the blind.

The workshops became one of the popular societies to which the charitably inclined left bequests.

As was customary in the field of charitable activity special fund-raising efforts were planned. Dr Campbell, superintendent of the Royal Normal College, toured the north of England giving concerts and gymnastic displays. A performance of Mrs Jarley's Waxworks was arranged by Miss Bottomley, who had already done this for St George's Church and the Prison Gate Mission for Men. This produced £70 for the library, clothing society and the brass band of the workshops. Miss Hobson raised £86 from a bazaar, concert and readings at Portrush, while a performance in the Working Men's Institute by a chorus and choir of sixty ladies and gentlemen with a small orchestra produced £15.[67]

In the early twentieth century the most popular form of entertainment in Belfast was the cinematograph show. There were picture houses scattered over the city with shows running from early afternoon to night. Although these shows were singularly inappropriate for the blind, the manager told the committee that he could arrange for two good cinematograph performances at the Y.M.C.A. at which the blind could sing. It would cost £8 to £9 to stage but a profit could be made. It raised £20, so two more shows were held in 1910 which were also profitable.

Table 5.8

Legacies to the workshops for the blind

Year	Testators	£	s.	d.
1874	H. Graham	500		
1895	Miss Pilkington	25		
1882	J. Bryce	300		
1883	Rev. C. Allen	50		
1889	R. Hardy	743	1	2
1889	Miss I. Morrow	115		
1889	W. Hughes	100		
1889	Sir W. G. Johnson	100		
1889	Mrs C. Shaw	100		
1889	Miss J. Law	50		
1889	W. Gilmore	40		
1891	Miss Hobson	10		
1893	A. Matier	250		
1894	A. T. Macaulay	1,000		
1894	J. Browne	30		
1895	Mrs Moore	50		
1899	Mrs May, Holywood	48	10	0
1899	L. M. Ewart	25		
1899	Miss R. Hamill	100		
1899	Miss C. Hamill	100		
1899	Mrs Henry	116	3	1
1900	Lady Shaftesbury	115	1	8
1901	Mrs Carlisle	200		
1902	Miss Benn	100		
1904	C. Ewart	25		
1905	Miss M. Rea	200		
1905	Miss S. Thorn	20		
1906	Mrs C. M. Mackey	50		
1907	Miss J. Y. Stanfield	392	15	6
1907	Miss Mulligan	100		

And of course, there were the ubiquitous bazaars. A small sale was held in the Ulster Hall in 1878 to reduce the debt outstanding with the Ulster Bank, and if there was a surplus, to put it to the new premises fund.[68] A very much more ambitious affair was 'Ye Olde Ulster Fancie Fayre' held in October 1882. This was (as usual) the project of 'Damozelle Hobson' who was determined to raise money for the Royal Avenue plan. The idea was to transform the hall into a totally imaginary medieval Belfast based on the drawing of High St with the Olde Market House.

All the programmes and information were put into excruciating olde Englishe doggerel. A sample was:

Come see our fayre, so olde, so newe its plan so wondrous deep,
Upon ye stalles on which we'll spread choyce goods in hepe on hepe
Fayre ladyes vende, gallants befriend, and buye their prettie nick nacks
Here learned things for 'blue stockyns', eke volumes for yr book rackes.
Thus have we brydged ye centuries inne oure adventures leape,
Transmogrifyed oure Ulster Halls into thys Antient Chepe.
To buylde ye Workshops for ye Blynde inne Royal Avenue,
Thys fayre unique wille eke ye golde – thys aime we have in view,
Yet still there are TWO THOUSAND POUNDS required atte thys Fayre
E're we can calle 'Ye Workshops' but a 'Castle in Ye Air'.[69]

It was very well organised. The ladies who ran stalls with such names as 'Ye Three Blynde Myce', 'Ye Brindled Cowe' and 'Ye Antient Crosse' were dressed in 'antique clothing'. The stalls were ranged along both sides of the hall and sold glass, china, needlework, flowers, fruit, toys and clothes for the poor. Music was played in the hall by the Prince of Wales's Own Regiment, concerts were given in the street and when tired the patrons could go to a conservatoire or drawing room.

Goods purchased at the Fayre were 'made up', there were fortune-tellers, and umbrellas, hats, coats and sticks were taken at 'Ye Travellers' Rest' at a moderate charge.[70] Goods were raffled at two stalls – the 'Maltese Crosse' and the 'Four-leaved shamrocke' – with such prizes as the embroidered dress won by Mrs E.J. Harland, a silver-mounted epergne and the doll and American trunk won by Captain Coote of Armagh. Railway companies gave favourable terms to travellers to the Fayre. It was a great success with over £2,000 raised, enabling the building to go ahead.[71] So by the end of the century the association, which in the spring of 1875 actually considered winding up its efforts because of financial difficulty, was in a solid and prosperous position. The premises in Royal Avenue, Charlemont St and Berry St were worth nearly £15,000.[72] The total assets in 1910 were £25,000.[73] This was just as well because new demands were being made on the workshops. Because it was a charity, the buildings had been exempt from the rates but it was now liable to pay them. A valuation of around £450 meant a charge of £160.

The success of any voluntary society depended on the manager, on the workers and, very importantly, the committee. The committee in the workshops delegated the day-to-day running of the institution to the manager but it was they who raised the money for its operation. The O'Neills were one aristocratic family which gave a great deal more to the association than their names. Lord O'Neill was a supporter from the beginning, giving concrete evidence of this by supporting two blind brothers from Antrim, Robert and George Pogue.

The main committee was composed solely of men but there was always an active ladies' committee associated with the workshops, whose members had two main functions. One was to collect money and the other to go daily to the workrooms and read to the blind, usually from the bible. The lady readers were not committee members. Miss Hobson, 'that valuable pillar in the good work of the ladies', was the ladies' secretary until her death in 1891.[74] Her domination of the committee became clear after her death, when a deputation from the ladies met the gentlemen's committee at Mrs Aickin's suggestion. Mrs Aickin, the new secretary, wrote that as during the years of Miss Hobson's association with the workshops she virtually *was* the ladies' committee, the remaining members were now perplexed as to exactly what their duties were.[75]

The Belfast Association for the Employment of the Industrious Blind was especially fortunate in its secretaries. The Ewart family were closely involved in the work. William Ewart was one of the founders and his son Lavens of Glenbank played the most active part in setting up the whole structure. He corresponded almost daily with Martin of Edinburgh from September 1870 as they planned the premises, the employment of manager and foremen, the admission of the blind workers and the products they were to make. L.M. Ewart was secretary until his death in 1898, devoting many hours of his time to correspondence and meetings.

But of course the dominant figure in the first years was Miss Hobson, if only because unlike the businessmen on the committee, she had no other occupation. By 1871 she was fifty years old, the spinster daughter of the prebendary of Connor and there was no paid work suitable for her, so she spent a great deal of time actively involved in the workshops. Having initiated the establishment of the workshops she devoted her life to their welfare particularly to raising money to keep the operation going. She was never on the main committee but she was in close contact with its members, most of whom were in some awe of her and wanted her approval for their actions. She spent much of her time in north Antrim but she wrote many letters to the committee keeping herself informed of what was going on and letting them know of her fund-raising activities.[76]

Her dedication to the workshops meant that she was not prepared to tolerate inefficiency in the staff which explains her vituperation against McBurney. Certainly her constant visits to Howard St and her close relations with the other staff and blind workers who themselves approached her in concern over the running of the premises, meant that she was aware of the problems. She did not hesitate to attack the committee of some of the richest and most important businessmen in the town, over their reluctance to dismiss McBurney.[77] She wrote acidly

I should indeed be immensely surprised if a number of men of business habits, such as are on the committee could possibly overlook McBurney's incompetence, with such a string of evidence in proof of it . . . it is amazing how the committee can shut their eyes to McBurney's total incapacity for his work . . . the committee look entirely to McBurney's interests and are acting as his patrons, seemingly determined to sacrifice the interests of the workshops for the blind to the personal interests of an utterly incompetent man.[78]

She dismissed the committee's fear that if they sacked McBurney they might not get any better – they must indeed be in a bad state if they could not get better than he. And of course she prevailed.

Her biggest objective was the extension of the workshops. The Howard St premises were not satisfactory for selling retail goods and her drive and energy were directed first to getting a central shop and then to building a purpose-built unit. The committee might have delayed but not Miss Hobson. The shop at 20 Castle Place was taken from Robinson & Cleaver, at a rent of £180 per annum. It prospered, but was only a small expansion so Miss Hobson continued her plans for development. During 1880 she began her campaign to persuade the committee of the practicality of the project. She organised a large meeting of ladies in February presided over by Rev. William

Johnston to arrange to start a fund for the new building (though Johnston thought it was to arrange a more efficient collection of subscriptions).[79] In November she wrote again to the committee urging them to proceed but they were unenthusiastic. Miss Hobson went ahead. On 7 November 1881 she made a suggestion of tendering for a site in the new street – again the committee displayed reluctance. She had taken great trouble in investigating cost and potential, so wrote to them repeating her idea, which they met to discuss.

Gentlemen,

The object for which you are meeting today is one of immense importance to the blind. It is to endeavour to provide more extensive premises. The blind now employed are working overtime while there are at least twenty outside who can get no work though most anxious to be admitted because there is no room for any more in Howard Street. The new street offers the most favourable opportunity for providing suitable workshops and a suitable saleroom without the expense of a second shop. The ground rent of lot 27 in the new street may be £140 per annum or less, and if a suitable building was raised there the cost would not exceed £3,000 – of this there is £1,300 subscribed already to which we hope another £100 will be added before the close of this year. The friends of the blind are willing to work up a good bazaar to be held about Christmas 1882 which if successful as it may be, will put the sum in hand over £2,000 which would leave only £1,000 more to be provided and if it were necessary, which we hope it would not be, to borrow £1,000 at 4_ per cent that would still leave the workshop under less rent by at least £100 than they are at present, the rent now being £280 per annum. The cost of building would be less than might be expected, by the use of the upper floor – if this plan is adopted we would have room for all the blind seeking employment, and would be at less expense than we are now with only thirty-six workers. I may add to this that it will be possible still further to reduce the ground rent by letting over our present shop.

Mary Hobson[80]

The committee could resist no longer though Rev. William Johnston later admitted that he had been against it when Miss Hobson suggested the scheme – though now he thought it was divine inspiration. When she laid the foundation stone in 1883 she was congratulated 'on this consummation of her life work'.[81] The achievement of her ambition did not stop her work. She collected much of the money for the extension in 1891. She wrote to the newspapers asking for contributions, to the mayor of Derry, Sir Robert McVicker, looking for his help in persuading local people to support the work, she supervised the quality of the goods, was always at the public meetings and gave her advice and support at all times.[82]

All this effort was ended by her death in November 1891, after she caught a cold at a concert in the Ulster Hall in aid of funds for the blind. This turned to pneumonia, fatal in pre-penicillin days. On her death bed she wrote to Lord Arthur Hill, M.P., asking him to use his influence to get an order for shoe brushes from the army. When successful she said 'Thank God, for that is my last action for the blind'.[83]   It must have been very satisfying to her that she could see the results of her effort in brick and prosperity, and to know that it was appreciated over the years. She was always spoken of with admiration, while her contribution to the workshops was recognised. Some comments were: 'to one lady they owe the very existence of the institution' – Rev. John Kinghan;[84] 'by her winning manner, and her anxious desire to promote the welfare of the charity, words could not convey the great benefit that had accrued to it from her exertions' – Sir John Preston; 'they cannot enough express their appreciation of her disinterested philanthropic spirit shown by her efforts since this charity began work' – the committee; 'she was always cheerful, hopeful and trusting, always trusting that money would be raised' – Lord O'Neill.[85]

The committee decided to have a portrait or bust of Miss Hobson to be placed in the building. Harry R. Douglas, a portrait painter of Royal Avenue, was commissioned. Although the picture was lost in the 1908 fire Harry Douglas repainted it and it is still in the Lawnbrook Avenue workshops. The blind were truly grateful to her. In 1886 they presented her with a handsome upholstered wicker chair, a table and some brushes, all made by themselves together with an address thanking her for her efforts for them.[86] When she died they asked the manager to place a statement before the committee recording their sorrow at their loss of

. . . their best and greatest friend, they feel that in her removal the blind have lost a loving, kind, sincere and dedicated advocate, whose love and faithfulness never flagged and to whose efforts they are mainly indebted, for the great blessing they enjoy in being enabled to earn their own livelihood.[87]

Miss Hobson would have wished for no better epitaph. At her funeral the coffin was carried from her home at 34 Donegall Pass on the shoulders of L.M. Ewart, A.P. Lemon, E.N. Banks and J.H. Hewitt with the blind workers following immediately behind in the cortege. She even merited an obituary in the *Northern Whig*.

As well as the workshops there were two other societies providing assistance for the blind. One of them was the Home Teaching Society which was closely (if sometimes uneasily) connected with the association. The blind children who went to the school for the deaf and dumb and the blind learned Moon or Braille type, but not all blind children got to the school, and of those who did, many lost their ability to read the raised type. The development of these types was an enormous benefit to the blind. Miss Gilbert, founder of the Berners St, London, workshops, said that Braille was the best system yet invented for it was devised by a blind man who was conscious of the needs of the blind. At the beginning the Home Society also used Moon but gradually dispensed with it so that in 1902 only one pupil learned it.[88]

It was to address this problem that a Home Teaching Society, which existed in most United Kingdom cities, was established in 1884 by Mrs R. B. Pim. The first meeting was held in September 1884, presided over by Lord Ashley and addressed by Dr Moon himself. A committee was convened, with Lady Ashley in the chair.[89] This would supervise the work of the society, of which Mrs Pim would take charge. Dr Armitage, on his visit to Belfast in 1885, was impressed by the organisation of the society. In 1887 Miss Hobson's ladies' committee and Mrs Pim's Home Teaching Society sensibly amalgamated.

The society's teacher went round trying to find blind people who were interested in learning to read. When he found them he paid visits, brought books to them, taught them to read or revived their knowledge of reading. At first about twenty people were on the books, men and women who were pleased to meet the teacher, and their number rose to over eighty. By 1889 there were eighty-six people being taught, though the older blind had great difficulty. Two pupils progressed to an advanced stage of learning history, elementary geology and English compositon.[90] There was a large age range.

Table 5.9

Ages of people taught by Home Teaching Society
    Over 70 years 6
            50 15
            35 20
            10-35 44
            Under 10 3

The teacher had a heavy work load, making over 4,000 visits in a year. A page from his daily diary shows what he did on a typical Saturday.

Called on W. McA, corrected Braille writing exercise
Taught McK Braille alphabet
Heard Mrs J. read St Luke's Gospel in Braille
Heard Mrs F. read St. John's Gospel in Moon
Heard A. V. reading Bob, the Cabin Boy in Braille
Heard A. J. read 1st and 2nd chapter of St Matthew's Gospel in Braille
Corrected a writing exercise for H. McM, heard him read 9th chapter on Revelation
Heard S. M. read 'Macbeth'
Heard J. G. read 'The Deserted Village', corrected writing of Shorter Catechism with proof
Visited J. C., read 22nd chapter on Revelation

On other days he attended the workshops between 1 and 2 pm, for many blind got lessons in their dinner hour in the reading room. On Saturday and Sunday he paid home visits.[91] Writing frames were provided for sale to the blind. Of the twenty-one sold in 1889, five blind paid the full price of 3s. Mr Shaw subsidised the remainder to sell at 1s. 6d. Dr Armitage gave Miss Hobson the address of Miss Elliott, secretary of Christian Letters, who sent forty-eight Braille letters to the blind. The blind who could read and write were paid to emboss books in raised type and these were bound by a pupil of the teacher. Several ladies actually volunteered to learn Braille so that they could help the workers.

The society could only afford to employ one teacher. The first appointment was of Richard Hardy who was given the post in 1884 and began with high hopes. However by 1885 the committee was deeply worried by stories that he was drinking rather freely, so they dismissed him. Hardy took this badly and threatened to do all the harm he could to those who reported him to the committee. In the interval between his dismissal and the choice of a new teacher, the ladies themselves filled the gap. In effect for some years until R. J. Leech was engaged, the Home Teaching Society was suspended.

Leech stayed for many years. When he began he found forty-two pupils able to read and write Braille and ten who could read musical notation. He started well but in 1896 he had severe health problems. He was off with a cold for some time, but more seriously he had a stroke and, when threatened with another, he resigned. His problem then was that he had no means of supporting himself, his wife could not go out to work because she had to look after him and there were no welfare benefits. So he appealed to the ladies for a pension. They were anxious about his case and planned to get a new teacher at a lower salary and give him the balance of money. The gentlemen's committee, while sympathetic, did not want to start paying a pension but agreed to pay his salary until May when they hoped he would start work again.

In 1897 he did return to work but he still suffered from ill-health and again the prospect of his resignation arose. In March 1898 the committee agreed to continue to pay Leech's salary if they got a report on his work and number of visits he made per month. Poor Leech was only able to do part of one week's work before he collapsed again. By May 1899 Mrs Aickin, the secretary, was in despair. She asked the committee

What is to be done? Would it be possible to set him up say as a newsagent? He is unable to work but he can still teach in his own home. Perhaps he could have private pupils . . .. I personally strongly object to the position I am in of being secretary to a virtually non-existent society and I should be glad to know exactly what your committee wish done.[92]

In 1899 Mrs Aickin wrote again explaining that she had been unable to get the committee together to discuss the matter, and proposing that a pension could be given to R.J. Leech if they gave up home teaching but kept the library (though this was the whole reason for the society). A.D. Lemon agreed that the committee would pay Leech until the end of the year and then consider the amount to be given to him. The difficulty was solved by the death of Leech in 1900.

In 1901 Miss Graydon was appointed to do the actual teaching at a salary of £25 per annum compared to Leech's £75.[93] Her first efforts did not really justify the expense of employing her, but Mrs Aickin was eager to keep her on until December 1901 to see how she progressed. Her work certainly expanded from the original contract of teaching. By 1905, she was visiting the sick blind in their homes and in hospital which was a great help to them for, 'a sighted lady can have a great influence for good and can get nurses etc. and report to the workshops'.

Miss Graydon willingly did this work, but the ladies' committee felt that 10s. per week was not enough for five hours work every day except Saturday, sometimes going long distances and into disagreeable surroundings. Therefore they asked the general committee to increase their contribution to help the ladies to pay her what she was worth. She was indeed worth a good deal, for she became involved in the daily life of her clients, reporting back to the manager on any of their problems as well as acting as a collector of funds. This was one job which she hated and at which she was unsuccessful, so she asked to give it up.[94]

This appeal for financial assistance to the committee touched on the biggest difficulty of the society, that of raising money. There were so many branches of the association's work that it was hard to persuade people to give to a special cause. At the beginning, the cost of operating the service was estimated at £50 per annum including the teacher's salary. The committee did give a small regular grant (about £10) supplemented by the efforts of the ladies' committee who organised a concert in the Ulster Hall at which Mrs L. M. Ewart, Mr E. Hill and the Misses Montgomery 'rendered instrumental selections', Mrs Ewart played a piano duo with Mr McCreary and Mr Hill played the flute. But these exercises were not able to make up what was needed, so the committee was approached again. Miss Hobson persuaded them to give £30 per annum to the Home Teaching Society – but only by two votes. Mrs Aickin expected the committee to give the money asked for by Miss Hobson as a token of appreciation for

... her efforts for the welfare of the blind are so unwearying and unvaryingly successful that some weight should be given to her. Successful teaching of the blind has been her object for sixteen years and in consideration of her services this should be granted to encourage the ladies' committee to carry out such work.[95]

The ladies asked for more in 1892 when the treasurer, Mrs Banks, stated the case for increased help of £20 per year. She listed the expenses.

Table 5.10

Expenses of Home Teaching Society 1892

	£	s.	d.
Teacher's salary	60		
Guides' pay	6	10	0
Writing frames	5	10	0

The committee gave half of the teacher's salary so the ladies had to raise the rest. Miss Hobson had done a good deal of this, collecting £77 in the year before her death, but after this the ladies were only able to raise a small sum. The committee agreed to give an increase because home teaching 'was a most valued and useful branch'. In 1898 the ladies had to ask the committee to pay all of the teacher's salary, for they found it impossible to collect subscriptions to cover the costs. They were quite willing to collect for the blind's guides, wages and money for the benevolent funds but money was also needed for Miss Walkington's library. The ladies and gentlemen resisted the temptation to stimulate sympathy and giving by describing some of the cases they encountered, for the blind 'are peculiarly sensitive' and they would not exploit their suffering. So the legacy of £200 from Lady Shaftesbury was most welcome.

The Home Teaching Society ran events to entertain the blind. In 1890 a Belfast Blind Temperance Society (much needed when the scenes of drunken debauchery are considered) gave an annual tea always presided over by Lady Shaftesbury and her daughters. In 1887 the idea of an annual concert given by the blind of the Home Teaching Society was applauded. As the editor of the *News Letter* wrote of the blind, 'having learned the blessing of reading for themselves their naturally inactive life is cheered and soothed by music.'[96]

After the trouble and decline of the early 1900s it is good to know that in 1910 the committee of the Home Teaching Society was revitalised by Miss Walkington, with a new treasurer, Miss Grimshaw, and enthusiastic workers. This service was important in that it helped to reduce the isolation of the blind who could not get into the workshops. Unfortunately it was bedevilled by problems. Until Miss Graydon came along the teachers were less than satisfactory, and the committee always felt that their first responsibility was to the workshops. This inevitably meant that after Miss Hobson's death the Home Teaching Society staggered from crisis to crisis, never able to consolidate its work. By the 1920s when the government took responsibility for the education of the blind even the limited function of the society was gone. Though the numbers involved were small, good work was done with those who were willing to learn. In 1888 of the fifty-seven members working in the workshops thirty-one could read, three could see something, seventeen could not read and did not want to and four were willing to learn. So although some of the blind were grateful for a chance, several could see no advantage in making an effort.

The second society which operated a service for the blind was the Homes for the Blind. There were nine blind asylums in Ireland, five in Dublin, two in Cork, one in Armagh and one in Limerick, all of which were residential. Only one town, Belfast, had workshops. The blind in general disliked the asylums because of the lack of freedom, but it was hard for them to find suitable accommodation in Belfast unless they lived locally. The workshops committee worried about this problem, indeed they sometimes discussed the idea of providing houses for the blind workers from where they could easily get to work and where the teacher could visit them.[97]

As well as concern for the shelter of the blind there was also an awareness of the need for special religious services. Mrs R. B. Pim founded a home mission for the blind with the motto 'For God's glory and the good of the blind'. There were sixty-seven people on the roll and it employed two biblewomen, a blind missioner and a teacher, Mr Mulholland. They found some sad cases of children to help. One blind boy had to support a drunken old woman (presumably his grandmother) by being put into public houses to sing, and a blind girl of three had drunken parents. The mission adopted three children and the deaf and dumb and the blind school took five.[98]

In 1891 Mrs Pim and her committee bought 30 and 32 Great Victoria St to give a home to ten blind women. In 1892 Mrs R. B. Pim presided at a meeting of the mission in the exhibition hall in Botanic Gardens, called to extend the work carried on in Great Victoria St. During the year of its existence the home mission had been successful, lending money to blind persons wishing to start in trade which, in almost all cases, had been repaid. The guardians had voted quarterly assistance for residents in the home. One bizarre object of charity they helped was J. Evans, a leper from Lisburn.

The premises were enlarged in 1895 but they still did not satisfy the demands for places. This led to a move to the Cliftonville Rd in 1901 at a cost of £3,000. In the new house, which cost £3,000, were thirty women and twenty men. The accommodation was described by Mr Milligan as the best in the United Kingdom. It was not free of course: the inmates paid 8s. 6d. per week. The plan was that the blind from the homes would get employment in the workshops, but there were some disputes between the two from time to time. The records of the B.A.E.I.B. contain many letters from Mrs Pim asking for admission to the workshops for people in her homes. The difficulty was that while Mrs Pim and her committee believed that the workshops would take in any men whom they sent, the workshops had their own waiting list.

When Mrs Pim found that the workshops would not take Robert Bolger and John Sands who had come to the homes from Dublin, she decided to set up an independent workshop herself, to compete with the one in Royal Avenue. The ladies' committee was deeply opposed to this plan and Mrs Aickin wrote asking that purchasers should be directed to the original shop.

The dispute was disturbing to both parties so in January 1902 Hewitt wrote to Mrs H.O. Wallace, secretary to the home mission, proposing discussions between the two institutions. These were successful, in that the B.A.E.I.B. agreed to take in those basket-makers who were going to be their competitors, so Bolger and Sands were admitted. Ironically after all this trouble Bolger soon left to join his friend Morgan with the organ.

Mrs Pim, a strong-minded woman in the mould of Miss Hobson, was an enthusiastic, active worker wanting to take men from the workhouse into the homes (even when there was no space) and continually pressing to get her candidates into the workshops.[99] The agreement made in 1902 had broken down by 1906 when Mrs Pim wrote to the committee saying that she did not want to get involved in a dispute, but she would never have given up her planned workshop if the committee had, as they claimed, not agreed to take in her men. The arguments went on from 1907 until 1911, when Miss E. M. Moore pressed the workshops to take in the men because they had become discouraged with waiting. The committee of the association continued to deny any agreement but for the sake of peace they did admit a few men in 1911.

Another dispute between the two institutions marred their relations. This concerned the collections made by the two groups, collections which subscribers could not always distinguish. In 1892, the ladies' committee complained that some of their regular contributors gave to the Homes for the Blind believing that it was to the workshops, and the homes would not return the money. The ladies did not want to antagonise any other institution, but equally they did not want to lose money. The committee of the homes was furious at these allegations, and R. L. Hamilton who was on both committees, wrote to the workshops categorically denying that there was any truth in the charges and demanding 'justice'.[100] Indeed E.N. Banks who had first raised the issue, now agreed that there was no truth in the accusations, but some bad feelings remained.

Then in 1900 when a legacy was left to the 'Asylum for the Blind' both institutions claimed it. As for the proposal to divide the bequest or to negotiate over it Mrs Pim refused point blank to do this, for she had all the information necessary to prove that they were the intended recipients – so they kept it. Mrs Pim's work was much appreciated by the blind who expressed their thanks to her on public occasions.[101] The Homes for the Blind still exist, now in Annadale Avenue, for the Cliftonville Rd was too near for comfort to areas of civil unrest.

After their first few years the workshops were a settled and successful going concern. At a time when society was increasingly looking to the government to provide welfare support, the management of the workshops with the National League for the Blind were also interested in getting state aid from national or local authorities. By the beginning of the twentieth century these municipal bodies could give assistance but Belfast was slow to adopt a scheme, though they provided educational aid for the sighted.

This was a perfect Victorian charity. The blind were clearly innocent of blame for their condition, they bore no responsibility for their disability and so were truly worthy of the help given to them. Not only that, the association did not hand out alms but taught the blind skills so that they could support themselves. This was welcomed not just because the ratepayers could avoid supporting the blind in the union workhouse, but it was believed to be better for blind men and women to feel independent. Belfast people could buy goods from the workshops and feel that they were giving assistance to those in need, while getting the products which they wanted. This gave a feeling of virtue easily achieved. The stories of unruly behaviour by the workers were not made public so Belfast's citizens did not have to censure the association for accepting such misbehaviour. It continued to prosper into the 1970s.

Emigrant party from the Home for Destitute Boys and Girls

6

'Do you really care for the wee cripples?':

THE CRIPPLES' INSTITUTE AND RELATED ACTIVITIES.

While most organisations concentrated on one area of need, the Cripples' Institute had several quite disparate bodies affiliated to it. These were three mission halls spreading the gospel to the poor, four seaside Homes of Rest in Bangor, the People's Palace on the Donegall Rd, Belfast which was an early example of a community centre, the Prison Gate Missions which aimed to rehabilitate discharged prisoners, lodging houses for men and women, two homes for destitute children, and day nurseries.

The only common feature of these very different forms of help was one family. This was the family of Lawson A. Browne, well-known in business and philanthropic circles in Belfast. One of his brothers, John, who was mayor in 1879 and 1880 was active in town relief, while the other, Thomas H., was secretary of the town relief fund of 1878.[1] L.A. Browne married the daughter of Alexander Crawford of Chlorine, Malone, and thus became the uncle of Major Fred Crawford of the Mission to the Adult Deaf and Dumb. Browne's daughter married A.W. Vance of Bangor, former banker turned philanthropist who was the motive force behind the People's Palace and the Homes of Rest. His son A. Crawford Browne who was involved with the Cripples' Institute and the homes for destitute children became the Unionist M.P. for West Belfast in 1931. It was therefore a classic, compassionate, Christian and Unionist family.

The Cripples' Institute regards its founding date as 1878, the year in which L.A. Browne, a devout methodist and member of the Evangelical Union, at his own expense opened a mission hall at Felt St. Browne was listed as its minister in 1892;[2] he supervised the Sunday school, held meetings, began a gymnastic class and later a national school was opened in the hall.[3] Education, religion, physical exercise, all regarded as desirable in Victorian times, were provided under one roof. After the Felt St Mission became firmly established,

143

another two missions were set up. One was in the Bethel, Sandy Row, once the home of a mission to the deaf and dumb, and the other was in Wylie St, just off Stanley St at the bottom of the Grosvenor Rd.

The missions were not residential nor did they give any material assistance, so they did not meet the full needs of the poor around them. The Homes of Rest in Bangor were the first practical part of the organisation, connected to the missions through one of their founders, Mrs A.W. Vance. The idea of holidays away from the cities and seaside outings for the industrious working class became popular at the end of the nineteenth century.

The crowded and insanitary conditions in the poorer areas of Belfast contributed to the ill-health prevalent in the town, so the homes were an attempt to give some of the working class a holiday in the fresh air. This was something that they could not have afforded without a subsidy. Young mill-girls were much affected by having to work in the hot rooms in the factories during the summer months of July and August. To spend sixty hours or so every week in such an atmosphere soon 'takes the bloom off the cheek.'[4]

The first effort of Mr and Mrs Vance who devised the scheme, was to take a house on the Donaghadee Rd Bangor, Grove Hill Cottage, but as it had only five double beds which severely limited the numbers who could benefit (only fifty per year), they decided to build a permanent home.[5] Mrs Forster Green laid the foundation stone of the Home of Rest for Women and Girls in Bangor in 1890.[6] This original building was extended in 1896 on the death of L.A. Browne when his family donated £375 for a memorial wing. Larger numbers were then able to go there – 3,000 passed through each summer enjoying the 'kindly influence, good food and plenty of fresh air.'[7] There was a strong evangelical Christian direction to the work of the houses which was seen in the expressions of gratitude of the beneficiaries, a gratitude which was printed and distributed in an attempt to encourage gifts.

From a poor factory girl

who had known nothing of the joy and love of life, but who when broken down in health obtained a holiday at this Home of Rest. While there, in the month of July, she heard of the Saviour's love. Receiving His Grace into her heart she went back to her factory and lived another year witnessing to her new-found joy, leading many others to follow in her footsteps. Her health rapidly fading she had to leave her work and two days before death wrote to the Lady Superintendent as follows:- Excuse this as I am near to the 'Pearly Gates' but *could not enter without a goodbye* for the sake of last July. Give my love to all the girls who were there. I love them all the same but King Jesus for me. Through great sorrow and suffering I shout 'Hallelu', 'Glory to the Lamb' slain for all who trust His blood to cleanse from sin. 3s. 6d. for the Home Box. Goodbye till the morning! No death but victory![8]

These tributes appear very mawkish to modern eyes but there is a sincerity about them which does indicate thankfulness on the part of the recipients. The homes are on a superb site on the shores of Belfast Lough, at Strickland's Glen, Bangor, and it is easy to see that they must have seemed like paradise to mill girls used to city streets, though it is difficult to believe that these effusions came directly from uneducated, poor factory workers.

It was the popularity and success of the girls' home which led to plans to open a similar house for women and children, the Mrs Forster Green Home, so-called as a tribute to her well-known philanthropy. An appeal was sent to potential contributors which gave a graphic description of the hard times and difficulty experienced by women with large families and small incomes. Their children had only the streets for a playground. The appeal said

My object in writing to you now is to ask you if you can extend these benefits to an even more needy class – the weary and limp wives and mothers. There is no class in the community with whom I have so much sympathy as the wives of our respectable working men, especially of the labouring class, and there is no class so deserving of consideration and attention. The working man's wife as a rule is first up and last to bed. She has all the cooking, washing, mending and marketing to do and when there is a family – and there usually is a large one too – all the nursing. Under these circumstances it is easy to imagine what a life of toil, worry and wearing anxiety theirs must be; and what *a boon and blessing* to such a one would be even a few weeks' rest once in a while, where she could have her baby with her, and where the charge would be within her means.[9]

Cases of women who had benefitted were cited. A girl crippled for five years, unable to walk unaided spending a dreary existence in a little back street, was sent by a lady. She was allowed to remain for a long period, finally returning to Belfast stout and rosy, so that her widowed mother pronounced her cure a miracle. Best of all, through the head of a Belfast firm who had seen her at the home and had been interested in her case, she obtained a job in his factory.

This still left the men and boys. With the opening of a home for men and lads where husbands could go, a whole family could now have a holiday. In 1898 a small house was rented in Dufferin Avenue, Bangor for July and August, a venture which was so successful that another permanent home was planned. A site was acquired beside the others at Strickland's Glen and money was subscribed for building a house. This was used not only for holidays but was kept open all year round, even at Christmas. Convalescent soldiers returning from the Boer War took advantage of it.[10] The charge for accommodation was reasonable and often, if the men themselves could not pay, some organisation or friends would help. The men too expressed their thanks to the committee of the Rev. J.A. Stewart Home for Men and Lads.

I enclose payment of your account for J. Smith, and beg to thank you for making the charge so reasonable; we are paying it for him as his father is dead and his mother cannot pay. The change of air and the great care you have so kindly taken of him have worked wonders; he is quite another man. When he left here I had grave doubts of his ever recovering, but he seems to be all right now.[11]

There was considerable support for the holiday homes, for the middle class could see the effects of life in the slums on workers. But the home for cripples had by far the greatest drawing power for funds, for it made the most emotive appeal to the charitable. In the nineteenth century all large cities had their cripples, visible on the streets exhibiting their various handicaps. Among them the children were the most pathetic. It was difficult to ignore their plight when it was brought to public attention and easy to inspire sympathy with carefully chosen case studies.

"I am quite useless!" has been the cry of many a poor maimed little sufferer in the courts and alleys of the great cities. No wonder that such a cry should rise from little lives cramped and confined, day and night, within the darkened walls of a desolate home, in a dirty and crowded street[12] ... little orphan cripples were perhaps the most helpless beings in our city. Without father or mother the only place in our modern civilisation that was available for them would be the Union, with all the unfortunate stigma that attaches to entrance in it.[13]

This was the sort of plea which was guaranteed to touch the hearts and open the pockets of the generous patrons of Belfast. A local branch of the League of Kindness to Cripples was formed with A.W.

Vance as superintendent and Miss Kathleen Clarke as secretary, who suggested that children bring gifts for cripples to a meeting where they could be distributed. William Fulton explained that the object of the league was to contact cripples in their homes, sympathise with them in their suffering and extend help where there was a need. Linked with it was the Fresh Air Fund for Crippled Orphan and Invalid Children which also supported the opening of the Mrs Stewart Memorial Home for Cripples, built with money donated by James Stewart. It may seem patronising to refer to the disabled in this way but the organisers genuinely cared for and wanted to help them.

The object of the league was to seek out and register cripples (in case there were imposters). Cases investigated included:

Minnie W – Aged 11. Was quite well until 2 years old. Suddenly on walking one day both legs were found to be paralysed. Father seems to work very little. Twelve other children, five living at home, three at work.

Robert S – Aged 10 years. Has been suffering from bone disease close to knee for over four years. Was in hospital for over four years and had two operations. The leg is now healed but he will probably be lame for life. Cause – a fall in the street. Father labours on the [Queen's] Island. Four other children two living at home; one brother delicate.

Annie H – Aged 19. Has been lame for nine years owing to stiffness of the muscles at the back of one knee, caused by a fall in the street. Father unable to work for three years due to blindness. Mother works in a factory. Two sisters both married.[14]

William H – Father blind. Makes baskets, very poor, works in Blind Asylum. 'Infantile paralysis' caused by a chill when a baby. He is now 16 years of age.

William C – Aged 12 years. Was run over by a bicycle when two years old and has suffered from spine disease ever since. Mother and eight other children living.[15]

The Mrs Stewart Memorial Home was free, for the children and their parents were in no position to meet the costs but the holiday homes which provided a chance to get away from the city were not 'carried out in the detestable principle of giving alms' so that parents and children could escape the feeling of taking charity.[16] The cost was very moderate – 7s. per week full board for men and 5s. for 'weak women and girls' (who also helped with the housework).[17] In later years the charges were raised to £1 for men, 15s. for mothers with babies and 14s. for girls.

The holiday homes were only able to take in a few needy men and women but Vance's next scheme was on a much larger scale. This was to build a 'People's Palace', in direct touch with the daily lives of the poor, which could combat the lure of the gin palace. L.A. Browne had been secretary of the Irish Temperance League in the 1870s and the Vance family were equally opposed to the public house which they regarded as the source of nine-tenths of the 'misery, wretchedness, depravity and ignorance of the lower quarters of our city' coming from these gates of hell.[18] Though considering the surroundings in which most of the patrons lived they can scarcely be criticised for wanting at least a temporary escape.

The scheme was ambitious in the extreme. It was planned to provide a training home and orphanage for crippled children, a residential house for factory girls, a medical mission and an old folks' home. The committee hoped to attract men from the surrounding districts to the social club, so a gymnasium and swimming bath and two lecture halls were built. The *Whig* commented that to some the scheme might appear too bold, but it was to be run in a business-like way and its office-bearers included men experienced in charitable work.[19]

A site for the new building was acquired on the Donegall Rd, bounded by Utility St, Eureka St and Felt St. The complex was designed to be a haven from 'the mean streets, the mud and the smoke' so the rooms were grouped round two courtyards with a rear garden laid out by the Botanic Park gardeners and with blank walls to the street.[20] To the right of the entrance there was a range of one storey buildings housing work-shops for crippled children. Opposite the entrance were the living rooms and dormitories, spacious, airy and well-arranged, providing accommodation for boys and girls, with a well-equipped kitchen in the centre. The offices divided the cripples' residence from the large hall on the third side with its open-work pitch pine roof and dado, at right angles to the minor hall. There were also rooms planned for the medical mission to the poor of the neighbourhood including a consulting room, a dispensary, male and female waiting rooms and cloakrooms.

In the second courtyard by the hall was the Cripples' Garden, surrounded on three sides by one storey buildings for particularly infirm cripples, with their own dining-room, sitting room and dormitories all on the ground floor. Near them was the day nursery. Intellectual interests were catered for by a museum and art gallery with a good collection of Irish birds, mammals, eggs and geological specimens. Labels for the exhibition for this 'Patterson Museum' were prepared by Robert Patterson with the help of the Naturalists' Field Club.[21]

There was always sympathy from the public for the crippled children, encouraged by the publication of photographs and emotive language used when talking of them. Supporters spoke of 'the white face of the suffering cripple, or the poor child who is obliged to face the world and its hardships with a pair of crutches as his principal stay.'[22] This sympathy reached its peak in 1903 with the Coronation visit of King Edward VII and Queen Alexandra. The Belfast Children's League of Kindness to Cripples organised a display for the royal party. They collected 200 children at the Bethel, Sandy Row, where they were clothed and given a substantial dinner. Next they were taken to Shaftesbury Square and assembled on the platform ready for the king and queen's arrival.

Until then the crowd was entertained by the military movements and the bands of the Inniskilling and Royal Irish Fusiliers, and the children on the decorated stand became more and more excited. Their majesties' carriage approached led by the Life Guards and drew up just beside the platform. Mrs Vance advanced carrying one of the most disabled children, little Nellie, an eleven year old orphan so deformed that she looked only about three years old. Nellie was carrying a bouquet which she presented to the queen. All of the cripples who were physically able to rose to their feet, cheered lustily and waved their Union Jacks.[23] Then the carriage moved off to the strains of the national anthem but the procession returned by the same route and the king appeared to look out for his 'little afflicted subjects', smiling at them and drawing the queen's attention to them again.[24] Queen Alexandra had been struck particularly with the basket of twenty infants brought to the scene.

Her motherly heart was deeply touched by the sight of the children; and the parents, who were accommodated in the adjoining stand, and who were keen observers of the touching scene, burst into tears when they observed the deep emotion of the Queen.[25]

The opening of the People's Palace was planned in 1903. By the end of 1904 it was completed and the lord lieutenant and his wife, the earl and countess of Dudley, on a vice-regal visit to the city agreed to perform the opening ceremony in December 1904. Elaborate preparations for the event were made. As well as the opening there was to be a zoo with a lion or a puma, alligators, monkeys and the smallest pony in the world, plus a cinematograph show and a sale of work including dolls dressed by the queen and the princess of Wales.

The weather was good, there was a large attendance, the court-yards were packed and the Donegall Rd was filled with an enthusiastic crowd. As the lord lieutenant said the only thing the organisers failed to allow for was the ladies' hats![26] Lady Dudley duly did her piece, opened the premises, made a short speech and praised the People's Palace's concern for the physical, social, moral and religious welfare of those under its care. She hoped that there would be support from all of Ireland. She then bought twenty dolls and accepted Capt H.H. Smiley's gift of an ambulance which was to bear her name.

The festivities continued after the vice-regal visit with five days of twice daily openings at 12 noon and 7.30 p.m. by local notables including Mrs Forster Green. The only slight disappointment in the whole event was the appearance of the vice-regal party for the opening, because the expected escort of the cavalry and guard of honour was dispensed with and 'the Belfast proletariat dearly loves a show of the kind.'[27] A reception was held on 3 January 1905 at the People's Palace to thank all those who had participated, particularly Mr and Mrs Vance. A large sum had been raised by the opening bazaar, £7,300. The cripples and the People's Palace had much more lofty support and interest than most of the other charities simply because of the objects of their care.

Other beneficiaries were less appealing, for example, the men and women who used the model lodging houses in Matilda St, spoken of as the Havens of Refuge rather than Rest. The first house was opened for men and in 1903 the demand for accommodation was so great that the original premises were handed over to the women, and fourteen houses on the opposite side of the street were taken and transformed for the men. The houses were opened because the lodging houses of the city were miserably squalid. The Matilda St houses were based on Lord Rowton's plan for providing clean, respectable and sober accommodation for homeless men at Vauxhall, London in an attempt (clearly unsuccessful in Belfast) to reform them.[28]

The men's house was divided into separate cubicles with clean, comfortable beds, a decent place to sit down and every requisite necessary for cooking for the twenty-five men usually in residence. The men's superintendent was an ex-soldier, Sgt Major Bell, assisted by George Varlow and a night man, Rooney. The need for strong discipline in the house was shown by a tragic incident in 1910 when one of the inmates, W. Mitchell, was charged with the manslaughter of another, R. McCutcheon. The report of the case made clear the sort of men who took refuge in the house and the problem of dealing with them.

The manager told the court that the two men had come in at 10.30 p.m., McCutcheon 'with drink taken' and he made him go up to bed. At 1 a.m. he found the deceased lying unconscious beside the general wash-basins, called the police and had him removed by ambulance to the Infirmary. The prisoner had been in a drunken, quarrelsome condition and was also sent upstairs, but he returned to the dining-room where a cripple, D. Morrow, was sitting. When McCutcheon came down again Mitchell had asked him why he had struck him earlier, but before he had time to reply the prisoner had knocked him down and when he tried to get up knocked him down again. As Morrow could not help, another man 'Blowheart' had to carry the drunken McCutcheon upstairs where he was eventually found. Death was due to a fractured skull.[29]

Life in the shelter could not have been very comfortable but it was at least better than the streets. The lodging house not only paid its way but actually recorded an operating profit, on average £70 p.a. The 'Model' as it was known locally continued to operate until its recent demolition – something that was welcomed in the area as the 'dundering' old building was regarded as a fire hazard because of the men smoking. It has been replaced by a smart modern building but it continues to serve the same purpose.

The Homes of Rest, the People's Palace and the lodging houses were the core of the Cripples' Institute. The other component parts of the society had come into existence independently. One of these was the Prison Gate Mission for Women. Most of the women imprisoned in Victorian Belfast were in for offences connected with drunkenness. The workers in the temperance field were very conscious of the pervasive nature of the problem and the difficulty of countering it. They tried talking to the pathetic victims:

"But why do you drink?" is said to a poor thinly clad, weary-faced woman, who is yet described by a lady who knows something of her home life as a "quiet inoffensive person". "Why do you drink? You know you were here a short time ago". "I was ma'am, I know it, but on Saturday night he had beaten me and I was hungry and cold and I could not help taking just one glass, and it went to my head and the police took me."[30]

The Belfast Women's Temperance Association was anxious to establish a Prisoners' Aid Society like those which had been successful to

151

some extent, in London and Dublin. They had no illusions about the difficulty of achieving their objectives, 'holding out a helping hand to endeavour to reclaim those whom society has been obliged to repudiate.'[31] However these women like Mrs Margaret Byers of the Ladies' Collegiate School, Mrs John Workman, Mrs R.W. Corry and Mrs L.H. Stevenson were undaunted and in 1876 they set up the Prison Gate Mission for Women. They had the support of L.A. Browne as secretary of the Irish Temperance League.

A committee was elected which set out the objects of the society. These were to provide a home and find employment for women discharged from prison and endeavour to restore them to sobriety and morality. It was decided to take a lease of Tudor Lodge, Crumlin Rd, a substantial dwelling house conveniently near the gaol, at a rent of £80 p.a. Women leaving prison were met and invited to the house for a cup of tea and a roll in the hope that they could subsequently be diverted from a life of crime. It cannot have been a very comfortable experience for the ladies to wait on the Crumlin Rd for the women being released, and select from amongst them those who would deserve or appreciate help. In the end it had to be stopped because the ladies' committee 'found with deep regret that the introduction of those who had not been previously subject to any softening influences impaired the comfort of the home and interfered with its order and discipline.'[32] Over 500 women were entertained between July 1876 and May 1877, an eloquent testimony to the numbers in need.

The committee hoped to increase the size of the accommodation for there was only room for ten or twelve women to stay and many of them had either no home to go to or had one with 'a fierce and drunken husband' who left them with bruised faces and scarcely healed wounds.[33] Having rented the house the ladies then had to persuade the women that sobriety was desirable, that temperance was a virtue, and there were many back-sliders. One woman having refused help at the prison gate had later to come to the home, having spent all her money and pawned her clothes to get drink, and there was no certainty that this would not happen again. Sometimes servants came in who had been started on their decline by being given an allowance of beer as part of their wages, and they were much at risk. Those who only stayed in the house for a short time were particularly vulnerable and the success rate was only about half of those who came in. Of course there were some good examples.

Mrs M – had been in the Home for five months and, having been sent a long distance to do laundry work, had received money and had returned safely without having taken drink. No-one could recognise the poor drunken outcast in the comfortably clad respectable-looking woman making her way to her place of work.[34]

Indeed when offered a drink she had asked for money instead and proudly handed 3d. to the matron. It was hard to keep the women when there was so much employment available to them in manufactories, regardless of their 'weakness' for employers never investigated their workers, but there was always a refuge even for the incorrigible drunkard. One woman having fallen by the wayside twice to the 'old enemy' was still received again and kept until her swift death.

What inspired these prosperous gentlemen and ladies to aid such low class women? First of all, it was a branch of the temperance movement which was very strong in Belfast in the last quarter of the century and of course, as the mayor said at the A.G.M. in 1879, they were all large taxpayers and it was cheaper to support the women in a mission home than in prison. Evangelical Christianity was also a strong influence. Over all the committee's assessment of the scheme was that, 'every woman drawn from a life of drunkenness and degradation is not only a direct saving to the state, but is a transformation into a contribution to the prosperity of the community'.[35] It would be wrong to think that this was a grim penitentiary, far from it. At Christmas 1900 the inmates had an entertainment when they decorated the bright and spotless rooms with 'God bless our matron', stretched in gay letters across the wall. And indeed the most important influence on the women was the matron. Most who came into the home were married women fallen into drinking habits who were transformed when they came in. The extraordinary spectacle

of a number of persons who the strongest measures had failed to control transformed in a short time into an orderly and happy household . . . with a peaceful atmosphere scarcely broken by a jarring word, clothed and in their right mind in busy smiling industry.[36]

was a tribute to Miss Funston, the matron. It is doubtful if the Prison Gate Mission Society for Women made much impact on the wider problem of women's alcohol abuse, but it was part of a larger effort to cut down the extent of it.

There was a parallel organisation, the Prison Gate Mission for Men which was founded at approximately the same time. It too met released prisoners, brought them for breakfast and tried to secure for them lodgings and work. The mission bought premises at Benwell St, Oldpark, in 1897 consisting of five houses, workshops, a stable, and a large yard used for cutting firewood. Two of the houses were used by the mission and they tried unsuccessfully to sell the other three houses.[37] Over a year several hundred men were helped with food, clothes, tools etc. as well as being employed in wood-cutting. The committee used an agent, Mr Harrison, whose wife was the matron. His job included visiting gaol every morning as well as attending the police courts. In addition there were lady visitors who paid no fewer than 590 visits to the home in a year. Miss Dunlop held classes during the week, bible classes for boys and evening classes on Thursday for reading and writing and singing.

Unfortunately Mr and Mrs Harrison, who were very good at their job decided to emigrate to Canada in 1906 at which stage the committee, led by A.W. Vance, now the most important figure in the Homes and People's Palace, proposed the transfer of the concern to the Cripples' Institute which was already supervising the Prison Gate Mission Society for Women. The men's mission had never commanded wide public support, operating in 1906 with an adverse balance of £383, so the office-bearers agreed that there was no point in trying to continue.[38] In 1907 the committee put in an insolvency application to the Charity Commissioners asking them to wind up the society but another blow came with the untimely death of Vance. The committee of the Cripples' Institute rescinded their agreement so in June 1907 the mission was transferred to the Church Army paying them £1,500 to include all the assets, leaving a debt of £600 which the committee had to raise.[39] The Church Army took over in July 1907, occupying 30 and 32 Oldpark Crescent. A work test was put to the men sent by clergy or the Charity Organisation Society to see if they were willing and deserving and if they passed they were employed in cutting wood.[40]

This charity operated on a small scale amongst men of the lowest social level. During 1906 118 were helped – 92 discharged prisoners, twenty-six destitute men, six of whom were admitted. They were in prison for petty crimes, larceny, drunkenness, assaults, vagrancy and house-breaking. Of the 118, eighteen were sent home, thirty-six to hospital, seven left, two were immediately re-arrested and twenty-two remained in the home. Even the R.M. had a certain sympathy for them. Speaking at the 1907 A.G.M., Mr Hodder spoke of his wide experience of incorrigible criminals for whom the mission was of short-term value, but he went on to say that when families were in a state of starvation one might almost excuse the offences common in such cases.[41] And after all, even if the mission only gave pleasure at Christmas to a few derelict men it was worth operating. In 1906 they had a Christmas dinner of beef, potatoes and plum pudding accompanied by a phonograph selection given by Harrison followed by a tea. The food was generously donated. The ordinary diet was less elaborate, costing an average of 6d. per day.

Yet another branch of the work was the provision of day nurseries. The scheme was started by Lady Henderson, when she was mayoress in 1873-4. Belfast's high death rate was due at least in part to infant mortality, much coming from neglect so Lady Henderson and other influential local women opened a nursery in Barrack St which was in the centre of the mills, for the babies of mothers of the industrial class. In it they could leave their children to be fed, sheltered and generally cared for while they were at work. At first the creche was not popular but gradually mothers were 'educated to its advantages' which were considerable. Infants could be left from 6.30 a.m. to 7 p.m. at a moderate charge of 3d. per day and there was room for up to twenty-seven each day.[42]

Certainly the report of a Saturday visit showed its attraction. The entrance in Barrack St (right in Belfast's centre) led on to a lawn almost out of place in the middle of streets and forests of chimneys. The rooms were lofty and well-ventilated, walls painted and covered with pictures. The floor was covered with cots some empty because of the half-day and the matron, Mrs Zebedee, and the nurses were clean and neat sitting with children on their knees. Just when it had become popular with its users, the lack of popular support led to the question of its closure, for it could not be self-supporting. Money was collected by the treasurer, Miss Bruce who lived at The Farm, Crumlin Rd, and the secretary, Miss F. M. McTear, from kind friends 'whose names might be stereo-typed so regularly do they appear in every philanthropic subscription list', but it was not enough.[43]

After a lapse of several years more nurseries were opened, the first and arguably the most successful at 188 Crumlin Rd in 1898. Another, controlled by Mr and Mrs Vance, was begun in the Bethel, Sandy Row in 1899. Mothers brought their babies as early as 6 a.m. on the way to work and they had to be away before 6.30 (it was not often that they were left late). As soon as they came in the morning they were bathed and clean clothes put on for the time they spent in the nursery, where there was a room crammed with toys, playroom, sleeping room and kitchen.[44] When A.W. Vance decided in 1904 to combine the day nurseries with the Cripples' Home, Lady Henderson thought it advisable to transfer the whole movement to this energetic committee. Lady Henderson opened a third nursery in 1906 at Wylie St and another was planned for Ballymacarrett. The People's Palace committee described some cases.

One man whose wife had died six months before, dressed and brought the baby to the Nursery every day himself. One poor woman whose husband left her two months ago had two children in the Nursery. The youngest one who was three months old had been neglected, and evidently dosed with laudanum. It weighed 8 lbs. and had much improved since it came.

One baby who had been called 'Scraps' because it had no proper name, was brought here by its mother without a stitch of clothing and the mother seems to care nothing about the child so she was warned that if she did not look after it better it would be necessary to inform the Inspector (NSPCC); now she is much better to him.

Another little boy when he came to the Nursery, was three years old and not able to walk, now he is able to run about.[45]

As well as the day nursery there was the 'Babies' Castle' in Matilda St, a great improvement on the Bethel. This had a large bright nursery with accommodation for thirty or more. Beside the nursery was a large space of ground used as a garden. Unfortunately the day nurseries were all closed by 1911.

The last charities provided by the Cripples' Institute were the Elim and Olivet Homes for Destitute Children in Belfast and Ballygowan. There was a visible presence in the new cities of the industrialised world of ragged, hungry, poverty-stricken children living by their wits and in danger of becoming habitual criminals. They were regarded with alarm by respectable citizens. People began to question their own responsibility,

how much is society to blame for its carelessness as to the fate of the helpless and neglected children who wander beneath the gas light in our streets, and seek a temporary refuge for their uncared for and weary bodies upon our stairs and doorsteps?[46]

It was easy enough to see the children, more difficult to find the solution. There was a general belief that juvenile crime and disorderly behaviour were the 'consequence of a squalid environment and an absence of moral and educative influences.'[47] But how to deal with it? The police tried, but with limited success, for there were simply too many children committing small crimes for them to catch many.

These lads were clearly destined for a life of crime and were thus outside the scope of philanthropic efforts. These efforts were designed to prevent boys from slipping into dependence on theft, for once a child was arrested and convicted of a petty crime it was usually sent to one of the reformatory schools. These had committees of men who were already involved in working for charities, but they were controlled by the government and are therefore outside the scope of purely voluntary societies. Money to run them did not have to be collected, although funds were raised to provide facilities and some entertainment. The juvenile offenders who had committed serious crime went to jail. In 1901 there were fourteen convicted male prisoners under twelve years of age (none from Belfast) and 102 male and ten female convicted prisoners in Ireland between the ages of twelve and sixteen. Of these nineteen boys and one girl were in Belfast.[48]

Those most at risk were waifs and strays who supported themselves precariously, by selling matches or newspapers. They were fiercely independent and scorned the idea of a residential home, so the aid they got was limited to a Christmas treat from the central Belfast churches and the homes. These were testing experiences for the generous friends who not only gave money for the entertainments but actually attended. The boys were not models of decorum and often the police had to be called, for example to Christ Church school when the newsboys became so unruly, clamouring for more tea and cake, that they were uncontrollable. The thought of facing 1,000 waifs, ragged and shoeless in cold December, who had been besieging the old circus in Hermon Hall, where six policemen had been called to keep order might have made the strongest spirit quail. But A.W. Vance played the harmonium for hymn singing, while magic lantern views with titles like 'Mother's Last Words' and pictures of animal life sent the boys wild. When in conclusion a picture of her majesty appeared, it nearly sent them off again.[49] The Methodist Central Mission fed hundreds of boys in the Grosvenor Hall every Sunday with a special Christmas treat, when there was hand-bell ringing, limelight views and the mandatory hymn singing.

Giving food weekly could not really contribute to the production of responsible, respectable adults but all were agreed that it was essential to catch the children young — prevention would be better than cure. It was of great importance therefore to stop the multiplication of the criminal classes. One large group of destitute children consisted of orphans and there was a desire to help them. There was of course, always the workhouse but this was never regarded as a desirable option. From 1862 Irish Poor Law Guardians could board out children up to five years old and Belfast had been doing this for a long time, as many of the foster-parents were known to the guardians.

The three main Churches in Belfast had orphan societies catering for their own denomination. St Patrick's Orphan Society was founded in 1840 under the patronage of Rev. Cornelius Denvir and managed by a ladies' committee. The objects of the society were 'to afford the means of support to destitute orphans, to bestow upon them a religious education, and to implant the seeds of virtue in their tender minds.'[50] It ran an orphanage on the Crumlin Rd, for in general the catholic hierarchy (particularly after Archbishop Cullen came to Dublin) preferred institutions. He believed that the Sisters of Charity, the Sisters of Mercy and the Presentation nuns were most successful in raising good catholic children.[51] As for the protestant churches both the Protestant Orphan Society of Down and Connor (episcopalian) and the Presbyterian Orphan Society fostered their own children. Money, collected from all over Ireland, was distributed by clergymen who selected families to keep the children and to sponsor orphans. The societies in this way helped large numbers of children; from its beginning the Protestant Orphan Society had 4,000 children on its rolls[52] and the presbyterian numbers ranged from 1,852 in 1875 to 2,596 in 1905.[53]

The children's homes associated with the Cripples' Institute grew out of the Boys' Industrial Brigade begun in 1875. These industrial brigades were started in London in the 1860s and were intended to remove street arabs from the perils and temptations of street life 'so that instead of becoming a terror to society, they became the centre of a system to assist boys to earn an honest living.'[54] The founder of the Belfast Brigade was Rev. B. Wallace. When he went to Kingstown David Henderson of Corporation St took over and rented two houses, 25 and 27 Malone Terrace. A letter to the *Whig* painted a pathetic picture of the sort of children taken in –

orphan children of degenerate parents, little outcasts from no fault of their own; those boys roam the streets by day picking up a precarious livelihood by their wits, and at night sleeping in gateways or in barrels, or trying to secrete themselves on top of the boilers in the newspaper offices which are open all night and think themselves very lucky if they can elude the watch and get creeping close to a brick kiln for the sake of the warmth.'[55]

Not that life in the home was too easy. The smallest children attended a national school but the bigger boys worked from 6 a.m. to 5.30 p.m., were taught the three Rs in the evening, made their own beds, cleaned boots, brushed rooms and scrubbed floors as well as attending daily bible class. Small wonder that the brigade found it hard to keep the boys in the home, for they resented the discipline.

There were some treats of course. Each year there was a Christmas party. In 1879 they were invited to Rev. Robert Montgomery's house at 3 Wilmont Place, where they found a tree covered with gifts. At the end of the evening the boys were marched back through the streets.[56] By 1883 the premises at Malone Terrace were too small, forcing the committee to reject some applicants. So new trustees were appointed who bought two large houses, Salem and Ardville at 41 Crumlin Rd at a cost of £1,250. This was called the Elim Home for Destitute Children and here nearly 100 children could be taken.

Girls were also taken into this home and the expansion necessitated a public appeal for funds. The committee succeeded in raising £1,055 of which Lady Johnson gave £200. The total annual income was around £500, mostly coming from voluntary subscriptions, though some people paid for the support for a boy or girl. Some young ladies 'connected with a boarding school' raised money through sales of work; these girls were the pupils of Mrs Byers's Collegiate school.[57] Most of the income was spent on food but the second largest amount went to assisted emigration to Canada. The home also got gifts of food, clothing, socks, vegetables, toys, etc. A tambourine, cornet and drum from Miss Henderson must have been welcome to the children, but the anonymous plate of dripping was more unusual.

Life in the home was highly regimented. Daily routine:-

6.00 a.m.	Boys and girls rise, have a bath and dress
6.45 a.m.	Housework
7.20 a.m.	Bell rings for bible class
7.30 a.m.	Bible class
8.00 a.m.	Breakfast

8.30 a.m.	Half hour in the playground
9.00 a.m.	School lessons
12.45 p.m.	Marching lesson
1.00 p.m.	Dinner
2.00 p.m.	Walk out with teacher
4.00 p.m.	Housework and play
6.00 p.m.	Supper
7.00 p.m.	Bible class
8.00 p.m.	Little ones retire to bed, elder ones clean boots, wash dishes, etc.
9.30 p.m.	Elder boys and girls retire to bed

In the homes the children were lovingly cared for by David Henderson and his wife, who became resident superintendents. Fifty boys and girls had been taken into the home and others aided

the transformation effected by a visit to the bathroom on arrival is usually remarkable; but it is still more interesting to observe the dogged boy and sullen girl grow brighter as it gradually dawns on them that they are not brought here simply to be clothed, fed, and taught, but that they are really loved.[58]

Children went on to employment, several to Canada: one became an engine driver on Canada's Grand Trunk Railway, and another became a sergeant in the Essex Regiment. For those who went to Canada the first stop was Miss Macpherson's Home at Stratford, Ontario. From there the boys usually went to a farm or occasionally to sea, while girls entered domestic service. They often wrote letters home paying tribute to the Hendersons' care in Elim and telling them of success in a new country. The committee was not going to publish any criticisms of the home but the fact that so many children wrote back is surely a tribute to it. This idea of sending children to Canada was used by several charities including the Orphan Homes of Scotland founded by William Quarrier and Dr Barnardo's Homes.[59]

In 1884 the Elim Homes received a generous gift from A.O. Reid, a partner in Robbs' store, who had built the Olivet, Ballygowan, as a memorial to his son. It was intended as a boarding school for two hundred pupils, and as it was built with the co-operation of the Presbyterian Church the minister expected to have a share of its running. However after a quarrel between Rev. T.S. Woods and Reid, the building was handed over with seven acres to the Elim Home. Many of the trustees of the Olivet were also trustees of Elim.

The Olivet still stands today, a huge three-storey building with a massive central tower constructed from local blue cut-stone with a yard at the back surrounded by a 12 ft wall. In the basement there was a laundry, drying room, bathroom, lavatories, kitchen, scullery, pantry and dining hall. The first floor contained two school-rooms with a large suite of rooms at each end for visitors and staff, with bedrooms above. At one end were the babies' nursery and the girls' dormitory, at the other end were the boys' dormitory and the master and matron's rooms[60] all equipped with 'warm comfortable beds.' It was intended that the youngest children would be transferred to Ballygowan, allowing Elim to be used as a training home.

In 1902 a national school was opened in the building, and gradually more children were taken to Ballygowan so after 1907 the Crumlin Rd premises were closed. However the Olivet was never successful as a charitable institution and increasingly the trustees wished to withdraw from their involvement so it was returned to the executors and trustees of Reid. They then offered it to the National Board of Education free, but after the board had received a report from their inspector the offer was refused.[61] There was considerable confusion over who actually was the manager of the school for A.C. Browne (appointed in 1907) had enlisted in Kitchener's army and handed over his responsibility to the minister of Ballygowan Presbyterian Church. In the end the building was sold to this church. These then were the component parts of the Cripples' Institute.

The articles of incorporation listed all the organisations described in this chapter and set out as the objectives of the institute to rescue, educate, maintain, train (religiously and industrially) and find employment for cripples, orphans, destitute children and young persons. To achieve these objectives it was planned to establish factories and schools, where the children helped were brought up in the protestant church. 'Criminal and immoral' women and girls would be rescued from inebriation and narcotics. Funds to sustain these efforts were to be raised by bazaars, entertainments and displays.[62]

The different parts did retain a measure of autonomy having their own vice-presidents: the Prison Gate Mission for Women actually had Lord Pirrie and G.W. Wolff on their list, unusual because the engineers were not often involved in charities. The services provided continued under the new institute. In the Cripples' Institute, the trades of shoe-making, umbrella repairing, tailoring, basket-making were all regarded as suitable for cripples and continued to expand. Hundreds of men, women and children had holidays in Bangor, the national school was successful, women passed through Tudor Lodge (which by 1913 had only a minority of discharged prisoners on its books), the creches prospered at first and the lodging house sheltered the homeless.[63] The Olivet continued, even if on a smaller scale, the work of rescuing 'orphaned, homeless and destitute street arabs and criminal boys and girls from the perils and temptations of street life.'[64] More attention was paid to the medical condition and treatment of cripples. Sir John Byers, whose mother was closely involved in the institute, had estimated that there were 300 cripples in Belfast, while 90 per cent of those in the Cripples' Home were afflicted by TB 'that fell modern plague of Ireland.' The medical advisers tried by giving good food and single care to prevent a recrudescence of TB.

Very unfortunate children were helped. One was a crippled girl of twelve years old, the eldest of five, whose mother was found by two workers of the People's Palace struggling to finish garments for which she was paid 1s. per dozen, sick and crying in a bare home, the father in consumption in hospital. A boy who would never walk was found pushing himself along on shrunken sticks of legs, paralysed but clever. He was taken to the Cripples' Home in Bangor where he was being educated.[65] Mr and Mrs Stevenson still provided the Christmas dinners which could now be held in the large hall of the People's Palace, when hundreds of children were collected in an ambulance, wagonette and bath chairs. They were given tea and buns with donkey rides, football (not very appropriate perhaps) and cinematograph shows with a programme of songs and recitations by the women of the Prison Gate Mission.

The need for increased funding after the amalgamation was acute. The sudden death at the age of forty-seven of A.W. Vance in May 1907 left the institute in a precarious financial position: there was a large debt to repay and it had lost its best fund raiser. Over fifteen years Vance had personally raised £25,000. Even before he died the debt was serious for, although £20,000 had been collected another £10,000 was needed and in 1907 the debt on the building was £13,000.[66]

The committee had to stage a number of events. Miss Kathleen Clarke suggested that a fund should be started to pay off the money as a memorial to Vance. By 1910 the debt was reduced to £8,204 and a legacy and donation of £1,000 as well as a large legacy of £5,000 added to the effort. Of course it was a never-ending demand, for the institute could not be self-supporting and every year there was a shortfall between income and expenditure which had to be absorbed. In a year when on average £6,000 was raised, only 70 per cent of costs would be covered.[67] The income from the inmates plus sales from products covered half the costs. From 1912 the Boys' Brigade made an annual house-to-house collection, something they still do today.

It was vital therefore that public sympathy should be sustained. The crippled children were the best group to encourage giving, and the Cripples' Choir, sometimes joined by A.W. Vance's Fellowship Choir, was always a popular entertainment. In 1906 their conductor Dr Koeller brought them to sing at the Keswick Convention, an evangelical meeting, where they were a great success. The wife of the lord lieutenant, the countess of Aberdeen, invited them to sing at Dublin Castle. So it was popular charity which could raise money, but was it successful in its objects? A holiday, a home, a training might not solve the problem of these disabled, deprived and poorer classes who turned to the institute for help, but they certainly at least alleviated some of the continuing distress. The same sorts of people who needed help then need it now, for even a modern welfare state cannot cope with all of the difficulties. The recipients of the charity were grateful and there were successes. The boy trained at the Cripples' Institute who was put in charge of a branch of a boot-repairing concern in Sandy Row did not need to go to the workhouse, and the people of the Donegall Rd used the facilities of the People's Palace until the middle of the twentieth century.[68]

The real interest in the Cripples' Institute was this wide variety of groups which made up the unit. Other cities had the same individual voluntary organisations such as the holiday homes, the missions to former prisoners, the lodging houses and the homes for destitute children. However, the linking of these disparate charities with work for cripples into one incorporated society appears to be unique. There is no record in any major study of Victorian and Edwardian charitable effort of such a body but perhaps it is waiting to be written.

Magdalene Church.

Magdalene Church, Donegall Pass.

'These fair messengers of mercy':

WOMEN IN CHARITY WORK

Another group who were the targets of charity were those women who were considered to be at risk in the new large industrial cities. Life in the countryside in a small community was not a very good preparation for work in one of these towns where there might be unscrupulous employers (both male and female) who could exploit young, unsophisticated country girls. In Victorian and Edwardian Britain there were two sorts of agencies of relief for this class of women – the charities run *for* women and charities run *by* women. Charities run for women were basically designed to prevent women and girls from falling into sinful ways by providing them with safe accommodation, by encouragement or by missions. Others provided refuges for those who fell from grace.

As a result of increased prosperity the Victorian era was the great age of the female servant. Any nineteenth century family with social pretensions had at least one domestic servant, and by 1901 'service' was the major employer of women in England.[1] In 1871 there were 1.2 million female servants in Great Britain and by 1901 their number had risen to almost 1.5 million – the largest occupational group of any kind – bigger than mining, engineering or even agriculture.[2] In a textile town (like Belfast) girls had the option of going into the mill where they had more freedom, shorter hours and better pay than in domestic service.[3] There were 7,610 female servants in the town in 1871 while there were 4,661 women working in cotton and flax and 3,503 working in mixed materials. However, by 1901 there was an overwhelming majority working in the mills. There were 7,852 domestic servants, up only 200 in thirty years, while 23,735 worked in cotton and flax and 1,852 in mixed materials.[4] Ladies found it difficult to recruit and keep servants, and they were anxious to protect the morals of their servants. It was in an attempt to encourage the supply of servants that a 'Society for the Encouragement and

Reward of Good Conduct in Female Servants' was founded in Belfast in 1836.

Such societies had already been founded in Cardiff, Manchester, London and other cities. Their main function was to give a small premium to any servant who stayed for an uninterrupted period of service. The amounts varied. The Belfast society was generous, giving four guineas at the end of four years, ten guineas at the end of seven years when the women presented a certificate from their employer testifying that -

A.B. has served me faithfully for 4 (or 7) successive years, during which time I believe her to have been sober and honest, and of good moral conduct.[5]

Mr and Mrs S.C. Hall put a high value on such a certificate, comparing it to the 'Waterloo medal we see so frequently glittering on the breasts of our brave veterans' and suggesting that they might even be left as a death-bed legacy to a dear relative or friend.

The object of another group of societies was to meet young girls, and give them somewhere to lodge until they could find their own accommodation. In this way it was hoped that they would not fall into temptation and become the prey of unscrupulous men or of drink. The Provident Home was based on the pattern of episcopalian homes in London and Dublin. The Dublin home had been opened in 1838 at Charlemont St for young women of good character who had no friends with whom they could stay. It dealt annually with approximately 100 girls. The ladies in the Dublin home tried to find employment for the girls, they gave them references for employers and maintained a lending wardrobe stocked with clothes donated by lady supporters to enable the girls to go for interviews.

The Belfast home which opened in Henry St in 1862 moved first to Kinnaird St and finally to 76 Pakenham Place, formerly the home of Mrs Byers's Ladies' Collegiate School.[6] The girls in the home were expected to work towards their own support for this was not a gratuitous body. Although it was run *for* women it was run *by* men. The home in Pakenham Place like that in Dublin insisted that its girls should have no stain on their characters for this was not a rescue home – prevention, they said, was better than cure. The girls who went to this home mostly did laundry work, indeed it sometimes seems that no-one in the town did her own washing so many laundries were attached to voluntary homes. If girls gave satisfaction at that, 'service or other respectable employment was procured.'

Next door at 74 Pakenham Place there was a superior home, the Lodging Establishment for Young Business Ladies. This was opened in 1875 and was also for girls who had no relatives in town. It offered

... at a modest cost respectable, neat and comfortable accommodation in an airy, healthful locality ... for the class of young persons, saleswomen, telegraphists, machinists, dress- makers, milliners, nursery governesses.[7]

This house was a cut above most of the others, catering for the 'new woman' with skills useful in an expanding mercantile economy but who might also be at risk. As there were several such homes for girls a Lodging House society was formed which tried to supervise them, to ensure the moral safety of the inhabitants.[8] The Benevolent Society which was active between the 1830s and 1850s had hoped to build a residential home for female orphans who worked in the town, but they failed in this endeavour. Instead the committee found accommodation for the girls with 'elderly, pious females.'[9]

The Midnight Mission founded in the 1860s had a full-time missionary, Thomas Clokey. A man was necessary for this work because it meant actually going out on to the streets late at night, meeting women often coming out of public houses and taking them to the Rescue House which was at first in Bradbury Place and then in four houses in Malone Place.[10] The secretary and agent, Thomas Clokey, who lived at 7 Byron St, gave his services free for years and with his wife helped 'that class of unfortunate fellow beings for whose benefit it was established', by providing midnight tea meetings.[11]

The trustees of the society were men but the committee was overwhelmingly female. Two clear pictures of the ethos which inspired the members came in the address to Thomas Clokey presented to him with a purse of sovereigns as a token of esteem from the ladies of the committee, and in the description in the 1877 directory. The address spoke of perseverance in the face of discouragement, of the attempts to provide Christian leadership to guide the fallen 'to restore them to virtue, peace and happiness.'[12] The directory said

It is the glory of Christianity that it passes no sinner, and no class of sinners by. None are too low and too degraded to be laid hold of, and brought home to God. It is a happy thought that through the exertions of the Agent of this Mission, and by some devoted Christian ladies, there is not a poor fallen woman in Belfast, who can possibly be reached, who is not kindly dealt with: from time to time, offered an opportunity of returning and pointed to the Lamb of God who taketh away the sin of the world.[13]

The people who worked with these women could not afford to retain high expectations of success because it was so hard to achieve. The mission had a hospital attached to the Rescue Home which received

. . . those afflicted with diseases which are the result of vice without claiming from them a promise of continued resistance under supervision.[14]

From 1901 a room was set aside in the house for the care of unmarried mothers. In that year one confinement took place but this number rose to ten in 1902 and 1903. Unmarried mothers stayed in the home until their babies were born and were helped afterwards to find a home and work. The babies were mostly put out for adoption. Eventually the Malone Place Home became a maternity unit taken over after some negotiations by the Northern Ireland Hospitals Authority, in 1948.

Of course these attempts at the prevention of immorality were often unsuccessful and women did fall into prostitution, the 'great social evil' of Victorian times. Some prostitutes were 'well conducted married females who have been diseased by their profligate husbands.'[15] They themselves often claimed to have been seduced as governesses or to have been clergymen's daughters trapped by a procuress. Henry Mayhew met one girl in London who had been a seamstress before she turned to prostitution and claimed to have been the daughter of an Independent preacher, only turning to sin because she could not earn enough to keep herself at sewing.[16] These claims were seldom true. General Booth estimated that the true reasons were:

	%
Seduction	33
Bad companions	27
Wilful choice	24
Drink	14
Poverty	2 [17]

There was a feeling at the time that servants were the most vulnerable class because they had no protection and if a servant lost her 'character' for some reason it was impossible for her to get another job. The Rescue Society estimated that 80 per cent of the fallen had been servants[18] while Pamela Horn writes of the 'alleged' immorality and casual prostitution among servant girls.[19] Judith Walkowitz estimated that in fact, just over 50 per cent of prostitutes had been servants or laundresses.[20]

Clearly then, there was no single reason why girls turned to prostitution. Pamela Horn suggests that only 'cruel and biting poverty' would have made women face the hazardous and precarious life on the streets. In fact for the unskilled daughter of unskilled parents life as a prostitute offered shorter hours and more pay than either the mill or domestic service.[21] The idea that a girl who became a city prostitute would inevitably sink into degradation has been challenged by Dr Acton writing in the second half of the nineteenth century and Judith Walkowitz suggests that the trade was highly seasonal and casual.

The very nature of prostitution makes an accurate analysis of its prevalence and the numbers involved almost impossible though there were efforts to do this in Victorian times. One such account was collated by 'A medical gentleman' in Edinburgh in 1851. His picture was one of unrelieved gloom, though it must be assumed that he was actually looking for the worst – and he found it. Stories of women walking the streets with their daughters were joined with one of poor Mary Anne R- whose decline began (improbably) with 'the secret and inflaming study of Ovid at school whose pages were devoured with unpalled appetite, the desire thus created brought a craving for more.' She was thus ready to fall an easy victim to the seduction of Mr R-, which in turn led to the lock hospital, consumption and early death.[22] This cautionary tale must be exceptional, but the author also produced a table which tried to establish the numbers involved in the trade and its cost.

Most towns and cities in the United Kingdom tried to assess the numbers of prostitutes in their districts; though these figures must be suspect. According to the judicial statistics there were 361 prostitutes over 16 years old, and 6 under 16 'at large' in Belfast in 1868 which does not suggest a serious problem.[24] In 1901 139 prostitutes were summarily convicted so assuming that the R.I.C. were not able to arrest all the prostitutes in the city the figure 'at large' must have changed little in thirty years.[25]

Table 7.1

Statistics of prostitution in Edinburgh

Number of houses known as brothels	290
Supposed number of private accommodation houses	170
Supposed 3 persons in each house	1,380
Landladies	460
Husbands of landladies, kept men and bullies – say	550
Supposed number who live on prostitution	2,390
Each girl has 12 visitors per week	16,560

Cost

	£	s.	d.
Two shillings per visit is about a fair average, as the receipts of the girls making	1,656	0	0
Each visitor on average will spend two shillings on drink	1,656	0	0
Total sum spent on prostitution	3,312	0	0

Robberies

	£	s.	d.
Robberies committed in brothels	1,046	0	0
Amount stolen (Edinburgh)	7,765	9	11
Robberies committed in brothels	1,332	0	0
Amount stolen (Glasgow)	5,091	13	8[23]

What was to be done with those women who did not reform? Contemporary statistics show that the prostitute had a career of three to four years on average sometimes even seven years by which time

... their strength is run out, their constitution gone. Late hours, exposure to wet and cold, intoxication to drown thought, ill-usage, disease, inevitable misery of mind and body, are enough in this space to break down the frail tenement of flesh and blood.[26]

The biggest problem for the women was the venereal disease from which many suffered. Many cities had their lock hospital (the word 'lock' is from the medieval 'loke' which referred to a lepers' refuge)

where prostitutes were isolated and treated. Some were very harsh in their treatment of their patients, for example in the Southwark Lock Hospital, London they were thrashed after treatment.[27] The women were discharged from hospital as 'cured' though in the nineteenth century the only treatment available (mercury) was not effective.

It was assumed that the women wanted to be rescued, that they were the innocent victims of exploitation and as David Owens writes 'among the causes benevolent Victorians found most irresistible were those having to do with the preservation of female virtue and the rehabilitation of those who had lost it.'[28]

Even before the rapid growth of Belfast began, it had its problem of prostitutes. In 1822 in an indenture between the House of Industry and the Charitable Society it was enacted that

every strolling prostitute to be taken up and confined to the house or hospital to keep them at hard labour and if they refuse or behave badly to inflict reasonable corporal punishment on the offenders.[29]

Belfast had a lock ward (of seven beds) in the general hospital opened in 1828-9 to keep the women separate from the other patients.[30] The ward was closed to make room for the cholera victims of 1832 and was never re-opened. After 1841 a lock ward was provided in the union workhouse and those women who were not paupers used the extern department of the Royal Hospital with the tacit acquiescence of the hospital management committee.

Although Belfast as a manufacturing town had plenty of employment for women, and should therefore have had fewer prostitutes there were three penitentiaries, a presbyterian one, an episcopalian and a catholic, for the churches played an important role in the work of reform. The Ulster Female Penitentiary opened in 1820 in York Lane, was non-sectarian and unconnected with any church but with a list of distinguished supporters. There was shelter for twelve inmates who received instruction in needlework, washing, spinning etc and a shop called 'The Bazaar' sold the work produced. The report of 1828 listed the work done in that year, on a limited scale.

In the course of last year, 47 unfortunate females have been in the Penitentiary: of these,

24 still remain in the house;

12 have returned to their friends or relatives;

3 have gone to service, (2 since married;)

3 have gone at their own request;
3 were dismissed;
2 eloped

Of those who have left the house,

8 were from the neighbourhood of Belfast;
2 from Armagh;
2 from Larne;
11 from Dundalk, Newry, Banbridge, Coleraine, Downpatrick,
   Randalstown, Ballymoney, and Portglenone.

The real beginning of the success of the penitentiary and its presbyterian influence came in 1839 when Rev. John Edgar, minister of Alfred Street Seceding Church, was asked by the committee to raise funds for a new building. If there is such a creature as a presbyterian saint, Dr Edgar must be a strong contender for nomination as a tireless worker for Christian philanthropy. It was his name which became identified for all time with the Ulster Female Penitentiary. The whole issue of prostitution was difficult for any minister to take on, as Dr Edgar's biographer said:

... how few would have the moral courage to enter on the discussion of so loathsome a theme! How few would venture to approach a respectable committee of males and females for the means of erecting a penitentiary. In a spirt of Him who came to save publicans and harlots, Dr Edgar undertook the task and was completely successful.[31]

In the space of a few weeks he collected £1,800 and afterwards nearly doubled that amount, enabling him to pay off the existing debt and build a solid brick building in Brunswick St with accommodation for fifty-four.

There was a separate apartment for each inmate containing a bed, table and chair so that the women had precious privacy. There was also a lending library (the home had a system of literary instruction because many of the women were illiterate) as well as a laundry where they worked. It was a sorry class of women who came to the penitentiary 'penitent victims of seduction',[32] 'wretched outcasts desirous of forsaking the evil of their ways ...... from the common jails, and *the low dens of infamy and crime*, its inmates are taken.'[33]

The institution prided itself on taking in 'all proper objects without distinction of sect or party', and no-one had been refused admission since its opening. In spite of the sort of people who came for help the penitentiary tried hard to give the women a caring environment. This was reminiscent of the atmosphere in the Tudor Lodge Home showing a Christian kindness and love instead of the censure and condemnation which might have been expected towards these 'undeserving' women.

Dr Edgar threw himself into the work with characteristic enthusiasm. Prudently accompanied by one or two policemen (in case of misunderstanding) he went off round every 'den of infamy' in the town discovering an estimated fifty-nine brothels with 236 abandoned female inmates.[34] Then he visited the principal penitentiaries in the three kingdoms, examining the laundries, for the penitentiary was not a charity and the women had to work for their support. In fact each girl earned a total of £10 per annum for the home by her labour. This income was essential if the penitentiary was to survive. Dr Edgar even crawled into the boilers to check them when the coal consumption appeared to be too high. Then he locked the coal hole and put the key in his pocket announcing that for some time the supply of fuel was to be taken out and distributed by him in person. For three entire days he tended the furnaces with his own hands thus discovering that through ignorance or neglect there had been a highly wasteful expenditure.

Dr Edgar, 'that great and good man', as Rev. William Park called him, died in 1866 but his work in the penitentiary was continued and his daughter Susan Edgar Park became secretary. In tribute to his work the name of the Female Penitentiary was changed in 1892 to the 'Edgar Home'. The committee was enthusiastic about the change both because of the recognition of Dr Edgar, and because the term 'penitentiary' conjured up a misleading association with retribution, with a sort of jail for females instead of what it was – a loving home.[35] It was under this name that the institution continued to operate, fittingly, for in the mind of Belfast's citizens it was Dr Edgar, 'Ireland's greatest philanthropist', who was its most important benefactor. The Edgar Home did not remain for long in the city centre. In spite of improvements of the premises making for better laundry work, by the end of the century the site had become unsuitable. And so a new 'Edgar Home' was opened in 1902 at 'Whitehall', Sunnyside St off the Ormeau Rd in 'beautiful and attractive surroundings', operating as a laundry until 1924.

The surroundings might be beautiful but what was life like in the home? Religious services were held by, among others, presbyterian ministers. Mrs Park held 'connective' reading classes and there was a weekly class for improving educational standards. Women were set to work in the laundry but they did have breaks. The usual festivities were celebrated at Christmas. A dinner was supplied by Samuel Kinghan, a tree by Mrs R.W. Corry of Benvue, prizes were given for committing scripture to memory as well as twenty-eight prizes from Mrs Park and a gift of fifty hand-written motto cards saying 'onward and upward' from the countess of Aberdeen. The matron asked for a piano for the home which would be useful for various entertainments and would brighten the home.

Money had to be raised to keep the house running. It might have been thought that because of the objects of the charity it would be hard to come by, but there was no major problem since the home had such a strong hold upon the practical sympathy of so many influential members of the community. Apart from interest on investments and the contributions of Christian people, the most important source of revenue came from the laundry work which became more and more mechanised and made sums ranging from £900 in 1892 to £1,145 in 1898 and £1,464 in 1906.

The number of women who passed through the home varied but was never large. There were fifty-four inmates in 1846 and forty-six in 1906.[36]

Table 7.2

Number of inmates of the Ulster female penitentiary 1840-1907

Year	Number of inmates	Number passing through home
1840	54	-
1866	40	-
1885	25	-
1892	-	83
1895	42	147
1906	46	129
1907	-	86

The committee was anxious to keep the women as long as possible and to give them a new life (often in Canada) starting them off with clothes suitable to a restored respectability. Special appeals were made to assist emigration and give outfits to the girls leaving. A careful account was kept of the destinations of those who left. 1895 was a typical year.

Table 7.3

Destination of inmates of the U.F.P.

Numbers in home	42
Numbers sent to Canada	14
Number finding employment	13
Number restored to friends	8
Number sent to hospital	6
Number left voluntarily	59
Number helped and sent on	5

Was the institution successful? The majority of cases who came into the Edgar Home were not hardened sinners but girls who had been left alone early in life without a real home and for them it became a true refuge and the matron and her assistant the most important factors in their rehabilitation. Some did seem to reform and their success was recorded.[37]

In 1859 Dr Edgar on a visit to the U.S.A. was stopped in the streets of New York by a former inmate who had obtained a good job with a good salary and was now highly respectable. He was very pleased that she felt such gratitude and recognised the value of the help she had got in the home. Only those who gave proof of a really reformed life were sent out to Canada after two years in the institution. Any success was attributed to the good care and devoted work of the matron and lady visitors who encouraged the girls to see the advantages of giving up a life of degradation and shame.[38] The other driving force was the committee composed very largely of presbyterian clergymen who gave years of service to this unsavoury work. Only Mrs Susan Park was an official on the committee though other ladies visited, provided goods and attended any festivities.

The second refuge for the fallen was the Ulster Magdalene Asylum. The term 'Magdalene' used in the context of the repentance of prostitutes dated back to Mary Magdalene, the prostitute who followed Christ. Belfast too had a Magdalene Asylum with a chapel of ease in Donegall Pass opened in 1849 for the 'reception of erring and repentant females reclaimed from a course of prostitution, whether being natives of or resident in Belfast, willing to work for their own support.'[39]

Just as Dr Edgar was deeply involved in the growth of the Ulster Female Penitentiary so Rev. Thomas Drew of Christ Church was the motive force behind the Magdalene. Initially there was an attempt to link up with the presbyterians in the project but the synod of Ulster declined this proposal, because they were already working on the Ulster Female Penitentiary, with the result that the Magdalene was always a Church of Ireland body.

Although the site had been acquired there was still not enough money to proceed and Dr Drew, disheartened by the lack of activity by the trustees, decided to carry on the work on his own responsibility. So

... early one gloomy morning in the Spring of 1838, Mr. Drew, alone, assisted by the ordinary workmen, laid the first stone of the Asylum in hope.[40]

No other person of note in the town could be found to lay it. The big problem about the whole project was there were in effect two separate objectives (the asylum and the building of an episcopalian church) and some local people would only support one and not the other.

The first to be finished was the chapel, completed in 1839 and opened on 1 December with the aid of a grant of £1,000 from the Church Accommodation Society. It took a long time for the asylum to be finished and opened. It was only through the generosity of the Dublin barrister George Tombe, who asked Rev. Thomas Drew in 1843 to suggest a suitable institution for a charitable donation that the work was done. Dr Drew seized the opportunity and suggested the asylum to which Tombe contributed £1,200.

Even in 1846 the building which had already cost £1,600 was unfinished and not being used for the purpose for which it was intended.[41] However in that year the chaplain who was connected with the asylum and its chapel of ease until 1880, Rev. E. J. Hartrick, took over. As a result of his energy the Ulster Magdalene Asylum, a grim brick building, was opened in 1849. It had a dormitory containing fifty beds with one storey reserved for another dormitory, with accommodation also for the employment of the inmates and for the reception of laundry – for this was another institution which relied on this work for its funds. It was closed in 1882 for repair and the women were either provided with employment or sheltered in the other penitentiaries.[42] When it was re-opened in 1883 it had double the space and much better industrial apparatus for the laundry.

The asylum was run by nine trustees, five clergy and four laymen of the Church of Ireland, for the benefit of women who could be reclaimed from a course of prostitution and who were willing to work. Guardians and visitors supervised the institution and appointed the matron and officials including the chaplain who had to be a married episcopalian clergyman. As for the inmates, only girls under twenty, or exceptionally, twenty-five, could be admitted. They had to undergo extensive daily religious instruction as well as doing laundry and needlework. Girls who behaved well for a sufficient time were encouraged to return to their friends or to emigrate to the colonies.[43]

The women were treated kindly but strict discipline was enforced. In Belfast the women who came in were predictably of the lower classes though the majority could read and write. Most had had jobs though a few were of the criminal class and almost all were addicted to drink. All were admitted without religious distinction. During 1887 they were:

Table 7.4

Religious denominations in the Magdalene

Religion		Education		Occupation	
Roman Catholic	39	Read & write	32	Millworkers	40
Church of Irel.	31	Read only	27	Domestic servants	21
Presbyterian	15	Nil	26	Nil	25
	85		85		85[44]

The Magdalene had the support of many important local people. Although the objects of the charity might have appeared to be 'undeserving' there was always hope of redemption, though many believed that the reform of prostitutes was hopeless.

Bazaars, so popular in Belfast, were needed because unlike the Ulster Female Penitentiary there was always a shortage of funds. Dr Edgar claimed that it was more expensive to run a Magdalene because it was attached to a church and sometimes there was confusion over whether the funds were being raised for the church or the asylum. The 1862 bazaar produced £400 from the sale of the endless variety of useful and ornamental work, but more substantial sums were raised by the laundry work. In 1887 £827.1.4 was earned, an average of £25.16.11 per inmate, more than they could earn outside. The total income that year was £968.0.7 but as the outgoings were £1,148.1.5 the debt was increased rather than reduced.[45]

Even though the debt was extinguished in 1914 the lack of endowments and the stress of modern industrial competition for the laundry, the high percentage of expenditure to income and the uneconomic nature of casual labour meant that the Asylum was a heavy burden on the trustees and the parish. So in 1916 the Ulster Magdalene Asylum closed. Between 1849 and 1916 it had given shelter to, maintained, employed, instructed and encouraged upwards of 3,000 women of all denominations.

The third refuge was that run by the catholics at the Good Shepherd convent, Ballynafeigh. In 1867 Bishop Patrick Dorrian invited the Good Shepherd sisters, whose role was the reclamation of the fallen, to come to Belfast. They took a small house at what was known as Convent Hill at the junction of the Ormeau and Ravenhill roads. Eight acres were rented from Mr Carolan and in 1869 a convent was built on the present site. New buildings were put up in 1893 and the current buildings date from 1906.

The nuns provided residential care for thirty teenage girls described as 'wayward girls who were in moral danger or disowned by their families.' Unlike the Ulster Female Penitentiary or the Magdalene Asylum, the Good Shepherd convent mainly took in young girls who were not necessarily prostitutes but who had committed an offence which was not serious enough to warrant a sentence at a reform school. However, most of them were unmarried mothers or reformed women seeking to escape from their surroundings. There was accommodation for 140 women and girls some of whom stayed for many years in the convent, ashamed to admit to the outside world that they had been inmates. One woman there today has been there for almost sixty years from the age of fourteen.

The nuns did not go out looking for girls at risk. Most girls were referred to the convent by parish priests or by their families who tended to put a pregnant unmarried girl out of her home. Most girls who came in were aged between fourteen and twenty-five and total confidentiality was maintained to protect both the girls and their families. Some even changed their names when they entered to shield their identity and the nuns did not know why a girl was in the convent. The work was funded mostly by collections from catholic churches, though they too held bazaars, the largest in 1907. The legend in the convent is that £7,000 was made on this occasion but this enormous amount seems unlikely when compared with the money raised by the Magdalene with a much richer group of supporters.

Like the other two refuges the Good Shepherd convent had a laundry which continued to operate until 1977, when, as a result of terrorist bombing of hotels which were their best customers, it became uneconomic.[46] The idea that laundry work was peculiarly suitable for penitent women was remarkably widespread and continued until the end of Queen Victoria's reign to be the industrial occupation of residential homes for fallen women. As Judith Walkowitz wrote 'clear starching it would seem, clears all sin, and an expert ironer can cheerfully put her record behind.'[47]

The second half of the nineteenth century was the heyday of the laundry trade, for many houses had inadequate space and facilities not only for washing but particularly for drying clothes. As the sanitary idea became more widespread, frequently washed and perfectly pressed linen was part of the appearance of gentility. Until the 1860s there was no mechanisation in the laundry business but after the steam laundry appeared in 1890 techniques improved and labour was saved. In 1891 the Good Shepherd convent installed the first steam laundry in Ireland. The sisters had been engaged in this work for many years as their French founder, St Mary Euphrasia, looked on it as a form of therapy. It needed discipline to get the work done in time, it gave employment to idle hands and there was a sense of achievement when it was done – all very important for the women and girls who came to the home, most of whom had had little success in life. The convent is the only one of the refuges still in existence though its operations have changed. It is still home for the old women who came in years ago as girls but residential care is less popular now. There are two homes in the grounds which provide temporary shelter for women in need. 'Marionville' is a home for pregnant unmarried girls (for there is still a stigma for illegitimacy in small Ulster communities), and 'Roseville' takes in battered wives. Most of the work of the Good Shepherd nuns is now done in the community.

The charities which looked after the morals of women and girls were run by committees of both men and women. There were, however, other bodies run almost exclusively by women with occasional professional help from men, which had as their object the welfare not only of women but also of their families. The three most important charities in this section were the Belfast Ladies' Clothing Society, the Society for the Relief of the Destitute Sick and the Society for Providing Nurses for the Sick Poor.

In a society which to-day has access to cheap fashionable clothes, which indeed shows conspicuous consumption, if not waste, in buying and discarding them, it is hard to imagine how important clothing was for the poor in nineteenth century Belfast and how difficult it was for them to keep warm. In 1832 during the cholera epidemic an overseer found eighty-eight individuals with only thirteen blankets between them.[48]

There were frequent references by the Belfast voluntary societies to the supplying of clothing and bedding, in times of exceptional distress, to the pupils of the Ulster Institution for the Deaf and Dumb and the Blind; to the children going to Canada from the Elim and Olivet Homes; to the need for men's clothes and boots by the Society for Providing Nurses for the Sick Poor; and to women from the various institutions looking for situations and needing to present a good appearance. In pre-Singer days after all, the clothes had to be made by hand, a slow and laborious process sometimes beyond the skill of the poorer classes, while workwomen had no retail structure through which to dispose of their products. Winter always led to a crisis. This particular form of charity fitted neatly into what was then perceived to be women's responsibility so, from the early part of the century when women usually played only minor roles in voluntary societies, they were involved in the clothing sales depots.

The long-term, efficient charity in this area was the Female Society for Clothing the Poor, later the Belfast Ladies' Clothing Society founded in 1819. This was the most important of the societies in Belfast run by local ladies. Its committee was made up of women from families associated with philanthropy and included an unusually high number of unmarried women – presumably because there was no moral danger in the distribution of clothing.

The committee was allowed by the town council to meet and give out clothes at the old House of Correction, Brunswick St, but when it was demolished in 1851 they had to open a depot at 129 Durham St. From there they moved to College St South and finally to 20 Carlisle St, following the population drift of the poor from the city centre. The ladies devoted considerable time and effort to the society. According to the rules they met weekly during the winter to distribute clothes[49] and, as they were anxious to avoid the stigma of charity, the recipients had to pay for the clothing and blankets, though they were charged less than half the correct price and in a few exceptional cases subscribers could recommend a gratuitous donation. Not just anyone could take advantage of the society. A line of referral from a subscriber had to be produced which would recommend 'an object of relief to the amount of the subscription.' The note presented by the applicant stated that he or she was a suitable subject for help and only the poor who were worthy of assistance and, particularly, not likely to pawn the clothes, were supplied.[50] This definition of the 'deserving' poor was not unreasonable for few subscribers would be happy if their donations ended up in the public house via the pawnshop.

There were frequent complaints from the committee of the facility with which recommendations were given to unknown people which made the work of selecting recipients so much harder, and gave them the disagreeable task of refusing unsuitable applicants.[51] The 'ungrateful poor' who lived in the 'entries and lanes in Belfast too offensive and dangerous to be entered, from the filth and immorality of the wretched outcasts of society that live in them' were hard to supervise.[52] In 1836 the matron reported that many recipients cheated and there was no way of preventing pawnbrokers from receiving articles and lending money on them. Once, in an attempt to stop this practice, she actually put brands on all the blankets but the pawnbrokers still took them, and she found five in one shop. She also used to visit people to check on the blankets but, having found that they had disposed of the covers, they appeared to be in such misery that it was difficult to blame them.[53] This was a common problem with all clothing societies.

These were unwelcome clients, for the Clothing Society really wanted to provide for families fallen on hard times. In the unparalleled disaster year of 1847 they had to give clothes for heads of families and children who would have been unable to go to work or school without this help. That year the committee bought some cast-off men's clothing to enable a few labourers to return to work and this was felt to be particularly beneficial to the industrious poor.[54] When the cholera was most severe in 1848 the committee supplied a large number of blankets to sufferers. Blankets were given to the Society for the Relief of the Destitute Sick for use by their clients.[55]

The scale of operations was small. In 1852 when Belfast's population was over 88,000 only 960 people were assisted with clothing.

Table 7.5

Clothing distributed by Clothing Society 1852

Articles distributed

Blankets	420	Flannel petticoats	200	Shirts	50
Cloaks	20	Black petticoats	190	Flannel waistcoat	130
Shifts	310	Bedgowns	70	Flannel drawers	70
Shawls	120	Frocks	50	Slips	69[56]

Similar articles were distributed in 1910 but in smaller amounts.

Table 7.6

Clothing distributed by Clothing Society 1910

Articles of serge, flannel, flanelette	320
Blankets	112
Shawls	38
Pairs of boots	44
Articles of underclothing	100
Sheets	24
Bed ticks	a few [57]

The money collected by the society came in small amounts from subscriptions and church charity sermons. By 1907 the church collections were stopped, for many congregations now had their own organisations among them St Anne's and the Roman Catholic Ladies' Clothing Societies. In 1907 in an attempt to stimulate interest and giving, the committee decided for the first time to go before the public and hold a meeting at which to report on their work and to show the efforts which they made. The charity may have operated on a small scale but, as the committee said, 'the poor would be ill-provided with blankets and clothing were it not for the exertions of the Clothing Society.'[58]

The Society for the Relief of the Destitute Sick was founded in 1826 after a stranger from Edinburgh, Mr Spalding, came to Belfast and visited his friend Dr Edgar. On a trip round the town to investigate life in the slums he found a sorry state of affairs. Spalding with that energetic philanthropist, Dr Edgar, developed the idea of sending out 'ministering angels' among these forsaken victims. This was the beginning of the society.

The benevolence of the organisation was directed exclusively towards cases of sickness and poverty united. It did not aim to give any medical treatment but to improve the environment in which patients were nursed. Its object, laid down in a scheme for administration and management, was

to afford relief to the Destitute Poor in the Town of Belfast in any time of sickness . . . but not to relieve old or superannuated persons unless suffering under sickness apparently of a temporary nature.[59]

While originally only intended to relieve workers and their families struck down by unexpected illness, the society revised its rules in 1878. After then chronic cases such as epilepsy, paralysis, consumption, rheumatism and bronchitis were taken on as well. The need for assistance came mostly from the wives and families of labourers and old men and widows, numbers of whom were unable or unwilling to go to the soup kitchen for rations, and who, in times of cold weather (as in the severe winter of 1878-9) were likely to succumb to an epidemic.

The operation of the charity was distinctly amateur. It was managed by a committee of ladies who personally visited and investigated every case brought before them. These ladies were voluntary helpers but by 1904 they employed one paid assistant at a salary of £15 per annum.[60] Most of the work was done by young ladies who collected the subscriptions and went into the back streets to investigate applications for help. Like the Clothing Society they divided the town into districts, and visitors were appointed to each so that they got to know every case.

No money was ever given in case it might be spent on drink or otherwise misapplied. Instead, every Friday, tickets were handed out, according to want, which could be exchanged in certain named grocers' shops to the value of 8d. to 1s., for coals and food for a week.[61] This amount scarcely changed through the century and the committee was disturbed by its inability to give more, for they could seldom afford to increase the shilling's worth of food even in the most severe weather. Often they even had to withdraw the weekly ticket in the summer, and replace it by a fortnightly one. The shops concerned submitted accounts monthly to enable the visitors to keep a check on the amount spent. As well as attending to the bodily needs of the poor and sick the visitors offered religious instruction, but they were careful not to obtrude their views.[62] This body had close connections with the Clothing Society with whom, for a time, it shared premises at 129 Durham St.[63]

The families which received aid were in dire straits. One case was of a man with cancer who had a delicate wife and large family, who got a special grant, and when he died his wife continued to get it. A young woman recovering from pneumonia received nourishment and aid for two weeks. There were particular hardships at Christmas and holiday times because, as there were no paid holidays, no money was coming in, and so the pressure on the poor was heavy. Things were even worse in harsh weather, when the undertaking gave coals (to the value of £3 in 1903). Applications for relief were made to the secretaries or lady visitors and if they were away the assistant would investigate and report back.[64] Some of the committee members were also on the committee of the Ladies' Clothing Society. There was (almost inevitably in an association with so many young unmarried women) quite a high turnover of members with only five out of the eighteen committee members still serving in 1904. The districts which they worked in were like those of the Clothing Society in the lower areas of the city, areas such as York St, Sandy Row, Cromac St, North Queen St and Nelson St.

The amount of money limited the aid which could be given. It was collected in small sums from individuals and firms. In 1904 the total income was £295.18.5, so it operated on a very small amount.

Table 7.7

Accounts of Destitute Sick Society

Income	£	s.	d.	Expenditure	£	s.	d.
Balance in bank	116	4	8	Miss Wright	15	0	0
Rosemary St Church	1	10	10	Printing reports	5	16	6
Collections	150	0	0	Acknowledgements			
				in papers		8	6
Interest on legacy	13	0	6	Postage etc.		16	8
Interest from P.O.	5	0	5	Relief of poor	158	6	6
				Balance in bank	115	10	9
TOTAL	295	18	5	TOTAL	295	18	5

In P.O. Savings Bank	200	0	0
In Provincial Bank	1000	0	0 [65]

184

In 1904 the finances were given a great boost with a legacy of £1,000 from J. Gray. Because of the low level of income few people could be assisted, in fact the numbers actually fell during the century. From 1826 until 1832, 3,684 sick persons were relieved, 577 in 1834, but by 1904 only 76 in winter and 43 in summer got aid.[66] In 1910 eighty were helped in the cold spring reducing to sixty in the autumn.

The undertaking was unpretentious, described by Rev. William Park, as

... one of the old-fashioned charities of Belfast that went about its work in the good old-fashioned way. It was founded at a time when people were not in a desperate hurry like those who live to day.[67]

The Society for the Relief of the Destitute Sick made no attempt to nurse its clients, for members were untrained volunteers. In the city there were families with a sick member who was not eligible for treatment in the hospital, and for whom the Destitute Sick Society could do little.

The Society for Providing Nurses for the Sick Poor was founded to aid chronic invalids among the poorest classes. The publicity given to the work of Florence Nightingale during the Crimean War stimulated a growing interest in the development of nursing as a profession rather than as a drudgery practised by the likes of Sairey Gamp.

Belfast had a nurses' home attached to the Frederick St hospital from 1872 and it was this home which made it possible for the Society for Providing Nurses for the Sick Poor to function, by supplying professional, trained nurses to work in the dispensary districts. The Royal Hospital would only take certain categories of sick people and

... anyone who has been present on a Saturday forenoon at the board of management of the hospital must have been often pained by witnessing the expressions of disappointment on the evidently sick countenances of those who were refused admission on the grounds that their ailments did not come within the objects of the institution.[68]

That being so, what was to happen to those people? One solution was the workhouse hospital, and in the case of 'desolate parties' without family or friends this was the best answer.

The foundation of the first Society for Providing Nurses for the Sick Poor in London was credited to Miss Annie Macpherson. The objects of the society were to nurse the sick poor in their own houses, to give instruction in disinfection and other sanitary matters, to teach the relatives of invalids the simple rules of nursing, how to prepare food in a wholesome manner and to supply nourishment for those who were too poor to get it for themselves.[69] In effect the society was the forerunner of the district nurse and the health visitor, dealing with the whole environment not just disease.

From 1874 the nurses were attached to a dispensary district, though at the beginning of the society there were only three districts with nurses, rising to five in 1879 (still not many for a population of 230,000) and then to nine.[70] They worked closely with the dispensary doctors who were described as the best friends and warmest supporters of the society, meeting weekly at the respective stations to receive instruction on the treatment of their patients. The treatment covered many areas. The nurses had to be prepared to work as home helps, even decorators, for the homes they worked in were often extremely dirty and bare. When they first went into the houses of the poor they had to put the room in order, cleaning, ventilating, whitewashing where necessary, a very difficult task. This in some ways was the hardest part of the work:

... nor is this to be wondered at when we consider the wretched dwellings in which many of our patients are obliged to live; the windows sometimes do not open, the chimney often smokes, and in one small room and perhaps in one bed the father, mother and several children sleep.[71]

The nurse taught women to cook and look after the household, and if her lessons of thrift, of cleanliness, of ventilation, of economy, of kitchenry were remembered she had planted the seeds of a proper future.[72] Lessons of cleanliness were taught to all who were visited and the sanitary and domestic arrangements of the houses much improved. The work of nurses would have been impossible if they had been unable to lend appliances which were quite beyond the means of patients to buy, such as air cushions, water beds, blankets, sheets and easy chairs.[73] The society was always looking for old clothes, especially boots and shoes, old flannels, old blankets, linen, carpets, indeed anything that would be useful and improve the comfort of the sick-room. In these cases local businessmen were generous. Sinclair's of Royal Avenue, the large department store, supplied blankets, and sheets for lending were replenished by W. Ewart & Sons.[74] In bad times when hunger was added to the suffering of the sick poor, food was also distributed. In the winter of 1878-9

13,800 quarts of new milk were handed out besides beef teas, arrow-root, beef-steak, eggs, puddings etc. contributed by suppliers. Wine and spirits constantly required for pneumonia sufferers were sent by Lyle & Kinahan, the Bushmills Distillery and others.

The association dealt with only a small number of clients. In 1879 there were 153 patients on their books being treated in their own homes, at any one time, 600 over the year. In that year 156 died, 56 of them on the Falls Rd.[75] The numbers of patients rose over the next thirty years. In 1909 the total nursed during the year was 1,521 to whom 38,884 visits were paid, an increase of 3,086.[76] The numbers treated depended on the funds available and like the Clothing Society and the Destitute Sick Society, the Sick Poor Society worked on very small amounts. Appeals were made to the employers of labour in Belfast, for the households where the nurses worked were those of the men and women by whose toil fortunes had been accumulated and the prosperity of the town built up. One of these employers (Thomas Sinclair) urged the claims of the society in emotive terms.

What! Have these poor girls coughing out their lives in earning our dividends, and shall we refuse what will help to soothe their dying pillows . . . [77]

for the girls toiled on to within a month from the end. Can the rich man, who thinks nothing of spending £100 or £200 to give relief to one dear, not give a few pounds to '. . . ease the short final conflict of those who almost to the end were building the fabric of his fortune?'[78]

The patients paid nothing, made no return of any material kind, for the time of illness could mean disaster for a family. Details of some of the cases were publicised in an effort to increase donations. Sometimes a family coming into the town to look for work fell on hard times. One example was of a mother and daughter in bed during the day because they had only one set of bed clothes which the father and son used at night. In this family one son and one daughter had died and another son was dying. Another man in distress was the father of six who was ill with consumption. The earnings of his wife (6d. per week) and one child (2d. per week) were the family's sole support. In one house the visitors found seven orphans supported by the eldest who was now ill. The younger children could hardly stand owing to exhaustion from hunger. Soup tickets were given to them.[79] During the first half of the twentieth century the society's nurses became more professional and eventually became district nurses supported by Public Health authorities.

Why were women personally and widely involved in charitable work in Victorian Britain? There is no single explanation but there are several which are important. The middle class men who prospered in business and industry had wives, daughters and sisters. When the men took an interest in philanthropy so did their families. Sometimes it was shown in attendance at Christmas parties for the poor or in providing food for these entertainments but this was only a beginning. These middle class women had money and leisure. Unlike aristocratic ladies they had no traditional pattern of occupations, unlike working class women they could not find suitable jobs, so charity work had considerable attractions. It occupied their time, gave them an interest and made them feel good because they were helping others. From making tea and collecting funds they progressed to serving on committees. This should not be surprising for, although the women might have been regarded as merely housewives, in the nineteenth century this job required considerable managerial skills. Servants had to be employed, supervised and made to conform to the house rules. Food had to be ordered and planned, cleaning had to be checked and children had to be cared for. With such experience, work among the needy seemed the obvious outlet for their spare time. As girls became better educated they were determined to use their talents more productively than by sitting at home. Then, it was quite exciting to go into the entries and courts of the towns and meet rough men and women, as long as they could go home to the leafy suburbs at night.

Why was so much effort devoted to attempting to eradicate vice? There were probably around 350 prostitutes in Belfast compared to 25,000 women working in textiles and almost 8,000 in domestic service in 1901 so vice cannot have been a real menace to society, and prostitutes cannot have thronged the streets. So why make such a fuss about it? One great attraction in the work was that fallen women could be reclaimed: there was a prospect of success. The deaf and dumb, the blind and the cripples would always remain handicapped no matter how much effort was made for them for, although their condition might be relieved, it could not be removed. Prostitution was patently a sin and there was the biblical authority of the rescue of Mary Magdalene to encourage the work. The help given at times of exceptional distress was only a temporary expedient lasting for a short time. The poor helped by the clothing societies and the nurses for the sick poor still remained poor, but the fallen women might possibly, just possibly, be raised.

Why did women not turn their attention to improving the housing of the poor? Octavia Hill's work in London to provide housing for labourers was one of the few societies in this field run by women.[80] In Belfast workers' houses compared favourably with other cities, for the greatest growth of the town came after bye-laws imposed some measure of restriction on building. This meant that it was the corporation, composed solely of men until the end of the Victorian era, which was most influential on housing.

The change in the position of women can be partly attributed to their work in philanthropy. This work brought them into the public view, they were seen to be competent and successful and their own self-confidence increased. They were now preparing to enter the professions, to take jobs in offices and become involved in politics. While it would be wrong to claim that it was only their work in charities which changed their status it would be equally wrong to ignore it. It was no accident that all of these societies had an urban setting. In rural areas there were not enough middle class women available to form any organisation of this kind while the picture of a Lady Bountiful carrying calves' foot jelly to the peasant did not appeal to the educated woman. The cities played a crucial role in providing schools for girls, as well as a concentration of interested women to meet and thus work effectively, even in supplying numbers of the lower orders upon which they could work. The nineteenth century gave women their first opportunities to emerge as independent workers and managers and it was then that they began to demand their rights to vote. How much was philanthropy responsible for this? It is very hard to assess the effects of it but it must not be ignored.

St. Patrick's Catholic Church, Donegall Street, c. 1820.

Rosemary Street Presbyterian Church, c. 1820.

8

'The other sort':

PROTESTANT/CATHOLIC
COLLABORATION (OR LACK OF IT) IN CHARITY WORK

One common denominator of these charities was the overwhelmingly protestant nature of their organisation. Only the Cripples'
Institute actually specified that aid should go to members of the
Church of Scotland or Church of England, but the management of
all relief bodies was almost exclusively protestant. The temporary
relief funds in the 1840s, 1850s and 1870s did have a few catholic
representatives but they were in a minority and when the crisis ended
the committees ceased to exist. Why was this so? Was it deliberate
anti-catholic bias? Were there no catholic charities? It was mainly the
result of Belfast's pattern of apartheid which affected most areas of
life in the city rather than a conscious decision to exclude catholics
from the societies. By the second half of the nineteenth century the
lines of division had been clearly drawn.

Housing and employment were inextricably linked in Belfast. The
spinning mills and weaving factories were mostly built on the west
bank of the Lagan, on the Falls and Shankill roads. The main area of
occupation for catholics was in the textile industry and as the mill
houses were constructed beside the work place, west Belfast had a
substantial catholic population. On the other side of the river the
shipyard and docks provided employment. As the workforce in shipbuilding and engineering was predominantly presbyterian, east Belfast was identified as protestant. Catholics and protestants preferred
to live in their own communities, surrounded by people of similar
traditions and interests. By 1901 the percentages of households which
lived in mixed streets was small. Forty-four per cent of catholics lived
in streets with more than 90 per cent catholic occupancy and 62 per
cent protestants in streets with fewer than 10 per cent catholic
occupancy.[1] By this time national schools were under denominational
control so many people knew little of life outside their immediate
surroundings of home, family and work. Inevitably this bred suspicion

and a fear of what 'the other sort' might be planning, and encouraged the development in both groups of a sort of siege mentality.

When it came to charity work it would have been surprising if joint efforts were made. It was not that catholics did not need help just as much as protestants but that the way in which they organised it was different. Because of the composition of boards of management of societies for the deaf, blind or cripples, catholics were rather wary of accepting aid. Deaf children were educated in Dublin and blind workers were always protesting against the rules which emphasised the protestant ethos of the workshops. In particular the reading of a chapter of the authorised version of the bible each day, provoked disagreement. Catholic workers claimed that their priests demanded that they should refuse to hear this, but the management would not compromise.[2] The town funds were distributed without regard to religious affiliation, the female refuges were of mixed denominations and no check was made on recipients of aid from the clothing and nursing societies, though once again office bearers were protestant.

This lack of contact came about because of the way in which the demographic pattern in Belfast altered over the years. Protestants made up 92 per cent of the population in 1801 but by 1861 this had fallen to 66 per cent and although their proportion rose to 76 per cent in 1901 the changes affected community relations.[3] The shared antipathy which manifested itself in the nineteenth century had its origin in events long ago. Since the plantation of Ulster in the seventeenth century the planters had feared (often with good reason) the Gaels. The Gaels in turn resented the alien rule of the English and although there had been a *rapprochement* in late eighteenth century Belfast between unitarians and catholics, this was limited and short-lived. From the Act of Union presbyterians and episcopalians united in support of the British connection and against catholic advances.

Traditionally catholics have often been perceived as being poor and disadvantaged compared with their protestant neighbours, but their prosperity grew with their numbers. The baker, Bernard Hughes, one of Belfast's leading catholics, spoke to the commissioners of inquiry into the 1857 riots of 100-150 catholic merchants and described catholics as the 'bone and sinew artisans of the town'.[4] In 1892 the *Irish News* wrote:

it is well known that many of the catholics of Belfast pay as much to the local tax as entitles them to rank among the highest rate payers of the city.[5]

In 1901 an examination of class structure based on male heads of household in the city showed that in classes I, II and III catholics and protestants were roughly equal.[6] Any doubt as to the growing wealth of catholics would be dispelled by the sight of their large Gothic style churches which rose in all parts of the town in the last quarter of the nineteenth century. A result of these displays of confidence and prosperity was that protestants felt threatened.

The two communities had very different perceptions of life in Belfast. Catholics saw themselves as oppressed and discriminated against. In 1885 Bishop Nulty of Meath spoke at St Patrick's, Donegall St, warning:

Catholics must ... make up their minds not to expect justice or fair play, but patiently submit to insult, injustice and wrong when employed as hands in the factories, the foundries, the workshops, the warehouses, the banks, the railways or in any of the various mercantile or industrial callings of this commercial community. In the Police, the Army, the Civil Service, and in the employment of great firms or companies their religion at once puts catholics under a ban; they must not expect promotion except when they cannot be passed over ... [7]

This attitude annoyed protestants who felt that no matter what catholics got they were never satisfied. They resented the fact that catholics who, up to the 1857 riots, had lived at peace with their neighbours, were now told that

the citizens amongst whom they lived were a minority trampling them underfoot, and that religion, manhood, prudence alike counselled them to put down the tyranny by an effort of physical strength.[8]

Even the refusal of Royal University students to stand for the singing of the national anthem on conferring day in 1905 seemed symptomatic of catholic disloyalty.[9]

The communal tension was partly the result of the peculiarities of Belfast's situation. In the town there were two minorities who were also, in different circumstances, majorities. Protestants were a majority in Belfast, a minority in Ireland and a majority in the United Kingdom; catholics were a majority in Ireland but a minority in Belfast and the U.K.. So neither community could behave normally as either a minority or a majority.

From 1886 the existing attitudes were intensified. Gladstone's home rule bill was a devastating blow to Belfast's protestants who feared absorption and subjugation in a catholic Irish state. Catholics in turn became increasingly confident and less prepared to accept protestant rule and this was reflected in the visible signs of the church's growth in the city and the country which was:

becoming clothed with new churches, convents and schools . . . churches rising up that rivalled in beauty of design and elegance of execution the proudest monuments of the zeal, the piety and the pride of our forefathers.[10]

Indeed to worried protestants the appearance on the streets of the nuns in their habits was another threat to them – there were even stories that the nuns took advantage of the weakened state of dying workhouse inmates to convert them to Rome.[11] The *News Letter* suggested that this practice could be stopped by excluding the sisters from the infirmary.

Effectively there was protestant charity and catholic charity. Catholics might not have been welcome on the committees of Belfast's main societies, but they made little effort to join, preferring to organise their own relief. As Dr Ambrose Macaulay has written:

. . . the catholic ghettoes grew stronger and could cushion their members, especially the migrants, against the harsh new realities of urban living, and . . . catholic charitable organisations made more effective provision for the destitute.[12]

Protestant societies operated with as much publicity as possible hoping to encourage donations and participation in their work. Annual reports were published, annual meetings were held and newspapers published detailed accounts of their activities: not so the catholic bodies. It is very difficult to document their work for they operated with a degree of secrecy and few records are available. The biggest difference between protestant and catholic charity is the comparative involvement of the churches. All of the main societies had clergymen on their committees but the main officials were usually laymen. By contrast, the catholic church in the form of parish priests and to some extent the bishops controlled catholic charity.

The two main forms of catholic charity were the layman's Society of St Vincent de Paul and the religious orders. The Society of St Vincent de Paul, founded in 1833 by the German student Frederic Ozanam, was established in Ireland in 1845. It was the main catholic agency for the relief of the poor.[13] The society aimed to encourage spiritual as well as material advancement and its active members were most often business and professional men, directed by the catholic parish clergy. Funds were collected in these individual parishes through bequests, donations, concerts, bazaars and church gate collections, and were spent within the parish.[14]

The society's special works were outlined by Bishop Tohill and included visitation of the poor, caring for the sick, visiting in the prisons, attending to the seamen, helping homeless men and boys, visiting the lodging houses, penny savings banks, hospital mainte-nance, propagation of the faith, distribution of literature and boys' clubs.[15] As for the spiritual function, the members were directed to circulate the teaching of the church on:

the fundamental questions of Education, Rights of Parents, Marriage, Property and Labour. Outside the catholic church all these questions are dealt with by a wrong point of view.[16]

The first conference of St Vincent de Paul was established in Belfast on 5 April 1850. The conference at St Mary's, Chapel Lane, consisted of twelve active and five honorary members. This foundation was followed by St Malachy's conference in 1851 and St Patrick's in 1856. Although the rule of the society forbids the publication of members' names most were prosperous doctors, spirit merchants or lawyers.[17] The society spread throughout the city to most of the parishes; St Peter's Pro-Cathedral in 1865; St Matthew's, Ballymacarett in 1869; Holy Cross, Ardoyne in 1869; St Vincent's, Ligoniel in 1869; St Joseph's in 1873; St Paul's in 1887; Holy Rosary in 1893; Most Holy Redeemer in 1897.

The work of the society was very varied, encapsulating in one body the work done by non-catholics in several organisations and carried out on a personal level. Like them, St Vincent's preferred not to hand out cash if this was possible but bought consumer goods in bulk, weighed them and distributed them to the needy poor.[18] In 1856 the president urged the workers to give advice on health, cleanliness, ventilation and vaccination.

Work done by the conferences was carried out anonymously and they kept no records of recipients, but several parishes had special interests. Blessed Virgin and St Vincent's, Ligoniel opened day and Sunday schools on the Falls Rd, in the Markets and Ligoniel. St Peter's distributed food tickets and fuel as well as articles of clothing. It was connected with the catholic boys' industrial school opened by Bishop Dorrian in 1869.[19] St Matthew's had a soup kitchen in the

1880s. Holy Rosary supported the maintenance of the Mater Hospital: Most Holy Redeemer was also involved in this as well as helping both the Nazareth Lodge Home for Boys and the catholic Deaf Mute Club. It was the first conference in the city to form a boys' club and a catholic scout troop.[20]

By 1889 the St Vincent de Paul Society had opened a home for boys and a night refuge in Academy St which provided beds and a meal of soup, tea or coffee for 1d.[21] Over a period of three years over 200 boys had been helped, not only catholic but, very occasionally, protestant boys who received religious education in St Anne's parochial school. In September 1892 there were thirty children in the home.[22] Boys could remain for a few weeks if they were 'worthy objects' – and they got a much needed bath. Because of the policy of confidentiality the numbers assisted by the Belfast conferences cannot be assessed. However, the accounts of St Paul's conference in September 1887 show that only very small amounts of money were involved, and there is no reason to suppose that it was different from the others.

Table 1. Accounts of St Vincent de Paul

	£	s.	d.		£	s.	d.
TO				FROM			
Balance on hand	2	16	8½	Relief in cash		3	0
Conference collections		4	3½	Relief in kind		10	1
Church doors		10	8	Balance	2	18	7
	3	11	8		3	11	8

The American White Cross fund also contributed to the work of St Vincent de Paul in Belfast giving £1,000 in 1920-22 at a time of civil unrest.[23]

St Vincent de Paul was a purely male organisation. Catholic women (like their protestant counterparts) also worked for charities. Lay workers and nuns collected money from their co-religionists which was distributed under the direction of the clergy. Women were sometimes active as auxiliaries for the Sisters of Mercy or Charity. There was a Belfast Catholic Ladies' Association and the Ladies' Society of St Vincent de Paul who did the same sort of work as the men. They visited the poor, giving tickets for food and spiritual guidance.[24] Funds were raised by dances and bazaars. In 1838, the ladies of St Patrick's parish founded St Patrick's Orphan Society under the patronage of Bishop Denvir. Its objects were to afford 'measures of support to destitute orphans, to bestow upon them a religious education and to implement the seeds of virtue in their tender minds.'[25] The operation of this society was taken over by the Sisters of Mercy when they came to Belfast, and they opened an orphanage on the Crumlin Rd.[26]

The female religious orders came to Belfast in the 1850s, invited first by Bishop Denvir and then by Bishop Dorrian. The Sisters of Mercy came in 1854 opening a convent, a school and a female penitentiary in Hamilton St. After a few years they expanded their work building an orphanage, school and convent on the Crumlin Rd. The purchase of Bedeque House beside the new convent led to the opening of the Mater Infirmorum hospital and increased their responsibilities.[27] In 1867 the Good Shepherd nuns took over the penitentiary which moved to the Ormeau Rd. They were followed by other orders each with a specific responsibility. The Irish Dominicans (1870) opened a convent and school beside St Paul's on the Falls Rd, the Bon Secours (1872) nurses opened a house in Alfred St, the Sisters of Nazareth (1876) founded a home for the elderly at Ballynafeigh and the Sisters of Charity (1900) visited the poor families in west Belfast.[28]

In general the involvement of catholic women in charitable effort dated from the second half of the nineteenth century when they began to take an interest in the material and moral welfare of the poor.[29] However, according to Fr L.J. McKenna (a writer on social issues) Irish women appeared to be less involved in this work than European catholics. Some of them apparently excused their lack of interest by claiming that social work was a 'protestant' thing and were put off by the 'repellent' protestant tone of the literature on the miseries of the poor.[30] This claim is not contradicted by Belfast effort.

Some historians have claimed that catholics and protestants had different attitudes to charity. T.P. O'Neill pointed out, for example, that the treatment of beggars was significantly more sympathetic by catholics.[31] He claimed that:

to the Protestant moralist the effects on the recipient and the results of alms-giving on the economy and society were of the greatest importance and so all charity had to be carefully examined to ensure that it did not create a new class of beggars or endanger the economic framework.[32]

Where is the difference between these 'protestant' ideas and the words of the first president of the St Vincent de Paul Society in 1833?

He advised its members

do not be content to dole out alms . . . give to each family what personal help your own better training enables you to give . . . in all cases help them to help them-selves.[33]

Actually the biggest difference was that catholics were content to leave the administration of charity to the church hierarchy and they were not concerned with the fact that catholic charity was for catho-lic people. Protestants seldom had any greater concern that the recipients of their aid were generally co-religionists, though a few, including Lord Londonderry, deplored the rule in the deaf school which made pupils attend a Church of Ireland or Church of Scotland church.[34] There were occasional quarrels between Church of Ireland and presbyterian interests over undue bias – also in the deaf school – where presbyterians were alleged to dominate[35] and the Kinghan Mission did seem to be a rival to the episcopalian Mission to the Adult Deaf and Dumb[36] but Rev. W.J. MacNaughten of Third Presby-terian Church clearly expressed the views of his fellows

if ever the time came when it would be an open battle between protestantism and Popery he "would be found with his back to the Cathedral".[37]

How much did denominational differences effect charitable work in the city? In some cases there was no effect at all. The House of Industry aided all sections of the community without any qualifica-tions as did the town relief funds. The dispute between anglicans and presbyterians did not damage the work of the deaf school or even the missions. But undoubtedly a more equitable distribution of charity would have been achieved if protestants and catholics had been able to work together. However, it is unrealistic to expect that co-opera-tion would be acceptable in just one area. If there is to be joint effort in philanthropy it must appear in other areas first.

'Labourers in the Vineyard':

THE PEOPLE WHO WORKED FOR CHARITY

The one common element which was absolutely necessary for all of these voluntary societies was the willingness of Belfast's leading citizens to give their time and money to charities, in order to make them work. The middle class men and women who were prosperous and who had status, had to be prepared to organise new structures which would attempt to relieve the poverty and distress of the working classes in this growing industrial town. Committees had to be formed, constitutions drawn up, aims and objectives identified, publicity given, some staff employed, funds raised and work allocated. None of the societies could have operated without the support of the prominent people of the town. Who were they? What were their businesses? Where did they live? How much were they involved? Was Belfast different from the rest of the United Kingdom in this philanthropic endeavour?

Over the seventy years of the Victorian and Edwardian eras almost 350 men and women regularly gave their time and effort to alleviating the distress of the poor in Belfast.

Table 9.1

Distribution by sexes of workers in charity 1840–1910

Sex	Frequency	Percentage
Men	266	77
Women	79	23

As the population of the city rose to over 300,000 by 1901, clearly only a small percentage of the citizens were prepared to devote themselves to worthy causes, but they were the richest and most influential members of the community. A significant number of men also took part in public life as councillors, guardians, magistrates or M.P.s. Of the men who worked for charity in Belfast, 31 per cent also appeared in these offices. They thus gave service to their fellows in two ways, much influenced by their religious convictions. As E.P. Hennock asked: 'Is it surprising that those deeply involved in the moral and philanthropic work of the churches . . . answered the call of the town council?'[1]

However, it was not only pure altruism which inspired them to stand for public office. In the new industrial towns considerable power and authority came from control of local institutions and the newly rich bourgeoisie found it very satisfying to participate in local philanthropy and municipal affairs.[2] Town councillors worked particularly hard in times of exceptional distress in 1847, 1858 and 1879, and they served on the lord mayor's coal relief fund every year. Of all the men who worked for charity 40 per cent were active only in this town relief. It is interesting that by the 1890s fewer philanthropists sat on public bodies, for the widening of the franchise gave more chance for electors to go outside the tight circle of leading families. Whereas 25 per cent of philanthropists sat on these bodies before 1890, afterwards the figure was only 6 per cent.

From the beginning of the nineteenth century it can be seen that the businessmen of Belfast did their best to tackle the problems of the growing town. However, it was the famine year of 1847 which really activated charity, and this was true of both men and women.

Table 9.2

Comparison of men and women in 1847 town relief

Sex	Frequency	Percentage
Men	80	30
Women	18	23

The businessmen came from many trades but the most common occupation was the textile trade. This included flax spinning and weaving, cambric manufacture, sewed muslin production and shirt collar manufacture.

Table 9.3

Table of occupations in charitable effort 1840-1910

Occupation	Frequency	Percentage
Textiles	66	25
Clergy	36	13
General merchants	34	13
Gentlemen	15	6
Solicitors	14	6
Physicians	12	5

It is not surprising that a substantial number of clergymen took part in this work, for after all this was what their master had told them to do, but the large numbers in textiles (almost twice as many as the clergy and five times more than physicians), does come as a surprise. By contrast ship-builders and engineers are almost completely unrepresented. The only industrial engineer on any list is Sir James Musgrave of Drumglass, in the Society for the Deaf and Dumb and the Blind, the People's Palace and the Mission to the Adult Deaf and Dumb. Sir E.J. Harland appeared once, on the committee for town relief in 1879, and this was when he was on the council and aiming to be mayor. G.W. Wolff occasionally graced a platform, the Pirries collected for the Royal Hospital but the Mackies of Jas. Mackie and Sons and the Davidsons of the Sirocco Works were never active in Victorian charity, though it is hard to know why this is so.

This too was the time when philanthropists were less likely to be on the council or board of guardians. As well, many of the engineers had come to Belfast from outside and thus were less involved in local duties. It is also clear that the engineers were not so interested in religious observance as the linen merchants, and as Christianity was a major factor in the charitable field, this also meant that they had a different attitude to charity. Besides in later years Harland, Wolff and Pirrie lived outside Belfast most of the time.

Most of these committee members are just names in an annual report or in a newspaper account of an A.G.M., but a few are better known. Vere Foster is famous for his copy-books designed to enable Irish youth to be equipped for a business career, but he was also a Belfast philanthropist. He did not come from the traditional com-

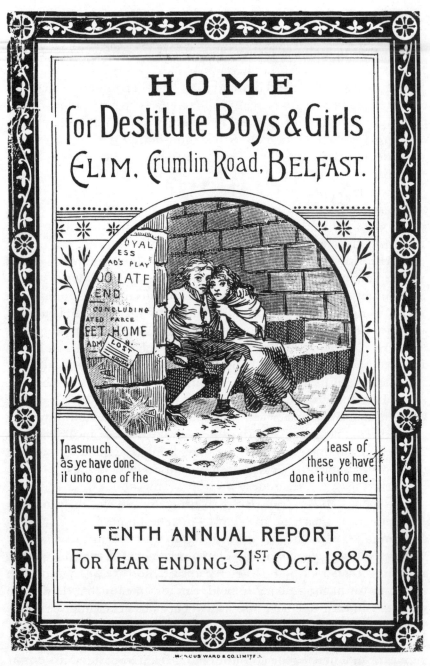

HOME
for Destitute Boys & Girls
ELIM, Crumlin Road, BELFAST.

Inasmuch as ye have done it unto one of the least of these ye have done it unto me.

TENTH ANNUAL REPORT
FOR YEAR ENDING 31ST OCT. 1885.

MARCUS WARD & CO. LIMITED.

Annual report of the Home for Destitute Boys and Girls.

mercial background of the other town committee members but from the Anglo-Irish land-owning class.[3]

He came to Belfast in the 1870s because the local publishers, Marcus Ward, were printing his copy-books.[4] Foster lived in the town for twenty years but he did not enter public life for his one object was to serve others and he was 'prominent in every Belfast movement that had the welfare of man for its object, provided that the charity was sufficiently all-embracing to exclude none on account of religious belief.'[5] This was why he was so involved in the running of the soup kitchen in 1879 as part of the town relief, for these were truly non-sectarian funds. As well as his philanthropic work he was one of the promoters and supporters of the Government School of Art which was sited in the north wing of the R.B.A.I., guaranteeing the headmaster's salary for some years.

Sir Otto Jaffe, lord mayor in 1904, sat on the committees of the town relief fund and the Ladies' Industrial School. The Jaffes were a German Jewish family who came to Belfast in the 1860s to set up a linen business. Otto married Miss Paula Hurwitz, also of Hamburg, and they were both prominent in good works. At the opening of a fund-raising bazaar for the Mission to the Adult Deaf and Dumb they were compared by the chairman to war-horses, always responding to the call. They raised £1,200 for a soup kitchen, large sums for the Royal Hospital and founded the Jaffe Memorial Schools in 1907. Belfast showed its ingratitude to the Jaffes. In 1915 a wholly disgraceful outbreak of racism and war-fever led a group of local ladies to refuse to subscribe further to the Children's Hospital if 'the Germans' remained on the committee. These Germans had lived in Belfast for sixty years spending their time and money on the welfare of its citizens, but this counted for nothing. Sir Otto was informed of this crisis and solved the problem by not standing for re-election to the committee.[6]

Forster Green, tea merchant of Derryvolgie House, a devout quaker attending Frederick St Friends' Meeting House regularly, was the city's most notable philanthropist from 1870 to 1903. Over the period of his long life (he was eighty-eight when he died) it was estimated that he gave the huge sum of £200,000 to charity. As well as showing this generosity which did not need any personal commitment, he gave time to the committees of the Prison Gate Mission for Women, the Midnight Mission (of which he was a trustee), the Workshops for the Blind and the Homes of Rest in Bangor. No charity in the city turned to him in vain and he served on the relief committees and even gave a soup kitchen to the citizens. In 1896 he founded the Forster Green hospital for TB patients at Knockbreda. In later life his health deteriorated and his sight began to fail, which made him more sympathetic to the Workshops for the Blind.

Then there was Sir Thomas McClure, M.P., tea and general merchant. He was a Liberal elected in 1868, when he and William Johnston of Ballykilbeg defeated Charles Lanyon and John Mulholland, when 'the Orangemen and the Roman Catholics have been united.'[7] He was given a baronetcy by Gladstone in recognition of his political support but he withdrew this support after Home Rule. Sir Thomas lived with his sister, Betty, for many years, a lady who was decidedly eccentric. Barney Telford who grew up in mid-nineteenth century east Belfast, recalled her in a letter in 1913. She and her brother were devout presbyterians, holding prayer meetings and a Sunday school in the laundry of Belmont House. Whenever Sir Thomas was away she used to send the Sunday preacher home in her car and instruct Barney to take her home. So when she told the boy to call to get a reward, he was appalled to receive a bottle green swallow-tail coat, cream vest and pearl-buttoned knee breeches. Understandably he was afraid to wear them in public in Belfast.[8] The £1 in an envelope from her brother was more welcome.

Sir Thomas gave £1,000 towards the building of Belmont Presbyterian Church, an offshoot of Fisherwick Place Church, and he and Miss McClure were regular attenders. Miss McClure clearly felt that she had some authority over the congregation so she always came in late, turned round and counted the number at the service and, if she felt a draught, put up her umbrella.[9]

When Sir Thomas had amassed a considerable fortune he bought the estate of the earl of Ranfurly at Belmont and built himself a mansion. His selection as an M.P. was surprising given the comments made about his powers of oratory. Barney described his attempts to make a speech at the Sunday school class where he was a 'failure'; for the children got fidgety because it took him so long to finish. F. Frankfort Moore agreed with this assessment. He wrote that McClure was an elderly wealthy merchant, good natured and with many friends but:

a man who could no more grasp the bearing of a Government policy than he could make a speech that did not violate every rule of grammar and pronunciation, but who could be trusted to follow his leader into the right lobby at a division and be always in his place to do so.[10]

As for his charitable work he was on the committees for town relief in 1847 and 1858 and the 'Gibraltar' training ship and was appointed first president of the Belfast Y.M.C.A., but his real devotion was to the Presbyterian Church.

It is surprising that men who held responsible positions in the world of business and the professions had time to spend on charities, though most only served on one committee and that was usually for town relief.

Table 9.4

Numbers of Men Active in Charities 1840-1910

Category	Frequency	Percentage
Men involved in one charity	191	72
Men involved in two charities	43	16
Men involved in three charities	19	7
Men involved in four charities	13	5

Only 2 per cent of the men working in charity were catholics. Men such as Arthur Hamill, Bernard Hughes and the bishops of Down and Connor remained aloof from committees which were in effect protestant, for example, the committees of the Deaf and Dumb and the Blind Institution and the Workshops for the Blind. These were the two most popular charities and many of the leading citizens sat on their boards of management.

Table 9.5

Distribution of Membership in the two committees 1840-1908

Category	Frequency	Percentage
DDB	33	12
WSB	42	16
Both	17	6
Others	173	66

A few men sat on as many as four committees, though out of the thirteen who did so, six were clergymen who had more time to spend on good works.

Fewer ladies than men were involved in philanthropy. In absolute terms of numbers men were three times more likely than women to sit on a charity committee, and even if the 106 men who were only active in town relief are subtracted from the total of 265, they were still twice as numerous as women. Although ladies began their public involvement in 1847 many more were interested in women's charities, particularly in the later years of the nineteenth century.

Table 9.6

Comparative Involvement of Women in Charity 1840-1910

Category	Frequency	Percentage
Women most active in 1847	18	23
Women involved only in women's charities	43	54

All of the governing bodies so far surveyed in this section have been exclusively male and most of the societies, even if there were many women in them, had men as administrators, organisers and decision makers. Ladies associated with them were mainly auxiliaries. Some women did hold influential roles in the running of charities – Miss Mary Hobson in the Workshops, Mrs Margaret Byers in the Prison Gate Mission, the Cripples' Institute, and the Victoria Homes, Miss Isabella Tod in the Ladies' National Association. It is no coincidence that these independent women were either single or widowed.

The first time that ladies appeared in public to organise relief was in 1847 when, somewhat to the surprise of the citizens, they inaugurated famine relief funds. The Belfast Ladies' Association for the Relief of Irish Destitution had a committee of one hundred women, though, of course, they were not all active. Once the worst of the Famine was over the two committees were disbanded, with only the Ladies' Industrial School remaining.

For the rest of the century the part played by ladies in the voluntary organisations was either active as in collecting subscriptions, running bazaars, reading to the blind, visiting applicants for relief or making tea, or else purely honorary, acting as patronesses for fund-raising events. Frequently ladies were linked with charities regarded as particularly suitable for women, such as the Nurses for the Sick Poor, the Destitute Sick Society and the Clothing Society but they were not

merely token members. A most important function was the collecting of funds, vetting of applicants for these societies, reading to the
blind and organising bazaars. Several ladies sat on both committees
and a paid assistant, Miss Wright, 129 Durham Street, ran the two
societies.

Dr Marion Andrews and her sister were visitors for the Society for
the Relief of the Destitute Sick. This society also divided up the town
into districts where ladies went to visit the homes of those who
applied for help. The Magdalene, too, had its lady visitors. These
were all married women for this was a charity where they would
prefer to keep their daughters at a distance from the fallen women.
The visitors supervised the running of the asylum, selected suitable
entrants and made sure that the laundry was working efficiently
though they did not go out into the homes of the women. The
executive posts of treasurer and physician as well as chaplain were
held by men.

In contrast, the lady readers for the Workshops for the Blind were
mostly unmarried girls. The girls found this task not demanding or
difficult, and they did not take it too seriously. In the summer the
service had to be suspended because so many were on holiday and
the ladies' committee had great trouble in keeping to the rules about
reading. The girls came from established families mostly living near
Queen's College. In 1876 there were thirty-one girls on the list. By
1898 the number of girls on the rota had fallen to sixteen though
numbers rose again when Miss L.A. Walkington took over in 1906.

Ladies helped to organise the popular bazaars which were a feature of Victorian fund-raising. An analysis of the names of the committee members for the bazaar held by the Society for Promoting the
Education of the Deaf and Dumb and the Blind in 1860 shows that
some were just 'names' while others were workers. The workers were
ladies who were on other bodies and, although they did not do all of
the planning or collecting, they did have stalls for which they collected goods and at which they served.

The part played by ladies in voluntary societies was of a limited
nature, though it would be wrong to disregard their contribution.
They were seldom publicly consulted about the operation of the
organisations, though undoubtedly they were influential behind the
scenes. Without them the charities simply could not have func-
tioned. There is no strong evidence that the ladies who took part in
charitable endeavour resented their ancillary role. Women who
wanted to take a prominent position (like Mrs Byers, Miss Tod and

Miss Hobson) were able to exercise an influence to the extent which they wished.

In many ways it seems more likely that clergymen should be interested in doing good than the businessmen, for their work was concerned in feeding the hungry, helping the helpless and sheltering the lost, if they were carrying out the lord's commands. Indeed many of Belfast's clergy did just that, though some were more interested in politics than charity, appearing only occasionally on platforms at A.G.M.s. Presbyterian ministers were the most visible in their efforts, and of these Rev. Dr John Edgar and Rev. William Johnston were by far the best known. Dr Edgar was associated with many Belfast movements. He was the son of Rev. Samuel Edgar of the Secession Synod who was professor of theology in the R.B.A.I.. John Edgar also became a minister of the Secession Synod, ordained in the Independent Chapel, Donegall St, after which he conducted services in a room in Commercial Court.[11] He raised enough money from supporters to build a meeting house in 1820 in Alfred St. In 1826 he was unanimously chosen to succeed his father as professor of theology for the Secession Synod of Ulster.

He was a founder member of the Society for the Relief of the Destitute Sick with which he was associated for many years. More publicly, he was the father of the temperance movement in Ireland. At that time (the 1830s) whiskey drinking was a major problem even among ministers of the church; it was estimated that one-seventh of the ministers of the Secession Synod had been suspended or downgraded for intemperance.[12] The most famous demonstration of his conversion came when he poured one gallon of whiskey out of the window of his manse in Alfred Street.[13]

Rev. John Edgar devoted a great deal of his time to the relief of famine in Connacht, and was instrumental in initiating the collecting of funds in the town in 1846 and he was also on the 1858 town relief committee. He was a member from its earliest years of the committee of the Society for Promoting the Education of the Deaf and Dumb and the Blind, until his death. His greatest work was for the Ulster Female Penitentiary. In spite of all his goodness he was a rough diamond and was not an attractive or even a popular figure in the town. W.D. Killen, his biographer, wrote of him that he was not very prepossessing, indeed he 'might have betokened a descent from one of the sable sons of Afric.'[14] Certainly some examples of his outspokenness seem rather strong. His description of Rev. J. Scott Porter of First Belfast as a 'stunted smoke-dried unitarian, to whom heresy has not left enough of feeling or principle to love what is good or admire what is Godlike and great', and as a 'wolf that digs the shrouded body from the grave' displays little Christian charity.[15]

He visited the United States in 1859 where his method of speaking exposed him to ridicule and abuse – 'he rides rough-shod over the stiff rules of rhetoric and principles of good taste. There is strength, rough and hairy in his play: his sport is the gambolling of the elephant.'[16] In a letter of introduction for him a lady wrote: 'You need not give yourself any trouble about paying him any attention, for he does not expect anything of that sort . . . till he is turned inside out he has little to recommend him, but I feel happy in the thought that in befriending and assisting him you are furthering the cause of the Gospel.'[17]

One incident shows the character of the man. This story was told by Robert Magill of the Sabbath School Society. One Sabbath evening, after the service at Alfred St Church, Dr Edgar asked his elders to meet at the penitentiary corner (Brunswick St) at 8.00 am the next day. Four elders, Robert Magill, John Arnold, H.H. Boyd, and Robert Workman, turned up and joined their minister. Dr Edgar rapped the penitentiary door. It was opened and they saw that near the door on a form lay a coffin.

Dr Edgar and the elders got it on their shoulders and carried it to a hearse which appeared at the door and then walked along beside it to the New Burying Ground in Clifton St. Here was Dr Edgar's own burying ground where some of his family were already buried. They found the grave open and the minister read the bible and prayed. The coffin was lowered and the grave filled. Mr Magill said 'the person buried was a poor woman who was a sinner who had come from England and had been respectably connected. Dr Edgar believed that she had been led to the Lord Jesus and he buried her in his own grave.'[18] Although he may have been impatient and rough, he was a true Christian to those in need and was prepared to show charity to the fallen.

Rev. William Johnston was equally, if not more, involved in good works than Dr Edgar and he was better known as well as being more popular. He too was a minister's son born at Tullylish in 1818. He was educated at the R.B.A.I. and Edinburgh, the classic progression for potential ministers, and ordained in Berry St Presbyterian Church in 1842. This was a church right in the centre of the town with a very poor congregation as well as non-churchgoers who looked to the minister for help. In 1847 he went to Townsend

St Presbyterian Church where he remained until his death in 1894.

Like Rev. John Edgar, Dr Johnston was interested in the work of the Ulster Female Penitentiary though unlike him, he was reluctant to identify the poor sinful women as his responsibility. He preached in the open air to groups of them, so effectively that on one occasion a 'considerable number of the fallen women' marched to the Ulster Female Penitentiary. One of these women, Jane I – lived near Townsend Street Church and came under the care of the biblewoman, Mrs Douglas. Jane had been in the penitentiary before but found the discipline too stern and unsympathetic so she refused to stay.

She really was a problem: she threw up situations found for her, she earned little even when she did work, she accused Mrs Douglas of taking money supposed to be given to the poor, and was 'both unreasonable and ungrateful.' Rev. Johnston became involved when Jane reformed and then got typhus from which she died. On her death-bed when he was praying for her she asked him to go to her funeral and to warn her previous companions that 'the wages of sin is death.' The minister provided a one horse hearse and two outside cars but, unlike Dr Edgar on a similar occasion, William Johnston did not drive in the procession for fear of being seen with notorious characters. He met them at the cemetery. Jane's friends complained to Mrs Douglas that they would have given her a 'decenter funeral.'[19] Rev. W. Johnston clearly was aware of the dangers in Belfast of being seen to associate with undesirables. This was the difference between these two ministers: Dr Edgar was more concerned with aiding the fallen than with public opinion.

Probably the most famous episcopalian clergyman in nineteenth century Belfast was Rev. Thomas Drew of Christ Church. It was his sermon preached on 12 July 1857 which allegedly caused the 1857 riots. In fairness to Drew, unless the hostile catholic mob from the Pound, which gathered outside, had actually attended the service, they could not even have heard what he said. As for his congregation, it contained about fifteen or twenty men who put on orange collars only when they got inside the church grounds on the other side of the railings (the Party Processions Act had prevented them from parading in the street), a sight which inflamed the Pound mob.[20] He could have been better remembered for his charity work. He joined Dr Edgar in attempts to direct funds to Connacht not only in 1847 but also in 1858 and he was on the committees of the temporal relief fund of the established church, the Day Asylum, the Ladies' Industrial school and, of course, the Magdalene Asylum. This institution would never have opened had it not been for him and his Church Accommodation Society, nor would its chapel of ease have been built.

Dr Drew's name still lives in Belfast today in the Drew Memorial Church standing on the Grosvenor Road in west Belfast in a one hundred per cent catholic district. It hangs grimly on, resisting vandalism and intimidation with a tiny, declining, elderly congregation – Dr Drew would have been proud of them. The part played by the clergy, particularly the presbyterians, had a very important role in the charitable life of Belfast. Not all of them had the time or concern to join societies but no charity was complete without its quota of long-serving ministers.

Apart from individual philanthropists there were some important business families which devoted themselves to helping others. A study of the families is made difficult by their regrettable habit of calling sons after fathers and nephews after uncles, often producing extreme confusion. However, the Browne/Crawford/Vance family did not have any names in common and many of them were involved in charity work. L.A. Browne was the lynchpin. As well as all of his links with the organisations which came together in the Cripples' Institute he was honorary architect and builder of the Homes of Rest, a founder of the Belfast Y.M.C.A., on the committee of the 'Gibraltar' and the Association of Christian Workers and was secretary of the Irish Temperance League.

Browne married the daughter of Alexander Crawford of Chlorine who ran Cromac Saw Mills owned by J.H. Browne, brother of Lawson A. Browne. Alexander Crawford was secretary of the Provident Home and his son J.W. Crawford, a starch and chemical manufacturer, served on the committees of the Homes for the Blind as well as the People's Palace. His son, Major F.H. Crawford, who had served as a captain in the South African War after he had finished his apprenticeship with Harland and Wolff and worked as an engineer for the White Star Line, sat on the committees of the Mission to the Adult Deaf and Dumb, Cripples' Institute and the Homes for the Blind.[21] This legendary gun-runner died at the advanced age of ninety-one in 1952.

As for L.A. Browne's own children, his daughter Mrs A.W. Vance shared his interests, and with her husband founded the first Home of Rest in Bangor in 1889. Alfred W. Vance, Mornington, Bangor, began his career as an employee of the Belfast Banking Company but he left it to devote himself to charitable work. He was very well-known in the city for his philanthropic effort and on his death in 1907, many tributes were paid to him in city pulpits. But for Vance the Homes of Rest would never have been built nor would the Model Lodging Houses for the poorer classes, and recently he had taken over the Prison Gate Mission.[22] Of course, his greatest achievement was the opening of the People's Palace whose gates were draped and arranged with palm leaves when he died. A. Crawford Browne continued his father's association with charity in the Cripples' Institute, and was manager of the Olivet National school at Ballygowan until he went to the war in 1915.

Not many people in the streets of Belfast today would be familiar with the Browne family but the Ewarts are still well-known. This family was one of the most active in philanthropy in the city. Their commitment began with William Ewart junior of the linen firm of W. Ewart and Sons. William Ewart was a councillor, mayor twice and M.P. for north Belfast which might have been regarded as enough work for anyone, particularly when he was also chairman of the family firm. However, he served on the town relief committees in 1858 and 1879, on the committee of the Workshops for the Blind, for whom he acted as agent in the purchase of their new premises, and the Prison Gate Mission for Women. In recognition of his services to the town he was made a baronet. His son and heir, Sir W. Quartus Ewart continued, even extended, his father's work. He too was a member of the corporation, sitting on the 1879 relief committee. In addition to this he sat on the committees of the Prison Gate Mission for Women and for Men, the Elim Home, Workshops for the Blind and the Cripples' Institute.

Sir W.Q. Ewart's brother, Lavens Mathewson Ewart, was most closely associated with the Workshops for the Blind of which he was a founder member, secretary and trustee but he was also on the committees of the society for Providing Nurses for the Sick Poor and was trustee of the Mission to the Adult Deaf and Dumb. L.M. Ewart was manager of Glenbank Bleach Green, part of the Ewart empire, but he was also an antiquarian, writing in the *Ulster Journal of Archaeology* on Belfast maps, and compiling a *Handbook of the Diocese of Down and Connor and Dromore*. He was a member of the Belfast Natural History and Philosophical Society and a member of the Royal Irish Academy. His sudden death in London in 1898 at the early age of fifty-three shocked his friends and colleagues. His wife was a keen member of the Girls' Friendly Society.

Another famous Belfast family, still operating in the city, were the Corries. They came from Dumfries to Newtownards in the 1630s. The Corries claimed to trace their ancestry back to Alfred the Great through Robert Bruce, but they made their mark in Belfast through Robert Corry and his three sons in the nineteenth century.[23] Robert Corry, who set up the timber business, was on the 1858 town relief committee but it was his sons who were most active. J.P. Corry was a Belfast M.P. and was defeated in 1885 but was then returned as M.P. for mid-Armagh in 1886. The list of committees on which he sat is long and varied and included seven committees of the General Assembly. His brother, R.W. Corry, was on the committees of the Prison Gate Mission for Women, the Homes for the Blind and the Cripples' Institute.

Then there was the Workman family. An accurate study of them is almost impossible because the same names recur so frequently. John and Robert Workman, brothers who came to the town from Scotland in the early nineteenth century to set up a muslin business in Upper Arthur St (R. & J. Workman), both had sons whom they called Robert and John. As Robert junior, son of John of 'Ceara', Windsor Avenue, had fifteen children (two of them called Robert and John) and Robert junior, son of Robert of Queen's Elms, had nine children, identifying them is difficult.[26] Robert, John and William Workman were all connected with the Lancasterian school and William became a trustee of the Ladies' Industrial school. John was on the 1858 town relief committee as well as the Workshops for the Blind and the Cripples' Institute while William was on the committees of the Mission to the Adult Deaf and Dumb and the Boys' Industrial Brigade. Mrs John Workman sat on the committee of the Prison Gate Mission for Women.

As for the answers posed at the beginning of this section about the nature of charitable response in the town, they have largely been answered in the accounts of the men and their families. In the main they were linen manufacturers, merchants and professional men who lived in substantial homes on the Malone Rd (particularly at Windsor) and the Antrim Rd. They were deeply committed to at least one and often more societies, to such an extent that it is difficult to see how they could have continued to earn their living. Others gave only limited time and effort to philanthropy. David Owen in his study of *English Philanthropy* identifies certain classes as being active in this field, financial, commercial and industrial, and certainly Belfast fitted into this pattern.[27]

Belfast charities suffered from having no rich resident aristocrat. The second marquis of Donegall did live in the town from 1802 in Ormeau House which he had built in Ormeau Park, but as he was so heavily in debt he contributed little to local charities. He appeared occasionally on platforms at A.G.M.s and laid the foundation stone of the Deaf and Dumb and the Blind Institution. The second marquis of Donegall died in 1844 and his son, although he visited the town and built a new Belfast Castle between 1867 and 1870 could not be classed as resident.[28] His daughter Harriet married the son of the eighth earl of Shaftesbury and she spent some time in the city. The countess was patroness of the Magdalene Asylum and sat on the committee of the Home Teaching Society for the Blind. Her son continued this local connection becoming lord mayor in 1907 and first chancellor of Queen's University, Belfast.[29]

As a result of this lack of landlord concern by most of the Donegalls, charities which wanted the status of having a landed aristocrat on their platforms had to look outside the town. The most assiduous supporting family were the O'Neills of Shane's Castle. Lord O'Neill was connected with the Workshops for the Blind as their president, with the 'Gibraltar' and the Cripples' Institute, actively working in them. Successive Lords Lurgan supported the Deaf and Dumb and the Blind Institution, and Lord Londonderry appeared as their chairman at one A.G.M., though with controversial results. The marquis of Downshire was associated with the 'Gibraltar' and the marquis of Dufferin and Ava opened the Kinghan Mission. However, it is a fairly thin representation compared with the work of the middle class. Their ladies also were patronesses of bazaars and fund-raising events.

These then were the people who made Belfast charity work, who were prepared to spend time and money on those much less fortunate than themselves. The middle class did not turn a blind eye to the needy around them and though not all of them, or even most of them, worked for the voluntary societies, and though not many people were relieved, the whole system of philanthropy had a major impact on the town.

'To do justly, to love mercy and to walk humbly with their God':

MOTIVES AND ASSESSMENT OF
CHARITABLE ENDEAVOUR IN BELFAST

All of the prominent people in Belfast who gave up their time to running charities in the town had to have reasons for their involvement. What were their motives? Why did they join societies which demanded considerable effort with little apparent reward? One class, believed to be superior, gave generously to another class, believed to be inferior, and it is their motives which must be assessed. Was it 'social control'? Was it the 'imposition of opinions and habits by one class upon another'?[1] Did it mean that the middle class wanted to make the working classes so dependent on their generosity that the workers would be obedient, docile, hardworking and orderly? Certainly the middle class preferred their workforce to be all of these things but it is very unlikely that this was their only incentive.

In the 1840s there was considerable concern about social unrest, with its danger of class conflict, which inspired middle class efforts to alleviate the misery in the cities by temporary relief. In this way they hoped to avoid revolution by saving the poor from the worst effects of deprivation. By the 1870s it was clear that there was not going to be a revolution in Britain, but relief was still given in the bad years of 1878-9. The middle class was not eager to see crowds of unemployed men on the streets even then, and 'concern for the plight of the outcast could shade off into fear of the criminal.'[2]

Some employers were anxious to provide relief work because homeless men slept in their premises, particularly in the brickfields where the kilns gave warmth. Middle class contributions to charity were influenced by the benefits that could be gained from philanthropy. In fact instead of the term 'social control' a more accurate description would be enlightened self-interest.

This animated almost every form of aid given. It was the motive force behind some of the first attempts to improve the environment. In the dirty and disease-ridden Victorian industrial cities fever did

215

not discriminate between rich and poor. Thus charities like the Belfast Society for Ameliorating the Condition of the Working Classes raised money to build baths and wash houses, to cleanse the people living in homes with no running water (most houses in Belfast in the 1840s) and help them to maintain improved sanitary standards. Besides, although the middle class had mostly moved to the suburbs to live they could not ignore the filth in the town. Any successes in the improvement of town life benefitted the poor as well as the rich. A pleasanter environment and the removal of street beggars was as welcome to the dwellers in the back streets as to the inhabitants of the Malone Rd.

It should also be remembered that charity to the poor could save money by keeping them off the rates, which would increase with the numbers in the workhouse. This theme is echoed in the reports of all the Belfast charities, for example, the Workshops for the Blind. The workshops' committee reported that they could run the workshops for 100 blind people for £500 p.a. which 'would be more economical to the people of Belfast than if these people were thrown upon the rates.'[3] After the Poor Laws were passed in 1834 and 1838 British citizens had no alternative but to support the poor – their choice was in which way to do it at least cost to ratepayers.

It might be thought that aspiring politicians with local or national ambitions would use their membership of voluntary societies to increase their vote, but this would be wrong. In the nineteenth century Britain was not a full democracy. There was no 'one man one vote' in local government elections. This meant that the voters had to be householders and therefore more unlikely to be the recipients of charity, so they would not be influenced by the candidates' good works. The electors were more concerned for their own personal advantage through patronage, or by the political interest which the candidate represented. There was no 'social control' in this area. Then there were many people who got pleasure from helping the needy and feeling useful. Richard Potter, father of Beatrice Webb, once said 'what a luxury it is to do good.'[4] And Edward Baines certainly thought that young ladies actually enjoyed their charity work rather than finding it a burden.[5] It is interesting that there were patterns in the biographies of philanthropists – they were often childless, or bachelors or widows who had time and money to spare and no one to lavish them on.[6]

Much effort was devoted to the moral reformation of the poor by charity organisations as well as religious bodies. 'Moral' in this context seemed to mean cleanliness, sobriety and thrift, but the implication that the middle class practised these ideas while the working classes preferred dirt, drunkenness and extravagance is ridiculous. In every class there were examples of hard work and idleness: every street in the town had its 'wee palaces' beside neglected hovels. The working classes were perfectly able to recognise for themselves that they were more likely to prosper if they were prudent than if they were thoughtless: they did not need to be controlled. 'Respectability' was seen as desirable by all classes. The middle class observers interpreted behaviour patterns in terms of the 'model' workman, temperate, respectable, self-improving, and so did the working classes.[7] The object of both classes was to keep the lower orders in a position to look after themselves with assistance in times of special need, and with a continuing support for the handicapped.

Independence was shown by the working classes in their means of helping themselves, for they much preferred to avoid any form of charity unless they were in dire distress. The poor often had to resort to the pawn shop or 'Mont de Piete' for temporary assistance, to take loans from money-lenders or families. The earnings of a wife or children might save the family in time of need and neighbours helped when they could.[8] Self help was the principal aim. By 1900 working class culture was different from that in 1800, not because change had been imposed by the middle class, but because the workers had their own values which had evolved from changing circumstances. The culture had altered in response to urban living and factory work with its discipline of time and place. Friendly societies, burial clubs and the informal social organisms of the streets, the neighbourhood and the community were positive developments for these workers.[9]

So any idea that philanthropy was able to make the working classes conform against their wishes is clearly wrong. It was in the interests of all classes to live in an ordered society with peace and prosperity. Employers might want to have a docile workforce but the way to achieve it was not by charity. Besides the numbers helped by organised charity were very small and could not have had a major influence on society. Was charity work a means of social advancement? Garrard agrees that philanthropy was the high road to social advancement.[10] In fact it seems as far as Belfast was concerned that it was the other way round – that the people who served on the charity committees already had an important social position. If they were not prosperous and prominent they wold not have been elected to

217

·MAIN·ENTRANCE:

The People's Palace, Donegall Road, opened 1904.

the boards of management. It is hard to believe that Sir William Ewart M.P., head of a great linen firm, or Sir Robert Anderson of Anderson and McAuley needed to be on the committee of the Workshops for the Blind or the School for the Deaf and Dumb and the Blind, to be important in Belfast.

Most of the members of the committees of the societies were already from the same urban elite who ran the organisations by 'subscriber democracy' and had become prominent figures in business and commerce. Social climbers may have followed the lead of their superiors in joining societies but without status they would get nowhere. The range of societies was designed to attract the sort of person who would be an ideal member of a stable thriving industrial community.[11] The abilities which produced a good society member also produced a good citizen, so it is not surprising that the two were frequently synonymous.

Admittedly it was gratifying to share a platform with a marquis, but that alone was hardly enough to justify monthly (sometimes even more frequent) committee meetings. Status could also be confirmed by such charitable involvement, even if status was not conferred by participation. Victorian cities had large networks of charitable organisations and there were detailed press reports of the programme of their activities which gave publicity to the philanthropists. Their friends could see how rich and generous they were, and with luck would try to emulate them. A list of charitable bequests was printed regularly in local newspapers and while the deceased got no gratification from this, the family basked in the reflected glory.

Was it a feeling of duty which encouraged philanthropy? Certainly this was one of the factors involved. Many of the middle class felt that they had a bounden duty to promote the welfare of the poor. In the words of the *Englishwoman's Journal* in 1858 'it is our plainest duty to feed the hungry and clothe the naked and afford shelter to the aged.'[12] Many people believed that patronage should be matched by duties of order and obedience by the poor. There was a feeling of guilt in the educated classes in the 1880s about working class difficulties which encouraged their efforts to alleviate poverty.[13]

Another form of duty was to appear on platforms at the A.G.Ms of voluntary societies. Aristocrats throughout Britain regularly presided on such occasions even if they gave little of their time to serious involvement, and leading citizens in the towns joined them. Sometimes this was not an attractive task. Sir Otto Jaffe presiding at a meeting of the coal relief fund in 1907 said: 'It is no pleasure to me to

219

stand here, but it is a matter of duty.'[14] Reformers knew that legislation alone could not make people good, but they felt that the law should show the citizen his duty. In late Victorian Britain legislation had been passed to root out brothels, to stop obscene advertisements, to raise the age of consent and to restrict drinking hours, and while the laws had limited success, the voluntary societies continued their efforts in local areas.[15]

Of course, as well as duty as a motivation there was also principle. Indeed this was one of the strongest reasons for charity work. Morality was not a Victorian invention. What the Victorian era did do was to elevate morality and organised religion to an essential virtue. The middle class men and women who were active in charity work were devout church members. So was religion very important in motivating charitable effort? In this case there is no doubt that it was the single most important reason which spurred middle class concern for the poor into action. The nineteenth century was the time when

the virtues of a Christian after the evangelical model were easily interchangeable with the virtues of a successful merchant or a rising manufacturer. To be serious, to redeem the time, to abstain from gambling, to remember the Sabbath day to keep it holy, to limit the gratification of the senses to the pleasure of a table lawfully earned and the embraces of a wife lawfully wedded are virtues from which the reward is not laid up in heaven only.[16]

The whole social relief movement in the south of England started with Church of England religious impulses, and though it became non-denominational and ended in the hands of secular professionals, in many ways and for many years, a religious bias continued. This was a time when, to an extent difficult to imagine today, religious observation permeated all areas of life and guided attitudes towards the poor and towards reform. The clergy were men of influence, admired by their congregations, and if they could not change society they could tell the upper class and the middle class how the poor lived and what could be done for them.

In Belfast political theory was not an important feature of charity work. Most of the middle class in the town were happy to accept the philosophy of the hymn:

The rich man in his castle
The poor man at his gate,

God made them high and lowly
And ordered their estate.[17]

Sermons emphasised the contrast between rich and poor so that donors got a spiritual blessing, and a thirst for souls was 'a very powerful influence on early Victorian charity.'[18] The notion that the existing social structure was the creation of divine providence persisted into the last decades of the nineteenth century. People believed that God decided people's status, his will was supreme, and thus the poor should not resist his decisions. Some preachers even argued that the poor had a spiritual advantage over the rich for they had less to answer for at the day of judgment.[19] It is not recorded what view the poor had of this.

This religious motive was very strong in Belfast. It was a major feature in the lives of the men and women who worked for charity. Many men like Sir Robert Anderson and Sir Edward Coey were ruling elders of the Presbyterian Church. Sir J.P. Corry was the superintendent of Elmwood Presbyterian Church Sunday school for many years – a job which had for him deep 'spiritual satisfaction'. The Ewart family were instrumental in the building of St Mary's, Crumlin Rd, and St Matthew's, Woodvale and Sir William Quartus was a member of the diocesan synod, the general synod, the C.I.Y.M.S. and the Boys' Brigade.[20] It was the aim of most of the charities not only to relieve the poor in the life they were enduring, but to bring them 'to the saving power of the gospel of the Lord Jesus.'[21] This aim was encouraged by those Christians who served the poor. Rev. Henry Montgomery of the Shankill Rd Mission, preaching at his church shortly after the death of Sir W.Q. Ewart, hoped 'that in future there would be in the coming generation a band of Christian men equally patriotic and equally devoted.'[22]

So what were their motives? Social control; social advancement; duty; principle; religion; all of these played a part in leading people to work in charity. Basically these men and women in Belfast were good, inspired like their English counterparts, with a genuine desire to help those in need. They sincerely believed that Christianity and schemes to help the poor to help themselves, were of benefit both to the recipients and to society. It is difficult to measure success in this field. The needs of the lowest stratum of the community must be identified and then the impact of the voluntary societies on these needs must be analysed. All of them stemmed from the basic problems of disease, poverty and ignorance, problems which could not be eradicated in Victorian times. They could nevertheless be alleviated.

In Belfast in the nineteenth century the people who looked for help fell into three main categories: the poor; the sick and disabled; and those who had fallen (for whatever reason) on hard times. The 'poor' were the men and women permanently unable to support themselves in their own homes. This class of poor was outside the scope of the voluntary societies who simply had not the resources to hand out money (even if they had wanted to) and they could not afford to build premises where the paupers might live. The union workhouse was the resort for the aged, widows with children or women deserted by their husbands and the sick, who were totally destitute.

The most active and best-supported of the charities were those for the sick and disabled where it is hardest to assess success. The blind, the deaf and the cripples could not be cured and they were always the most incapable of earning a living without help. But it was in this field that charity was most beneficial. Voluntary societies were able to ameliorate the conditions of life for the disabled in several areas which can be measured. The committees of the main charities for the handicapped – the Society for Promoting the Education of the Deaf and Dumb and the Blind, the Belfast Association for the Employment of the Industrious Blind and the Cripples' Institute – set themselves realistic targets. They knew that they could have only a limited effect, but nevertheless considerable time was spent in providing services.

The aim of the School for the Deaf and the Blind was to educate all the children in Ulster who qualified for admission. If this was not achieved it was not the fault of the committee. They opened their doors to any child who cared to come to the school but not all parents were prepared to let their children go, even though Rev John Kinghan encouraged them. The school was invaluable to its pupils for without education they would have been burdens on their families or the community. When the children grew up, the workhouse would almost inevitably have been their only resort. In this case the committee and subscribers could see a result from their efforts at the public examinations and in the list of former pupils who were employed and independent. Thus it can be considered a success inside its limited objectives.

Of all the charities in the city the one which appeared most successful was the Workshops for the Blind. The aim of the founders was to enable blind men and women to earn their living and above all keep out of the workhouse, by giving them a training in a trade, and employment in that trade. The main restriction on the achievement of this aim was shortage of space in the workrooms to take in all of the blind who sought entry. The committee extended its premises as often as possible but the site was finite. Another restriction was the extent of a market for the products of blind workers, but allowing for this, the workshops in general achieved their objectives. Blind workers could support themselves in the community, a fact which gave them great satisfaction. This organisation can also be described as a success in the context of its aims.

The workshops gave a continuity of education to former pupils of the School for the Deaf and the Blind, for most blind workers had been taught there. The missions to the adult deaf and dumb continued the religious instruction begun in the school. Deaf and dumb men and women could easily have lost their religion if they were only able to attend church in a hearing environment, which excluded them from participation in the service. In addition the missions gave a social framework for the deaf; it is interesting that they did not prohibit intermarriage of the deaf as did the Workshops for the Blind to the blind. The missions too were successful in maintaining a Christian framework for their members.

As for the Cripples' Institute its main focus was on providing residential care for crippled children, and seaside holidays for the poorest class in Belfast. The Mrs Stewart Memorial Home in Bangor and the People's Palace on the Donegall Rd, Belfast had accommodation for long-term child inmates, though this was probably the least successful charity for the handicapped. Most of the children taken in by the institute were so physically damaged that it was very difficult for them to be trained to earn a living, though the quality of their lives was much improved by opportunities of education and good surroundings. Holidays by the sea for men, women and children from the narrow streets were not just for cripples or the chronic sick, and were a real boon to tired city workers. Most people in Belfast could not have afforded to go away on holiday so the Homes of Rest were successful in what they set out to do.

Perhaps the best confirmation of the success of these bodies is the fact that they still exist today, even at a time when the state has largely taken responsibility for care for the disabled. The School for the Deaf and Dumb and the Blind continues its residential function for deaf and dumb Ulster children at Jordanstown. The Mission to the

Adult Deaf and Dumb, now the Ulster Institute for the Deaf, and the Kinghan Mission are still operating in College Square North and Botanic Avenue. The Workshops for the Blind are a part of Ulster Sheltered Employment Ltd, doing the same sort of work as before. The Cripples' Institute maintains a hostel for disabled girls in Belfast as well as three homes in Bangor: the Stewart Memorial Home which gives respite care, West Bay House which used to be a home for disabled men and is being renovated into a shelter for disabled people, and Stricklands Centre used by religious and missionary groups for conferences.

By contrast all of the other societies, which treated the sick in their own homes and supplied clothes and bedding to the needy, have disappeared long ago. The structure of modern life is now so different that there is no place for the lady visitors of the Society for the Relief of the Destitute Sick. The treatment of illness is the responsibility of the National Health Service and, whether at home or in hospital, nurses and doctors are paid by the state. It is not that the services they gave are no longer required. The Society for Providing Nurses for the Sick Poor may have gone, but these nurses have been replaced by health visitors who do much the same tasks. The Ladies' Clothing Society is defunct but Oxfam and War on Want shops sell clothes at exceedingly low prices to the sort of people who used the Clothing Society.

While the voluntary societies existed their aims were modest. They believed that it was mothers who needed most help, not to change society, but to feed and clothe their families and this is what they tried to do. They may not have been totally successful but the 900 items of clothes and bedding distributed by the clothing society in 1852 gave at least a small amount of comfort to their recipients. The ladies who ran the organisations which were family-directed did not have the capacity to provide better housing or jobs but inside their competence they were able to alleviate distress.

None of the charities working for the sick and disabled dealt with large numbers. The School for the Deaf and the Blind and the Workshops for the Blind each had approximately one hundred people in their institution at any time. The Cripples' Institute in Belfast had accommodation for fifty children as did the Mrs Stewart Memorial Home. The clothing given out to the poor reached about 300 families in the year, while the Sick Poor society had around 150 patients on its books in most years, about the same number as the Destitute Sick society. It was impossible for the charities to reach a mass need and so they did not attempt to. The quality of their efforts probably gained from the ability of philanthropists to concentrate their endeavours on a few charities, rather than dissipate them on many.

The third category, those who had fallen on hard times, was by far the largest. It was made up of several different groups of peoples including homeless men, the temporarily unemployed, ex-prisoners, destitute children and fallen women. The aims of the societies which directed their attention to these groups had in common the desire to prevent crime, and to keep down the poor rates by reducing the numbers in the workhouse. It seems unlikely that the charities had a major impact in either of these areas.

The sort of criminal activity which worried Belfast businessmen was an unformulated fear of civil disorder which might well result from lack of food and lack of shelter, but this fear was much exaggerated. In 1847 public opinion in Belfast was considerably exercised by the stories of the famine in Connacht which, they feared, could soon bring hunger and death to Belfast if peasants from the west sought refuge in more prosperous regions. In retrospect this was highly unlikely given the distances involved, but hindsight makes such assessment easy. At the time when there were hundreds of homeless men and women in the town who had come in to Belfast, not from Munster or Connacht but from surrounding counties, it is clear that the citizens had some cause for their alarm. The poverty-stricken crowds seemed to represent a potential threat to stability, and it was this fact which encouraged the growth of local charities, in a reaction to the problem.

The Night and Day Asylums were specially established to meet the demand for shelter and to prevent men from sleeping in the streets at night and roaming about during the day, surrounded by temptation to break into houses, to steal or to beg. There were places for only about one hundred in each institution so that the refuges alone could not possibly have stopped disorder if there had been a serious danger of trouble. Nevertheless the citizens were convinced that the two shelters played a crucial role in keeping the peace. In fact the men who came looking for work were not organised, had no leaders and above all they were not intent on making a disturbance. After the asylums closed in 1847 there was only one similar institution opened, and that for a short time.

In 1858 and 1879 it was unemployment rather than homelessness which aroused concern. A trade depression left hundreds of local men and women in destitution, and thus a risk to law and order. They did not want to go to the workhouse and the business community, as personified by the town council, hoped that if temporary work could be organised it would tide the poor over until the economy improved. It was this feeling which led to the establishment of the town relief funds, though again the effect of the funds was limited. The only sort of relief work which could be given was unskilled, and local businessmen objected to any work being done under the scheme which might have been done by a commercial firm for profit. This was a major restriction on the success of the plan. Men were set to the unproductive task of stone-breaking and in 1879 were put to work levelling roads and making paths in Ormeau Park. Women were employed to sew garments in the Ladies' Industrial school-room and the Townsend St school. This had a dual benefit: women could earn some money and clothes for the poor were made.

Only small numbers benefitted from the relief work. The corporation paid 300 men in the park while the relief fund paid 450, and there was employment for about one hundred women. At the times of most distress in 1847, 1858 and 1879 soup kitchens were opened where cheap soup was sold to suitable customers. Of course no family could have survived on the soup alone, but it did give a useful supplement to their restricted diet. In none of these years was there serious trouble, though it is questionable if charitable effort prevented it. Always it was a very small number who were in great need and they could be helped, in any case there was no mass discontent, for most families could manage until times were better.

It is clear that the Prison Gate Missions for Men and for Women made little impact on the problem of ex-offenders. For a start they only came into contact with the few men and women who were prepared to try to reform and their resources were small. The Tudor Lodge home could take twenty women and the rate of lapsing was high. The men's hostel could admit even fewer, only six men could be accommmodated at any time, though over one hundred men were assisted in a year. Most of the offences committed by these men and women were alcohol-related, so really they were the targets of the temperance movement. The two charities were amongst the least popular and least successful in the city. It was possible to stimulate sympathy for the blind or crippled children but it was much more difficult to present former criminals in an attractive light. There were therefore two limits to their success, the reluctance of the former prisoners to accept the discipline of the homes and the reluctance of the citizens to support them.

There was a similar lack of success in solving the problem of destitute children. There were orphans of respectable families who were supported by the Protestant Orphan Society, the Presbyterian Orphan Society and the Sisters of Mercy and thus did not sink into destitution, but there were many more who were street arabs. The great danger was that abandoned children would become habitual criminals and it was this fear which encouraged efforts to rescue them. The guardians had to support orphans out of the rates but there was every chance that they would turn to crime when they got out of the workhouse. Boys who committed minor misdemeanours were sometimes sent to the 'Gibraltar' training ship, but there were a few children who might become upright citizens. It was these children who were taken into the Elim and Olivet Homes run by the Cripples' Institute.

The Elim Home received more public support than the Prison Gate Missions but there were two limitations on its operations. There were perhaps 1,000 street arabs in Belfast in the last two decades of the nineteenth century, according to the number who turned up at the entertainments provided for them at Christmas, but they were very reluctant to give up their freedom to enter a strictly run home. The other limitation was the amount of money available. Any success depended on a residential home and this was expensive to provide, so there were just fifty children in each home at the peak of the operation. The greatest success in the Elim Home was the assisted emigration given to twelve children each year. The boys and girls went off to Canada and while some were undoubtedly exploited, many others got a new life with much better opportunities than they would have had in Belfast. Both the Elim and the Olivet Homes had to close in the early twentieth century: neither was successful over a long period though, of course, some benefit was given to some children.

Finally what degree of success had the refuges for fallen women? These had to be residential if they were to have any impact but it is doubtful if they were successful. What were their aims? Penitentiaries generally were the next stage after women suffering from venereal disease had been discharged from hospital treatment, before they tried to re-assimilate themselves into society. The women who entered them did not intend to stay for long (except in the case of the Good Shepherd convent) but to give themselves a chance of rehabilitation. Although the women had made a conscious decision to reform this was not easy in a tight-knit community like Belfast, where everyone knew what the neighbours were doing. They could not disappear into the anonymity of a huge city like Manchester or Birmingham. The fact that the two protestant refuges closed in the early years of the twentieth century was not due to the fact that the problem of these women had gone but that they could more easily support themselves in new jobs. Laundry work was out of date.

It is clear then that the voluntary societies had a mixed amount of success in their work, but overall it was considerable given the limitations imposed upon them. A great deal of time and effort was spent in the charities even though comparatively few people actually benefitted. What the societies did in Victorian Belfast was to cope with problems which the state was not yet ready to tackle, and to lay the foundation of professional structures which became state-run. The committee members were realistic in their objectives. Arguably the middle class in the town should have made attempts to change the structure of city life but most of them saw no need for this. What they hoped to do was to make life better for the poor and needy, even to help them out of their poverty and need, preferably by their own endeavours. This is not to denigrate charity work. After all there still remain the problems of the disabled and the unemployed in the welfare state. The ladies and gentlemen who devoted themselves to philanthropy were pleased with what they did and were satisfied that the recipients appreciated their benevolence.

There is something even more difficult to assess than the success or failure of the charities. Were the people helped grateful or did they resent the patronage of the bourgeoisie who served on committees? It is almost impossible to measure this accurately. The sort of people who turned to charity for aid did not write about it afterwards, so their feelings about the societies are not recorded. The only information readily available (and this is very little) comes from the annual reports of such societies or from reports of A.G.Ms printed in local papers. These accounts give a uniform picture of gratitude, couched in enthusiastically evangelical terms. Obviously these accounts of the feelings of the people who were assisted were carefully chosen and were indeed often written in language which does not sound natural for the working classes to use, but it is reasonable to assume that the examples quoted in previous chapters did reflect the feelings of the writers. Why would they not appreciate help? It certainly did not make the poor obsequious. The Belfast working class may be accused of many things but deference is not one of them.

Beneficiaries often tried to exploit and take advantage of their benefactors, but they knew that without the help freely given to them life would have been even more difficult. Parents of children at the School for the Deaf and Dumb and the Blind, factory workers at the Homes of Rest, customers of the soup kitchens were all aware of the advantages of the institution and the fact that many of the charities required a contribution from their users helped to reduce the stigma of charity. The inevitable restrictions on the success of the charities were basically the amount of money which could be raised, the numbers of active workers who could be recruited and the amateurism of their efforts. The biggest charities did employ trained staff in the School for Deaf and Dumb and Blind children and in the Workshops for the Blind, for example, but it was difficult for the inexperienced ladies and gentlemen to supervise them.

Of these restrictions probably the most important was the availability of money. In general this was not a major problem because most of the societies were continually involved in fund-raising. The businessmen in the town were the committee members and they were experienced in financial management, indeed this was their biggest contribution to philanthropy. These gentlemen had the right contacts among the prosperous middle class, they knew who to ask for subscriptions and they knew how to invest their funds. It is therefore not surprising that in the generation of money from a variety of sources they were largely successful. This was an area where the ladies too developed a considerable expertise. One great satisfaction for them was that success could be measured in practical terms.

Many of the charities had their own particular way of raising money. The Workshops for the Blind produced and sold goods, the Society for Promoting the Education of the Deaf and Dumb and the Blind was grant-aided by the Poor Law Guardians and got a great deal of support from their auxiliaries, the female refuges ran laundries and the missions for the adult deaf collected for themselves. However, subscriptions were given by the general public though the amounts raised in this way were comparatively small. Without the special methods of providing income the charities could not have surivived. More substantial amounts came from life memberships which most of the organisations gave.

There was a steady income for most societies, who collected in districts delineated round the town and from protestant churches.

Charity sermons preached in these churches brought in sums in 1844, ranging from £1 in Ballymacarrett church to £33 from the wealthy congregation of Fisherwick Place. Ladies handed out 1d cards to their friends and fellow church members. The cards were divided into squares which were pierced with a pin for each 1d subscribed. The cards only produced 25s over a year but many were handed out so that the cumulative total was quite respectable.

As well as private individuals some firms gave money to charity every year, particularly the businesses owned by philanthropists such as W. Ewart and Sons, Dunville and Co. and Forster Green. Finally, there were the ubiquitous bazaars and sales of work. The biggest one was Ye olde Ulster fancie fayre for the Workshops for the Blind which brought in £2,000, closely followed by the British empire bazaar for the Magdalene Church and Asylum in 1909.

All of these efforts paid dividends in that most of the voluntary societies could continue their work well into the twentieth century. J.H. Hewitt of the Workshops for the Blind was proud that they always managed to keep the blind workers on full-time and the School for the Deaf and Dumb and the Blind could open its doors to any child who wanted in. However it was not a completely successful picture. The Elim and Olivet Homes had to close from lack of funds and it was a contributory factor in the closing of the penitentiaries. By their nature the temporary relief funds were always in a precarious state. There was a small balance left after the 1847 funds were wound up which was passed on (if rather reluctantly) to the 1858 fund. Unfortunately money for this effort ran out and the relief work stopped, and in 1879 Otto Jaffe and Vere Foster had to guarantee £750 to keep the work going. The money not used to pay workers was used to distribute food and clothes. Fuel was given through the lord mayor's coal relief fund which was run every year and which was able to collect sufficient money to help the very poorest.

Belfast subscribers in the nineteenth century had to limit their contributions for they would have spent enormous amounts if they had supported every cause which asked for money. One way of stimulating their giving was the publication of subscription lists in annual reports and newspapers. In Belfast (and no doubt in other similar cities) the first thing many society or church members do is to look up the amount given by their friends and compare it to their own subscription. It is always very gratifying to them to find that they have given more than most other members. Status required that the level of contribution should be maintained if not increased. Although obviously, there was a finite amount of money available, lack of it was not crucial until the government began to take responsibility for the maintenance of the needy.

A greater difficulty was the small number of men and women who were prepared to become involved actively in charity work. It was much easier to hand over some money than to spend time in committee meetings or checking on applicants for aid. The time-consuming nature of charitable endeavour meant that men who ran their own business or were in the professions found it hard to combine philanthropy with earning their living. Committees usually met every week, sub-committees at least as often, and the secretary and treasurer had considerable work to do. As a result it was only those who were inspired by duty or Christianity who were able to commit themselves, and this put limits on the scale of operations of the charities. This was true of the ladies as well, for although they did not have jobs outside the home, running a Victorian establishment demanded time.

Apart from fund-raising and financial management the gentlemen had no experience of professional care for the poor, nor did the ladies. It was the ladies who most often came into contact with the recipients of their bounty. Few of these middle class ladies were competent to assess the needs of the poor women who came to them, so they were often cheated by their clients. Trained nurses were much better at this work so that gradually a new profession of health visitor evolved from the early attempts at aid, eventually cutting down most of the voluntary effort. The ladies were not even experienced in financial affairs. They had to run their households and purchase food and clothes as well as supervising servants, but this was done on a budget fixed by their husbands. Unmarried girls who had always lived at home were even less able to organise a society, though by the end of the nineteenth century girls were more independent and were more often earning their living.

However, in the last analysis the greatest limitation of all on charity work and barrier to success, was the inability of the members to change the environment in which the poor lived. Inside that framework the men and women who ran the committees had a considerable degree of success. They did not change the world: they reached only a few people but Belfast was the better for their work. While the voluntary societies – that is 'any organisation devoting money, time, thought or energy to relieving the miseries of the poor, the neglected or the oppressed' – had some success, during the last three decades of the nineteenth century questions were being asked about their value.[23] It was widely accepted that the Poor Law left many gaps in meeting the varied needs of the poor, but between them, the guardians and charity kept the mass of the population from starvation and homelessness. However, society was becoming increasingly concerned about the whole system of philanthropy.

The early founders of charitable societies had no theory of philanthropy. They were not setting out to judge the worth of each applicant for aid, but they did dislike the idea that it was mainly the dishonest who benefitted. Not that the working classes had a philosophy of deliberate dishonesty in their relations with charity. It was just that the poor saw men and women much richer than themselves who could well afford to give generously, the sort of feeling shown in the Belfast expression 'it is coming off a broad board', which excuses people who take more than their entitlement. A report of the Poor Law Board in London in 1869-70 even found that some of the poor had so refined their methods of getting assistance that they were earning wages, getting outdoor relief to supplement them and receiving aid also from private charities.[24]   Some of the middle class disapproved of charity *per se* as undermining the self-reliance of the workers, but the sheer size of the need of large numbers which the Poor Law could not relieve, made private help essential and the years between 1820 and 1860

in the areas of medical relief, aid for the physically handicapped, the relief of the destitute and helpless, treatment of the delinquent saw the energies of the philanthropists reach a high, almost a frenetic pitch.[25]

The biggest problem was that philanthropy was an amateur response to an obvious need, but without a structure or an organisation which could administer help efficiently. It was this which led to the attempts by committee members to curtail the amount of help given without any check. If Victorian philanthropists had regarded moral inadequacy as the reason for distress and if they had stuck strictly to the concept of the deserving poor, few would have got any assistance. In fact the aid given to different groups was on such an *ad hoc* basis that it was almost inevitable that some got too much. The multiplicity of voluntary societies meant that their efforts were duplicated for it was almost impossible to ensure a fair distribution of help.

One favourite method of supervision was the sending of visitors to the houses of applicants for aid. This was certainly done in the early nineteenth century by the Belfast House of Industry. Its visitors tried to call unexpectedly, so that applicants had no time to clear their homes of all their possessions, which they did to accentuate their poverty. This was a common feature of charity in all of the United Kingdom industrial cities.

Confusion in the operations came about because the circumstances in which help was given were quite different from any which obtained before. This was the first time in history that large industrial conurbations had grown in many parts of one country and it was also the first time that the affluent in such a city were faced with the visible results of deprivation, and, for whatever motive, tried to alleviate them. How could these middle class people possibly know the best way to go about this work? There were no precedents which they could follow and so the nineteenth century saw a series of trials and errors, as they tried to work out an appropriate structure. The first charitable efforts were reactions to specific problems: street begging, temporary unemployment, sickness and disability, women at risk and destitute children, and gradually the organisers learned from their mistakes. They did not turn away from their Christian desire to help the helpless, they just wanted to target it to the most needy.

In the 1860s the belief that indiscriminate charity was actually producing a widening social gulf led to the setting up of statistical societies like the Manchester and Salford society, which gathered evidence about the needs of the Manchester poor. Surveys around the country revealed dire poverty in all cities. Some societies began to keep records of their clients in an attempt to keep some control over the distribution of aid. One consequence of this activity was the foundation in 1869 of the Charity Organisation Society (C.O.S.) in London. C.L. Mowat in *The Charity Organisation Society* makes the aims of the society clear. These were to co-operate with the Poor Law and other charitable agencies; to investigate applications for aid; to assist deserving cases; to promote habits of self-reliance and sanitary principles; to repress mendicity. There was a disagreeable odour of sanctity about the C.O.S. which limited its effectiveness, but it was an important transition stage between uncontrolled charity and state provision.[26]

It was the great cardinal principle of the C.O.S. that only the 'deserving' merited aid, which led them to spend so much time and money on investigating claims for assistance. Indeed, when the Cardiff C.O.S. was founded in 1886, local people expressed the hope that it would not emulate the London society by spending more on investigation than on relief.

It took a long time for a branch of the C.O.S. to be set up in Belfast. It was not until 1906, some thirty years after the society's methods were already being called into question, that an office was opened at 28 Ocean Buildings in the city centre. In the *Belfast Directory* its objects were listed showing that, like the London branch, the organisation wanted to co-operate with other agencies and administer charity more efficiently. The general public was urged to let the C.O.S. know if they were approached for help and to look for investigative tickets from the C.O.S. asking them to take action. Cases of begging were publicised. James Brown, a fifteen year old boy, had been begging successfully at Malone, giving false names and addresses.[27] The public were asked to use the C.O.S. tickets to try to stop him. A committee of ladies and gentlemen already engaged in 'social work' was established in three districts of the city: east, north and west Belfast. South Belfast was presumed to be in less need of charity.

The C.O.S. operated differently from other voluntary societies. While they had continuous fund-raising programmes, the C.O.S. asked for subscriptions for special cases which had been investigated. The C.O.S. would decide whether or not the cases referred to it warranted aid and this aid would depend on the state of their funds at that particular time.[28] Many of the cases concerned children. At a conference in 1910 the society described the four classes which needed to be reformed and rescued. These were:

juvenile criminals under sixteen who would have been imprisoned if they were adults, and who were simply sent back to bad homes;
juvenile street traders whose parents found their work necessary;
ill-treated or neglected children;
the children of widows.[29]

Then there were needy families for whom special appeals were made. One of these was a tradesman who had been in a sanatorium, who had a wife and six children to support, who could not get work; another was a family of four with the mother as the main breadwinner; and an old couple who had grandchildren to support. In their appeals the C.O.S. guaranteed that all money collected would go only to the cases which the public chose to support. From time to time it published warnings of people to avoid – for example, a German beggar who was in the city.

When cases were passed to it the C.O.S. applied strict criteria in deciding whether or not to give help. In 1906 out of fifty-five cases forty-four were not assisted, six were assisted, four were withdrawn, one was referred to the church. The reasons given for non-assistance reflect the ethos of the C.O.S.. There were fifteen who were 'unsatisfactory characters', nine were Poor Law cases, seven gave the wrong address, six did not really need help, three were out of work and four were 'other causes.' The society made no attempt to explain how the 'unsatisfactory character' was identified nor why some were Poor Law cases. The secretary commented that it was instructive to see how many importunate there were and how many gave false information. By 1908 the secretary, Rev David Purves of Elmwood Presbyterian Church, reported that 229 cases had been assisted though 575 had been refused and 77 had withdrawn their applications, not surprising given the low level of numbers assisted.[30] The poor did not appreciate the stringent tests given to the destitute.

It is hard to assess how important the C.O.S. was in Belfast. At this first A.G.M. in 1906 the dowager marchioness of Dufferin and Ava presided, and such familiar personages as Lady Jaffe, Miss Walkington, C.H. Brett, Sir John Byers and R.W. Corry were on the platform, so it seemed to be attractive to the charitable community. Thomas Sinclair of Hopefield presided over a society in 1909. There was encouragement for the idea of close collaboration with such societies as the Ladies' Clothing Society, of which Miss Bruce, who was in the C.O.S., was a committee member. The clothing society had been asked to elect representatives to the C.O.S. and Miss Annie Bowman was chosen. However, an editorial in the *Northern Whig* in 1907 commented that the C.O.S. was at first 'misunderstood' and there is no evidence that it became much more popular in later years. At subsequent A.G.Ms the people on the platform were less prominent.

Certainly the C.O.S. was never as popular as well-established societies, even if its members were told in 1910 that it had met with general approval.[31] More money was always needed, as well as personal efforts by ladies and gentlemen. The society reported in 1908 that £500 was necessary each year to carry on the work, but in the previous year only £300 had been collected.

The big problem in Belfast, as in most centres, was that public attitudes to charity were changing. The idea that only the 'worthy' poor deserved help was becoming repugnant to philanthropists. Agents of the C.O.S. who appeared to be sharp and suspicious when they vigorously pursued their investigations, aroused hostility in some recipients.[32] David Owen in *English Philanthropy* quoted the brickmaker's ultimatum to Mrs Pardiggle – 'I wants an end of these liberties took with my place I wants an end to being drawed like a badger.'[33] There was also tension sometimes between the C.O.S. and the voluntary societies. For example, the Manchester societies resented the local C.O.S.'s criticism of their indiscriminate giving, for no-one liked the imputation that he was naive and gullible. Belfast citizens disliked it as well. People preferred to direct their efforts to a specific need, to be involved with it on a long-term basis when they could appear on platform at A.G.Ms and on subscription lists. They were more ready to do this than give to an anonymous family who, although regarded as worthy by the C.O.S., might not appeal to the donors.

The C.O.S. was an important development in a social policy which wanted efficient regulations and more contact with the poor, which began case studies of the needy and was a basis for social reform. It did do good work in exposing fraud but from the 1880s there was a recognition that the resources of the state would be needed to cope with destitution. Canon Barnett of St Jude's, Whitechapel, one of the founders of the C.O.S., which always resisted state intervention, by 1883 had come to believe that the government would have to help.[34] Also in the 1880s Joseph Chamberlain's urging that local authorities should provide relief works and payment for the temporarily unemployed 'carried implications that the state or municipality bore a responsibility to the unemployed.'[35] Socialist ideologists like Sidney and Beatrice Webb bitterly attacked the C.O.S. and its policies, for these political theorists believed that the state should take much more responsibility for its citizens.

The Liberal government of 1906 began the process of wholesale state involvement in aiding the underprivileged classes and took over a field which had previously been dominated by private charity, to support children, the sick and disabled and the unemployed. Once the government took action in legislation and, more importantly, put money into schemes, the voluntary societies found it more difficult to collect subscriptions. Already it was only a minority in the cities who actually gave money or personal service, and they and other less active philanthropists were reluctant to give twice, once through their taxes and once through donations. It was because so few did take action in charities that the state had to become involved. It was only by forcing the citizen to pay tax, willingly or not, that sufficient funds could be raised to provide the structure of support which had become common throughout Europe in the early twentieth century. Most countries had health insurance, labour bureaux and primary education as well as old age pensions, and charity could not supply enough money for these.

The next five decades saw the spread of government involvement and acceptance of responsibility for its citizens until the Labour government of 1945 promised to support the people 'from the cradle to the grave.' The 1980s have seen the time when a dependency culture, allegedly produced by the removal of responsibility for one's own needs, has led to a transference of this responsibility to the 'government' now regarded as all-providing. The state is now advising the needy to turn to charity – the wheel has turned full circle.

The nineteenth century was arguably the most confident and prosperous time in Belfast's history. The city was conscious of its British identity and it followed the pattern of cities on the mainland in local government, public health, and housing, and charities were no exception. Dublin had many charitable societies but they were different from those in U.K. cities such as Glasgow or Liverpool in that they were either eighteenth century survivals, for example the Sick and Indigent Roomkeepers Society, or run exclusively by the Catholic Church. By contrast voluntary societies in Belfast were the same as in Great Britain, for example the school for the deaf and workshops for the blind. Even if their success was limited by the circumstances of the beneficiaries they were an important part of Belfast's life.

Philanthropists were prepared to devote much of their time to good works and they were pleased if the recipients benefitted. The poor did appreciate the help they were given, for the giving and receiving of help created a sort of bond between classes. Even today the middle class continues to support charity – societies to provide funds for medical research and aid the third world are popular and well-supported. The state still cannot do everything.

NOTES

Chapter 1: The Growth of Belfast in the Nineteenth Century

1 *Belfast News Letter* (hereafter B.N.L.) 2 Jan. 1801.
2 Ibid.
3 P.G. Cleary, *Spatial expansion and urban ecological change in Belfast 1861–1917* (Ph.D., Q.U.B., 1980), p. 324.
4 L.A. Clarkson, 'The city and the country' in J.C. Beckett et al. (eds.), *Belfast: the making of the city* (Belfast, 1983), p. 156.
5 Emrys Jones, *Social geography of Belfast* (Oxford, 1960), p. 342.
6 Jonathan Bardon, *Belfast* (Belfast, 1982), p. 126.
7 Ibid., p. 303.
8 Ibid., p. 303.
9 P.G. Cleary, *Spatial expansion*, p. 345.
10 Emrys Jones, *Social geography of Belfast*, p. 250.
11 *Henderson's commercial chronicle*, 1849.
12 Emily Boyle, 'Linenopolis' in J.C. Beckett et al. (eds.), *Belfast: the making of the city* (Belfast, 1983), p. 43.
13 Francis Geary, 'The rise and fall of the Belfast cotton industry' in *I.E.S.H.*, viii (1981), pp 30–49.
14 *Belfast directory* 1880.
15 D.A. Armstrong, 'Social conditions in the Belfast linen industry', in *I.H.S.*, vii (1951), p. 267.
16 M. Moss and J.K. Hume, *Shipbuilders to the world* (Belfast, 1986), p.11.
17 Ibid., p. 14.
18 Ibid., p. 20.
19 *Guide to Belfast* 1913.
20 *Belfast and adjoining counties* (British Association, 1902).
21 Emrys Jones, 'Late Victorian Belfast' in J.C. Beckett & R.E. Glasscock (eds.), *Belfast* (Belfast, 1967), p. 110.
22 From a report of Capt. Gilbert on the proposed extension of the boundaries of the borough of Belfast 1852–3. *Problems of a growing city*, PRONI (Belfast 1973), p. 125.
23 D.J. Owen, *History of Belfast* (Belfast, 1921), p. 294.
24 *Illustrated guide to Belfast* 1899.
25 Robin Sweetnam, 'The development of the port' in J.C. Beckett et al. (eds.), *Belfast: the making of the city* (Belfast, 1983), p. 70.
26 *Chamber of Commerce report* 1877.
27 Ibid., 1890.
28 *Illustrated Belfast 1899.*
29 A.S. Moore, *Belfast today* (Belfast, 1907), p. 83.
30 *Irish builder* 1873, p. 56.
31 B.M. Walker & Hugh Dixon, *In Belfast town* (Belfast, 1985), p. 30.
32 *Northern Whig* 4 Nov. 1879.
33 C.E. Brett, *Buildings of Belfast* (London, 1967), p. 45.
34 G.M. Young, *Portrait of an age* (London, 1936), p. 25.
35 Eric Midwinter, *Victorian social reform* (London, 1968), p. 7.
36 David Owen, *English philanthropy 1660–1960* (London, 1965), p. 134.
37 *Report of select committee on the state of Ireland*, p. 1, H.C. 1830 (637), vii, 150, p. 150.
38 George Nicholls, *The history of the Irish poor law* (London, 1856), p. 187.
39 George Nicholls, *The Irish poor law*, p. 204.
40 Evidence given to viceregal commission on poor law reforms in Ireland, ii, 1 [Cd 3203], H.C. 1906, li, 441, p. 33.
41 M.E. Bruce, *The coming of the welfare state* (London, 1961), p. 107.
42 Michael Farrell, *The poor law and the workhouse in Belfast* (Belfast, 1978), p. 75.
43 Joel Mokyr, *Why Ireland starved* (London, 1983), p. 1.
44 *Report of the select committee on the employment of the labouring poor in Ireland*, p. 1, H.C. 1823 (561), vi, 331, p. 445.
45 S.J. Connolly, 'Religion, work discipline and economic attitudes: the case of Ireland' in T.M. Devine and D. Dickson (eds.), *Ireland and Scotland, 1600–1850* (Edinburgh, 1983), p. 235.
46 Mr & Mrs S.C. Hall, *Ireland, its scenery and character* (London, 1843), p. 53.
47 *Third report of the commissioners for enquiring into the condition of the poorer classes in Ireland*, p. 1, H.C. 1836 (43), xxx, 1, p. 38.
48 J.A. Pilson, *History of the rise and progress of Belfast* (Belfast, 1846), p. 24.
49 Rev. W.M. O'Hanlon, *Walks among the poor of Belfast* (Belfast, 1853), p. 30.
50 Ibid., p. 34.
51 *Third report of the commissioners for enquiring into*

the condition of the poorer classes in Ireland
(hereafter *3rd report*), p. 1, H.C. 1836 (43),
xxx, 1, p. 38.
52 Rev. W.M. O'Hanlon, *Walks among the poor*,
p. 3.
53 Rev. W.M. O'Hanlon, *Walks among the poor*,
p. 4.
54 Rev. A. McIntyre, 'Diary of visits to the poor
in Belfast 1853–6', p. 1, PRONI D1558/2/3.
55 Ibid., p. 24.
56 Ibid., p. 33.
57 For a detailed account of the Charitable
Society see R.W.M. Strain, *Belfast and its
Charitable Society* (Oxford, 1961).
58 Indenture made between the trustees of the
Committee for the Employment and Relief of
the Poor of Belfast and the president and
committee of the Belfast Charitable Society.
PRONI D1905/2/200.
59 Letter issued by the Charitable Society.
60 *B.N.L.* 27 July 1804.
61 *B.N.L.* 13 June 1809.
62 Ibid., 11 July 1809.
63 *Belfast Monthly Magazine*, 11, June 1809,
p. 481.
64 *Belfast almanac 1810.*
65 *Northern Whig*, 7 June 1841.
66 *Belfast almanac 1810.*
67 *3rd report 1836*, p. 11.
68 *3rd report 1836*, p. 34.
69 *3rd report 1836*, p. 11.
70 *3rd report 1836*, p. 11.
71 *3rd report 1836*, p. 11.
72 *Report of the House of Industry* 1813.
73 *B.N.L.* 31 Oct. 1809.
74 *Northern Whig*, 8 Aug. 1839.
75 Ibid., 30 Nov. 1839.
76 Ibid., 9 Feb. 1841.
77 Ibid., 1 June 1841.
78 *Report of George Nicholls, esquire, to his majesty's
principal secretary of state for the Home Department on poor laws in Ireland*, p. 1, H.C. 1837
(69), li, 201, p. 210.
79 Sermon by Rev. H. Cooke (Belfast, 1815).

Chapter 2:   Relief in times of exceptional distress

1   R.J. Morris, 'Voluntary societies and the
British urban elite', *Historical Journal*, xxvi,
1983.
2   *Northern Whig*, 7 Jan. 1841.
3   *Northern Whig*, 7 Jan. 1841.
4   Ibid., 12 Jan. 1841.
5   Ibid., 4 Dec. 1841.
6   *Banner of Ulster*, 9 Jan. 1844.
7   Ibid.
8   *Banner of Ulster*, 3 Feb. 1843.
9   *Northern Whig*, 4 Nov. 1847.
10 *Northern Whig*, 13 Apr. 1847.
11 Ibid., 23 Feb. 1847.
12 Ibid., 3 Apr. 1847.
13 *Belfast People's Magazine*, i, no. 5 (May 1847),
p. 71.
14 *Belfast People's Magazine*, i, no. 5 (May 1847),
p. 120.
15 Ibid., 17 July 1847.
16 Ibid., 6 May 1847.
17 Michael Farrell, *Poor law and the workhouse in
Belfast* (Belfast, 1978), p. 65.
18 *Northern Whig*, 31 Mar. 1849.
19 W.D. Killen, *Memoir of Dr Edgar* (Belfast, 1867),
p. 198.
20 *Northern Whig* 16 Feb. 1847.
21 *B.N.L.* 5 Jan. 1847.
22 *B.N.L.* 8 Jan. 1847.
23 *B.N.L.* 26 Jan. 1847.
24 *Northern Whig*, 16 Feb. 1847.
25 *Northern Whig* 30 Jan. 1847.
26 *Northern Whig* 16 Feb. 1847.
27 *Northern Whig* 11 Mar. 1847.
28 *Belfast People's Magazine*, i, no. 3 (Mar. 1847),
p. 71.
29 *Belfast People's Magazine*, i, no. 1, (Jan. 1847),
p. 19.
30 *Northern Whig* 18 Feb. 1847.
31 *B.N.L.* 23 Mar. 1847.
32 Ibid., 8 Apr. 1847.
33 Ibid., 3 June 1847.
34 *Belfast Commercial Chronicle* 1 Jan. 1848.
35 *B.N.L.* 15 Dec. 1857.
36 For the background to the crisis in the linen
industry in these years see Philip
Ollerenshaw, *Banking in nineteenth century
Ireland* (Manchester, 1987), pp 72–81.
37 *B.N.L.* 15 Dec. 1857.
38 *Northern Whig* 24 Feb. 1858.
39 *B.N.L.* 28 Jan. 1858.
40 *Northern Whig* 9 Feb. 1858.
41 Ibid., 19 Apr. 1858.
42 John Scott, *A moral mirror for the use of the mayor
and his relief committee and the town council*
(Belfast, 1858), p. 1.
43 *Northern Whig* 3 Feb. 1858.
44 *Northern Whig* 9 Feb. 1858.
45 Ibid., 12 Feb. 1858.
46 *Report of the town relief fund 1878–9*, p. 7.
47 *Northern Whig* 14 Jan. 1879.
48 Ibid., 17 Jan. 1879
49 Ibid., 15 Feb. 1879.
50 *Northern Whig* 17 Feb. 1879.
51 *Report of town relief fund*, p. 12.
52 Ibid., p. 14.
53 *Northern Whig* 4 Feb. 1879.
54 *Northern Whig* 20 Jan. 1879.
55 Ibid., 20 Feb. 1879.
56 *Report of relief fund*, p. 15.
57 *Report of relief fund*, p. 15.
58 *Report of relief fund*, p. 12.
59 *Balance sheet of relief fund.*
60 *Balance sheet of relief fund*, 1879.

Chapter 3:   The Ulster Society for Promoting the
Education of the Dearf and Dumb
and the Blind

1   *Belfast Almanac*, 1823.
2   *Belfast Commercial Chronicle*, 27 Apr. 1831.
3   'Historical sketch of the Institution for the
Deaf and Dumb and the Blind' in *Review of
Deaf Mute Education*, Jan.-Apr., 1891.

4 Ibid.
5 *DDB annual report*, 1837.
6 Advertisement printed by the committee, 1 June 1844.
7 Minute book of the society, 9, 21, 22 Dec. 1842: 2, 9 Jan. 1843.
8 *DDB annual report*, 1841.
9 C.E. Brett, *Buildings of Belfast* (London, 1967) p. 24.
10 *DDB annual report*, 1843.
11 William McComb, *Guide to Belfast* (Belfast, 1861), p. 31.
12 *DDB annual report*, 1843.
13 *Belfast directory*, 1895.
14 Recollections of Mr James Anderson, former pupil.
15 Report of national deputation, 1856.
16 Recollections of Mr James Anderson.
17 *B.N.L.*, 4 Feb. 1891.
18 Statement from committee to subscribers, 21 Nov. 1848.
19 Ibid.
20 *Protestant Defender*, 21 Nov. 1848
21 Statement by committee to subscribers, 21 Nov. 1848.
22 *Protestant Defender*, 21 Nov. 1848.
23 Ibid., 1 Dec. 1848.
24 *Northern Whig*, 27 Dec. 1879.
25 *DDB annual report*, 1854.
26 *Northern Whig*, 4 June 1857.
27 J.G. McClelland, *The development of educational facilities for handicapped children in Ireland with particular reference to the deaf in Ulster* (M.A., Q.U.B., 1965), p. 113.
28 Ibid., p. 17.
29 K.W. Hodgson, *The deaf and their problems* (London, 1953), p. 254.
30 K.W. Hodgson, *The deaf and their problems*, p. 233.
31 J.G. McClelland, *The development of educational facilities*, p. 130.
32 Ibid., p. 135.
33 Information from Mr Anderson.
34 *Northern Whig*, 4 June 1857.
35 Ibid., 28 June 1889.
36 Ibid., 4 June 1857.
37 *Banner of Ulster*, 16 July 1859.
38 Ibid., 16 July 1859.
39 *DDB annual report*, 1838.
40 Rev. Burnside at Newry Auxiliary, 5 Sept. 1857.
41 *DDB annual report*, 1839.
42 Letter from Mr John Kinghan to committee, 28 Dec. 1859.
43 J.G. McClelland, *Development of educational facilities*, p. 138.
44 *Northern Whig*, 25 June 1886.
45 Letter from Mr John Kinghan to the committee, 30 Dec. 1859.
46 *Report of the national deputation*, 1856.
47 *DDB annual report*, 1843.
48 Ibid., 1842.
49 Application book, vol. 1.
50 Application book, vol. 5.
51 *DDB annual report*, 1875.
52 Printed appeal, 15 Apr. 1863.
53 Rev. James Morgan at the opening of the new building, 24 Sept. 1845.
54 *B.N.L.*, 18 Mar. 1899.
55 Ibid., 18 Dec. 1894.
56 Report of meeting of board of guardians, *B.N.L.*, 1 Oct. 1862.
57 *DDB annual report*, 1855.
58 Application form queries.
59 Appendix to annual report, 1843.
60 *DDB annual report*, 1839.
61 *Commercial Chronicle*, 28 Dec. 1849.
62 *DDB annual report*, 1837.
63 Minute book, 5 July 1837.
64 *DDB annual report*, 1840.
65 *DDB annual report*, 1842.
66 Minute book, 24 July 1846.
67 Ibid., 30 July 1846.
68 Minute book, 1 Aug. 1846.
69 Ibid., 18 Sept. 1846.
70 Ibid., 1 Oct. 1846.
71 K.W. Hodgson, *The deaf and their problems*, p. 197.
72 *Crockford's clerical directory*, 1880.
73 *Northern Whig*, 19 Dec. 1848.
74 *Belfast Commercial Chronicle*, 28 Dec. 1849.
75 *DDB annual report*, 1846.
76 Ibid., 1849.
77 *Quarterly Review of Deaf Education*, Apr. 1891.
78 Recollections of Mr Anderson.
79 *Northern Whig*, 18 June 1897.
80 Ibid., 2 Sept. 1895.
81 *DDB annual report*, 1896.
82 Ibid.
83 *The Messenger*, Talladega, Alabama, 14 Oct. 1897.
84 Ibid.
85 *DDB annual report*, 1897.
86 *Northern Whig*, 28 Mar. 1901.
87 *Endowed Schools Commission report*, 1858, iii, 42.
88 K.W. Hodgson, *The deaf and their problems*, p. 159.
89 *Glasgow Herald*, 19 Aug. 1899; *Daily Telegraph*, 21 Aug. 1899.
90 *DDB annual report*, 1886.
91 *Banner of Ulster*, 23 Feb. 1869.
92 *DDB annual report*, 1869.
93 *B.N.L.*, 14 Aug. 1855.
94 *Enniskillen Chronicle*, 5 Sept. 1844.
95 *DDB annual report*, 1837.
96 *B.N.L.*, 30 Sept. 1879.
97 *Belfast Commercial Chronicle*, 28 Dec. 1849.
98 *Journal of the Statist. & Social Enquiry Society of Ireland*, vii (1876), p. 33.
99 6 and 7 Vic., c. 92, s. 14.
100 Letter from the Poor Law Commissioners, 28 Nov. 1867.
101 Memorandum book of the society.
102 *Northern Whig*, 23 Dec. 1879.
103 *Census of Ireland for the year 1851 (report on the status of disease)*, p. 1 [Cd 1765], H.C. 1854, iii, 1.
104 *Census of Ireland, 1891 (province of Ulster, summary tables and indexes)*, p. 959 [Cd 6626–ix], H.C. 1892, xci, 959.
105 *DDB annual report*, 1897.
106 *B.N.L.*, 12 July 1905.
107 *DDB annual report*, 1905.
108 *DDB annual report*, 1840.

109 *Belfast Commercial Chronicle,* 29 Dec. 1849.
110 *Northern Whig,* 25 Mar. 1902.
111 *Northern Whig,* 22 Dec. 1882.

Chapter 4: Missions to the Adult Deaf and Dumb

1 Statement by Rev. W.H. Davis, *Northern Whig* 5 Mar. 1892.
2 K.W. Hodgson, *The deaf and their problems,* p. 165.
3 Ibid.
4 Robert Allen, *Soul of a silent mission* (Belfast, 1943), p. 7.
5 *Annual report of the Bethel 1878.*
6 Ibid.
7 Letter book of Edward Coey, PRONI D2926/1/2.
8 *Northern Whig* 5 Mar. 1892.
9 Leaflet published by the Mission to the Adult Deaf and Dumb 1898.
10 I am indebted for this information to Mrs Maude Morton, daughter of Mr W.E. Harris, head assistant at the Ulster Institution and later superintendent of the mission hall.
11 Minute book 4 Jan. 1892.
12 *Northern Whig* 5 Mar. 1892.
13 *Adult Mission to Deaf and Dumb annual report 1906.* (Hereafter *Deaf and dumb annual report).*
14 *Northern Whig* 5 Mar. 1892.
15 Recollections of Mrs Maude Morton.
16 *Northern Whig* 5 Nov. 1906.
17 Ibid., 26 Oct. 1889.
18 *Deaf and dumb annual report* 1907.
19 *Belfast Evening Telegraph* 16 Mar. 1910.
20 Minute book 7 Dec. 1888.
21 Letter from governor of the Ulster Institution, *B.N.L.* 21 Mar. 1895.
22 *Deaf and dumb annual report* 1888.
23 *Deaf and dumb annual report* 1909.
24 *B.N.L.* 8 Jan. 1898.
25 *Deaf and dumb annual report* 1908.
26 Ibid., 1909.
27 Ibid., 1888.
28 Ibid., 1889.
29 *Deaf and dumb annual report* 1910.
30 *Northern Whig* 26 Oct. 1889.
31 *Deaf and dumb annual report* 1888.
32 *Deaf and dumb annual report* 1906.
33 *Northern Whig* 26 Oct. 1889.
34 *B.N.L.* 4 Nov. 1893.
35 Ibid.
36 Ibid.
37 *Northern Whig* 26 Oct. 1889.
38 *B.N.L.* 26 Nov. 1894.
39 Ibid., 29 Nov. 1894.
40 Robert Allen, *Soul of a silent mission* (Belfast, 1943), p. 7.
41 Leaflet printed for 11 Fisherwick Place, 3 Oct. 1898.
42 Minute book 7 Feb. 1899.
43 Minutes of the general assembly 1897, p. 306.
44 *Annual report of the Kinghan Mission* 1899.
45 Minutes of the general assembly 1900, p. 1012.
46 Ibid., 1901, p. 100.

47 *Annual report of the Kinghan Mission* 1899.
48 Minutes of the general assembly 1909, p. 8802.
49 *Annual report of the Mission to the Adult Deaf 1904.*
50 *B.N.L.* 10 Mar. 1905.
51 Printed leaflet addressed to the committee of the Kinghan Mission, 12 Jan. 1908.
52 *Northern Whig* 2 Oct. 1904.
53 Ibid., 20 May 1907.

Chapter 5: The Workshops for the Blind; the Home Teaching Society; the Homes for the Blind

1 David Owen, *English philanthropy,* p. 170.
2 Martin to L.M. Ewart D3563/BC/5, 20 Feb. 1871, PRONI.
3 Report of meeting D3563/AA/1, 16 Feb. 1871, PRONI.
4 Ibid., 9 May 1871. Minute book of the Belfast Association for the Employment of the Industrious Blind D3563/AA/1, 12/4/1871, PRONI.
5 Ibid., 21 Nov. 1871.
6 Letters of application, D3563/DA/1, PRONI.
7 Testimonial to Alexander Youngson 1871, D3563/DA/1, PRONI.
8 Ewart to Youngson, D3563/BC/3, 14 Nov. 1872, PRONI.
9 Martin to Ewart, D3563/BC/5, 16 Oct. 1872, PRONI.
10 Address to Robert Erskine, minute book D3563/AA/1, PRONI.
11 McBurney to committee, D3563/BC/7, 2 Sept. 1878, PRONI.
12 R.L. Hamilton to committee, D3563/BC/4, 30 Sept. 1878, PRONI.
13 Hewitt to committee, D3563/DA/4, 26 Jan. 1881, PRONI.
14 Manager's report, D3563/BA/3, 5 Jan. 1898, PRONI.
15 Manager's report, D3563/BA/2, 5 Mar. 1890, PRONI.
16 Manager's report, D3563/BA/3, 11 Feb. 1893, PRONI.
17 Minute book, D3563/AA/3, 1 Apr. 1903, PRONI.
18 Ibid., 10 Feb. 1881.
19 Ibid., 7 Nov. 1881.
20 *Centenary volume of the workshops for the blind* (Belfast, 1971).
21 Minute book, D3563/AA/2, 14 Mar. 1883, PRONI.
22 *Belfast News Letter,* 14 Mar. 1883.
23 *Report 1884,* D3563/AK/1, PRONI.
24 Manager's report, D3563/BA/3, 7 Dec. 1898, PRONI.
25 Manager's report, D3563/BA/4, 2 Nov. 1904, PRONI.
26 Ibid., 1 Sept. 1908.
27 Manager's report, D3563/BA/2, 2 Dec. 1886, PRONI.
28 Ibid., D3563/BA/4, Mar. 1905.
29 Manager's report, D3563/BA/3, 7 May 1905, PRONI.

30 *Northern Whig*, 6 Jan. 1879.
31 Manager's report, D3563/BA/4, 17 Aug. 1904, PRONI.
32 *Report 1883*, D3563/AK/1, PRONI.
33 Manager's report, D3563/BA/3, 7 Jan. 1891, PRONI.
34 Ibid., D3563/BA/4, 4 Nov. 1907.
35 *Report 1890*, D3563/AK/1, PRONI.
36 Manager's report, D3563/BA/4, 1 July 1903, PRONI.
37 Minute book, D3563/AA/4, 11 Apr. 1900, PRONI.
38 Minute book, D3563/AA/2, 15 Nov. 1883, PRONI.
39 Manager's report, D3563/BA/4, 3 June 1908, PRONI. Ibid., 6 June 1872.
40 Minute book, D3563/AA/1, 6 June 1872, PRONI.
41 Manager's report, D3563/BA/2, 5 Apr. 1885, PRONI.
42 Manager's report, D3563/BC/7, 1873, PRONI.
43 Ibid.
44 Ibid., D3563/BC/7, 1873 PRONI.
45 Minute book, D3563/AA/1, 10 Sept. 1873, PRONI.
46 Report 1897, D3563/AK/1, PRONI.
47 Ibid., D3563/BA/4, 2 Sept. 1903.
48 Manager's report, D3563/BA/3, 4 May 1892, PRONI.
49 Manager's report, D3563/BA/4, 2 Aug. 1906, PRONI.
50 Minute book, D3563/AA/5, 2 Sept. 1908, PRONI.
51 Manager's report, D3563/BA/1, 8 Apr. 1874, PRONI.
52 Ibid., D3563/BA/3, 2 Nov. 1898. Manager's report, D3563/BA/4, 6 July 1904, PRONI.
53 Ibid., D3563/BA/2, 6 May 1886.
54 Minute book D3563/AA/3, 4 July 1888, PRONI.
55 Ibid., D3563/AA/4, Dec. 1889.
56 Sub-committee report, D3563/BC/4, 15 Dec. 1876, PRONI.
57 Minute book, D3563/AA/1, 14 Nov. 1876, PRONI.
58 Manager's report, D3563/BA/3, Nov. 1890, PRONI.
59 Ibid., 3 Dec. 1890.
60 Ibid., 7 Nov. 1893.
61 Ibid., D3563/BA/4, 4 Dec. 1901.
62 Manager's report, D3563/BA/4, 6 Jan. 1909, PRONI.
63 Manager's report, D3563/BA/3, 22 Feb. 1893, PRONI.
64 *Annual report*, 1892, D3563/AK/1, PRONI.
65 Manager's report, D3563/BA/4, 1 July 1909, PRONI.
66 Manager's report, D3563/BA/3, 1 Sept. 1897, PRONI.
67 Workshops for the Blind B.P.B., 1891.11.
68 *Northern Whig*, 12 Apr. 1878.
69 *Book of fancie fayre*, B.P.B., 1882.8.
70 Ibid.
71 *Centenary volume of the workshops of the blind* (Belfast, 1971).

72 Manager's report, D3563/BA/4, 4 Dec. 1907, PRONI.
73 *Annual report*, 1910, D3563/AK/1, PRONI.
74 Minute book, D3563/AA/2, 13 Mar. 1885, PRONI.
75 Ibid., D3563/AA/3, 5 Oct. 1892.
76 Miss Hobson to committee, D3563/BC/3, 8 Sept. 1878, PRONI.
77 Ibid., D3563/BE/1–2, 1878 undated.
78 Ibid., D3563/CB/1, 29 Aug. 1878.
79 Minute book D3562/AA/2, 27 Feb. 1880, PRONI.
80 Ibid., 25 Nov. 1881.
81 *Annual report*, 1883, D3563/AK/1, PRONI.
82 Ibid., D3563/AA/2, 17 Mar. 1887.
83 *Centenary volume* 1971.
84 Minute book, D3563/AA/1, 22 Feb. 1877, PRONI.
85 Ibid., D3563/AA/3, 11 Mar. 1892.
86 *Northern Whig*, 18 Jan. 1886.
87 Manager's report, D3563/BA/3, 2 Dec. 1891, PRONI.
88 Annual report, D3563/AK/1, 1902, PRONI.
89 Ibid., 1884.
90 Ibid., 1885.
91 Ibid., 1889.
92 Mr Aickin to committee D3563/BC/6, 2 May 1899, PRONI.
93 Miss L.A. Walkington to A.D. Lemon D3563/BC/6, 25 Feb. 1905, PRONI.
94 Manager's report D3563/BA/4, 3 July 1907, PRONI.
95 Mrs Aickin to committee D3563/BC/6, 12 June 1888, PRONI.
96 *B.N.L.*, 29 Nov. 1887.
97 Ibid., 14 Mar. 1884.
98 *Northern Whig* 5 Mar. 1907.
99 Manager's report D3563/BA/4, 4 Sept. 1905, PRONI.
100 Hamilton to committee D3563/BC/7, Jan. 1903, PRONI.
101 *N.W.* 15 Feb. 1892.

Chapter 6: The Cripples' Institute and related activities

1 *Northern Whig* 1 July 1896.
2 *Belfast directory* 1892.
3 Arthur Irwin, *Lights along the way* (Belfast, 1941), p. 96.
4 W.J.W. Roome, *For his sake* (Belfast, 1907), p. 32.
5 Arthur Irwin, *Lights along the way*, p. 98.
6 W.J.W. Roome, *For his sake*, p. 24.
7 Ibid. p. 23.
8 Ibid. p. 26.
9 W.J.W. Roome, *For his sake*, p. 42.
10 Ibid. p. 35.
11 Ibid. p. 37.
12 W.J.W. Roome, *For his sake*, p. 50.
13 Ibid. p. 53.
14 W.J.W. Roome, *For his sake*, p. 51.
15 Ibid. p. 52.
16 W.J.W. Roome, *For his sake*, p. 93.
17 Ibid.

18 W.J.W. Roome, *For his sake*, p. 77.
19 *Northern Whig* 6 Dec. 1904.
20 *Northern Whig* 6 Dec. 1904.
21 Ibid.
22 Ibid. 27 Dec. 1904.
23 *B.N.L.* 28 July 1903.
24 W.J.W. Roome, *For his sake*, p. 59.
25 W.J.W. Roome, *For his sake*, p. 59.
26 *Northern Whig* 7 Dec. 1904.
27 Ibid.
28 W.J.W. Roome, *A brighter Belfast* (Belfast, 1898), p. 100.
29 *Belfast Evening Telegraph* 7 Jan. 1910.
30 *Report of Belfast Female Prison Gate Mission* 1877 (hereafter *P.G.M. report*).
31 *P.G.M. report* 1877.
32 *Northern Whig* 8 May 1879.
33 *Report of the Prison Gate Mission Society* 1877.
34 Ibid.
35 *Northern Whig* 8 May 1879.
36 *P.G.M. report* 1877.
37 6 Feb. 1904, PRONI FIN 1/2/5.
38 *Northern Whig* 11 May 1907.
39 Minute book Cripples' Institute 20 June 1907.
40 *Belfast directory* 1910.
41 *Northern Whig* 11 May 1907.
42 *Northern Whig* 10 Dec. 1879.
43 Ibid.
44 *Northern Whig* 6 Dec. 1904.
45 W.J.W. Roome, *For his sake*, p. 69.
46 *Northern Whig* 10 Apr. 1878.
47 A.J. Kidd, 'Outcast Manchester' in A.J. Kidd and K.W. Robert (eds.), *City class and culture* (Manchester, 1985), p. 59.
48 *Judicial Statistics*
49 *Report of the Elim Home for Destitute Children* 1885 (hereafter *E.H. report*).
50 J.A. Pilson, *History of Belfast* (Belfast, 1846), p. 52.
51 J. Robbins, *The lost children* (Dublin, 1980), p. 293.
52 *Northern Whig* 10 Dec. 1906.
53 J.M. Barkley, *The Presbyterian Orphan Society 1866–1966* (Belfast, 1966), App. A, table 3.
54 *Belfast almanac* 1876.
55 *Northern Whig* 18 Dec. 1879.
56 *Northern Whig* 18 Dec. 1876.
57 *E.H. report* 1885.
58 *E.H. report* 1885.
59 Olive Checkland, *Philanthropy in Victorian Scotland*, p. 264.
60 Inspector's report 1915, ED2/836, PRONI.
61 Inspector's report ED2/836, PRONI.
62 *Articles of incorporation 1906.*
63 *Irish Christian Advocate* 16 May 1913.
64 *Belfast directory* 1890.
65 Ibid. 27 Dec. 1906.
66 *Northern Whig* 12 Nov. 1907.
67 *Northern Whig* 22 Dec. 1906.
68 *Irish Christian Advocate* 30 Jan. 1914.

Chapter 7: Women in Charity Work

1 Pamela Horn, *The rise and fall of the Victorian servant*, (Dublin, 1975), p. 13.
2 Ibid., p. 13.
3 Ibid., p. 27.
4 1901 Census
5 Mr and Mrs S.C. Hall, *Ireland*, p. 63.
6 *Belfast almanac* 1863.
7 Ibid.
8 *Northern Whig* 28 Feb. 1879.
9 J.H. Smith, *Belfast and its environs* (Dublin, 1853), p. 28.
10 R.E. Pelan, *The Malone Place Hospital 1860–1981* (Belfast, 1981), p. 2.
11 *Northern Whig* 17 Feb. 1870.
12 *Northern Whig* 17 Feb. 1870.
13 *Belfast directory* 1877.
14 *Ladies' National Association report* 1877.
15 *Report of the General Hospital committee*, 1828–9.
16 *Morning Chronicle*, 13 Nov. 1849.
17 H. Evans, *The oldest profession* (Newton Abbot, 1979), p. 107.
18 *Report of the Rescue Society*, 1871.
19 Pamela Horn, *The rise and fall of the Victorian servant* (Dublin, 1975), p. 133.
20 Judith Walkowitz, *Prostitution and Victorian society*, (Cambs, 1980), p. 5.
21 Judith Walkowitz, op.cit., p. 14.
22 A medical gentleman, *Low life in Edinburgh* (Edinburgh, 1851), p. 97.
23 Ibid., p. 118.
24 *Criminal and judicial statistics, Ireland, 1868*, p. 1 [Cd 4203], H.C. 1868–9, lviii, 737, p. 87.
25 *Judicial statistics, Ireland, 1901*, p. 1 [Cd 1208], H.C. 1902, cxvii, 395, p. 92.
26 'Female penitentiaries' in *London Quarterly Review* (1848), p. 361.
27 R.S. Allison, *Seeds of time* (Belfast, 1972), p. 14.
28 David Owen, *English philanthropy*, p. 173.
29 *Indenture between House of Industry and Charitable Society*, 1822, D 1905/200, PRONI.
30 R.S. Allison, *Seeds of time*, p. 14.
31 W.D. Killen, *Memoir of Dr Edgar*, p. 130.
32 *Belfast almanac*, 1840.
33 Mr and Mrs S.C. Hall, *Ireland*, p. 62.
34 W.D. Killen, *Memoir of Dr Edgar*, p. 134.
35 *Northern Whig*, 17 Feb. 1892.
36 J.A. Pilson, *History of Belfast*, p. 61.
37 W.D. Killen, *Memoir of Dr Edgar*, p. 138.
38 *Northern Whig*, 12 Dec. 1907.
39 *Belfast almanac* 1840.
40 *History of Magdalene Church and Asylum booklet of union bazaar 1895.*
41 W.S. Leathem, *History of Church of Ireland in St Mary Magdalene Parish* (Belfast, 1939), p. 36.
42 Ibid., p. 38.
43 *Report of the Ulster Magdalene Asylum* 1887 (hereafter *M.A. report*).
44 *M.A. report* 1887.
45 Ibid.
46 I am indebted to Sister Teresa and Sister Otran for information on the Good Shepherd convent.
47 Judith Walkowitz, *Prostitution and Victorian society*, p. 221.
48 *3rd Report*
49 *Belfast directory, 1890.*
50 *Northern Whig*, 11 May 1907.
51 *Clothing Society report* 1850 (hereafter *C.S.*

52 Ibid., 1852.
53 Ibid., 1836.
54 *C.S. report* 1860.
55 *Northern Whig*, 11 Apr. 1910.
56 *C.S. report* 1852.
57 *Northern Whig*, 11 Apr. 1910.
58 *C.S. report* 1836.
59 *Report of the Destitute Sick Society* 1904
   (hereafter *D.S.*).
60 Ibid.
61 *3rd Report* 1836, App. C, p. 15.
62 *Northern Whig*, 27 Feb. 1897.
63 *D.S. report* 1893.
64 *D.S. report* 1904.
65 *D.S. report* 1904.
66 Ibid.
67 *Northern Whig*, 11 Apr. 1910.
68 *Report of the first annual general meeting of the
   Society for Providing Nurses for the Sick Poor*,
   D3480/21/1.
69 *Northern Whig*, 25 Apr. 1878.
70 Ibid., 16 May 1879.
71 Ibid., 25 Apr. 1878.
72 *Report of the first annual general meeting S.P.
   Society*.
73 Ibid., 14 Nov. 1895.
74 *Report of the first annual general meeting S.P.
   Society*.
75 *Northern Whig*, 3 Feb. 1879.
76 *Belfast Evening Telegraph*, 26 Feb. 1910.
77 *Report of the first annual general meeting S.P.
   Society*.
78 Ibid.
79 Ibid., 7 Feb. 1879.
80 G. Kitson Clark, *Churchmen and the condition of
   England* (London, 1973), p. 217.

Chapter 8: Protestant/Catholic collaboration (or
lack of it) in charity work

1 Brenda Collins, *Selected social characteristics
  of Belfast*. Paper given at QUB Teachers'
  Centre 1984.
2 Workers to Committee of Workshops for the
  Blind, D3563/DB/1.
3 Ian Budge and Cornelius O'Leary, *Belfast:
  approach to crisis* (London, 1973).
4 *Belfast News Letter* 27 Oct. 1857.
5 *Irish News* 15 July 1892.
6 A.C. Hepburn and Brenda Collins, 'Industrial societies: the structure of Belfast 1901'
  in Peter Roebuck (ed), *Plantation to partition*
  (Belfast, 1981), p. 225.
7 *Northern Whig* 12 Dec. 1885.
8 *Belfast News Letter* 27 Oct. 1857.
9 *Irish News* 8 Nov. 1905.
10 E.R. Norman, *The Catholic Church in Ireland in
   the age of rebellion* (London, 1965), p. 1.
11 *B.N.L.* 12 Dec. 1857.
12 Ambrose Macaulay, *Patrick Dorrian* (Dublin,
   1987), p. 26.
13 M.E. Daly, *Dublin, the deposed capital* (Cork,
   1984), p. 93.
14 Ibid., p. 94.
15 *Report of St Vincent de Paul*, 1913.
16 Ibid.
17 *Centenary Volume of St Vincent de Paul*, 1950,
   p. 8.
18 Ibid., p. 12.
19 Ibid., p. 15.
20 Ibid., p. 27.
21 *I.N.* 26 July 1892.
22 Ibid., 17 Sept. 1892.
23 *Centenary Volume of St Vincent de Paul*, p. 23.
24 *I.N.* 13 Mar. 1905.
25 *Belfast almanac* 1842.
26 *Centenary Volume of the Sisters of Mercy*, p. 24.
27 Ibid.
28 Ambrose Macaulay, *Patrick Dorrian*, p. 122.
29 Fr L.J. McKenna, 'An Irish Catholic Women's
   League' in *Irish Monthly*, 45 (1917), p. 353.
30 Ibid., p. 361.
31 T.P. O'Neill, 'The Catholic Church and the
   Relief of the Poor' in *Archivium Hibernicum*,
   xxi (1973), p. 134.
32 Ibid., p. 133.
33 *Report of St Vincent de Paul Society*, 1913.
34 *Banner of Ulster*, 1 Jan. 1857.
35 *B.N.L.* 29 Dec. 1848.
36 See chapter 4.
37 J.W. Kernohan, *Rosemary Street Church: the first
   200 years* (Belfast, 1973), p. 55.

Chapter 9: The People who Worked for Charity

1 E.P. Hennock, *Fit and proper persons* (London,
  1973), p. 143.
2 J. Garrard, 'The middle class in 19th century
  national and local politics' in J. Garrard, D.
  Jarry, M. Goldsmith and A. Oldfield (eds.),
  The middle class in politics (London, 1978),
  p. 36.
3 M.A. McNeill, *Vere Foster* (Newtown Abbott,
  1971), p. 16.
4 M.A. McNeill, *Vere Foster* (Newtown Abbott,
  1971), p. 37.
5 S. Shannon Millin, *Sidelights on Belfast history*
  (London, 1932), p. 151.
6 H.G. Calwell, *The life and times of a voluntary
  hospital* (Belfast, 1973), p. 77.
7 J. Morgan, *Recollections of my life and times*
  (Belfast, 1874), p. 348.
8 Barney Telford to Mr Lowry, June 1913,
  PRONI T 515.
9 Anna McDermott, *History of Belmont
  congregation* (Belfast, 1950).
10 F. Frankfort Moore, *The truth about Ulster*
   (London, 1914), p. 42.
11 John McDermott (Dr Edgar) in *Three great
   leaders* (Belfast, 1899), p. 22.
12 Rev. William Patton, Address to Ballynahinch
   Boys' Sunday School, 1880.
13 P.T. Winskill, *The temperance movement*
   (London, 1891), i, p. 50.
14 W.D. Killen, *Memoir of Dr Edgar*, p. 16.
15 Correspondence between Dr Edgar and Rev
   J.S. Porter (Belfast, 1844).
16 W.D. Killen, *Memoir of Dr Edgar*, p. 283.
17 John McDermott, *Three great leaders*.

18 Rev. William Patton, Address to Ballynahinch
    Sunday School, 1880.
19 S.L. Prenter, *Life of Rev W. Johnston*, p. 94.
20 Evidence of Head Constable Henderson in
    the *Report of the royal commission on the origin
    and character of the riots in Belfast in July and
    September 1857*, p. 1 [Cd 2309], H.C. 1857–8,
    xxvi, 1, p. 201.
21 W.T. Pike (ed.), *Ulster contemporary biographies*,
    (Brighton, 1910), p. 79.
22 *B.N.L.*, 20 May 1907.
23 John Caughey, *Seize then the hour: the history of
    J.P. Corry* (Belfast, 1974), p. 202.
24 *Evangelical Witness*, vi (February 1867).
25 Case over the death of Thomas Sinclair,
    Grainger collection A1.
26 M.A. Garner, *Robert Workman of Newtownbreda*
    (Belfast, 1969).
27 David Owen, *English philanthropy*,
    introduction.
28 W.A. Maguire, 'Lords and landlords' in J.C.
    Beckett, *Belfast*, p. 38.
29 Ibid., p. 39.

Chapter 10:   Motives and Assessment of
                  Charitable Endeavour in Belfast

1   F.M.L. Thompson, 'Social control in
    Victorian Britain' in *Economic History Review*,
    xxxiv (1981), p. 190.
2   A.J. Kidd, 'Outcast Manchester', p. 49.
3   Minute book of the workshops D3563/AA/2,
    14 Mar. 1884.
4   David Owen, *English philanthropy*, p. 164.
5   G.B. Hindle, *Provisions for the relief of the poor*,
    p. 177.
6   H.W. Schnupf, 'Single women and social
    reform in mid nineteenth century: the case
    of Mary Carpenter' in *Victorian Studies*, xvii
    (1974).
7   R.Q. Gray, *Labour aristocracy in Victorian
    Edinburgh* (Oxford, 1976), p. 136.
8   K.V. Gregson, 'The Poor Law and organised
    charity' in M.E. Rose (ed.), *The poor and the
    city: the English Poor Law in an urban context*
    (Leics., 1985), p. 2.
9   F.M.L. Thompson, 'Social control in
    Victorian Britain', p. 207.
10 J. Garrard, *The middle class in 19th century
    politics*, p. 54.
11 R.J. Morris, 'Voluntary societies and British
    urban elites', p. 115.
12 Patricia Hollis, *Women in public* (London,
    1979), p. 231.
13 Brian Harrison, 'Philanthropy and the
    Victorians' in *Victorian Studies*, ix (1966),
    p. 144.
14 *Northern Whig*, 21 Nov. 1907.
15 Brian Harrison, 'State intervention and moral
    reform' in Patricia Hollis (ed.), *Pressure from
    without in early Victorian England* (London,
    1974), p. 304.
16 G.M. Young, *Portrait of age* (London, 1936),
    p. 2.
17 C.F. Alexander.

18 Brian Harrison, 'Philanthropy and the
    Victorians', p. 144.
19 J. Hart, 'Religion and social control in the
    mid-nineteenth century' in A P Donajgradaki
    (ed.), *Social control in nineteenth century
    Britain* (London, 1977), pp 108–11.
20 *Northern Whig*, 21 Oct. 1919.
21 *Northern Whig*, 29 Nov. 1906.
22 Ibid., 20 Oct. 1919.
23 Brian Harrison, 'Philanthropy and the
    Victorians' in *Victorian Studies*, ix (1965–6),
    p. 351.
24 W.L. Burn, *The age of equipoise*, p. 125.
25 David Owen, *ibid.*, p. 170.
26 C.L. Mowat, *The Charity Organisation Society
    1869–1913* (London, 1961).
27 *Northern Whig* 16 Jan. 1907.
28 Ibid., 9 Nov. 1906.
29 Ibid., 20 Apr. 1910.
30 *Witness* 19 Dec. 1908.
31 *Belfast Evening Telegraph* 3 Feb. 1910.
32 G. Kitson Clark, *Churchmen and the condition of
    England*, p. 272.
33 David Owen, *English philanthropy*, p. 140.
34 R.C. Birch, *The shaping of the welfare state*, p. 93.
35 G. Stedman Jones, *Outcast London*, p. 398.

BIBLIOGRAPHY

Guides to Belfast (Central Library and Linen Hall Library Belfast):

Belfast almanac 1804–90
Belfast directory 1819–1910
McComb's Guide to Belfast (Belfast, 1861)
Smith, J.H., *Belfast and its environs* (Dublin, 1853)
Vinycomb, J.H., *Guide to Belfast* (Belfast, 1896) *Belfast and adjacent counties* (Belfast,1902)

Newspapers and periodicals:

Archivium Hibernicum
Belfast Commercial Chronicle
Belfast Health Journals
Belfast Monthly Magazine
Belfast Evening Telegraph
Belfast People's Magazine
Belfast Weekly Telegraph
British Journal of Sociology
Bulletin of the Royal National Institute for the Blind
Christian Advocate
Current Sociology
Economic History Review
Evangelical Witness
Glasgow Herald
Henderson's Monthly Magazine
Historical Journal
Historical Studies
International Review of Social History

Bibliography

Irish Ecclesiastical Gazette
Irish Economic and Social History
Irish Presbyterian
Irish Quarterly Review
Journal of Interdisciplinary History
Journal of the Royal Statistical Society
Journal of the Statistical and Social Enquiry Society of Ireland
Local Historian
London Quarterly Review
McComb's Presbyterian Almanac
Orthodox Presbyterian
Quarterly Review of Deaf Mute Education
Shield
Social History
Ulster Journal of Archaeology
Victorian Studies
Vindicator
Witness
YMCA Magazine

Annual reports:

Belfast Chamber of Commerce
Belfast Clothing Society
Benevolent Society
Cripples' Institute
Elim Home for Destitute Boys and Girls
House of Industry
Kinghan Mission
Ladies' Industrial School
Magdalene Asylum
Mission to the Adult Deaf and Dumb of Ireland
Prison-gate Mission for Women
Rescue Society
Society for Promoting the Education of the Deaf and Dumb and the Blind
Society for Providing Nurses for the Sick Poor
Society for the Relief of the Destitute Sick
St Vincent de Paul's Society
Town Relief Fund

Minute books and original papers:

*Belfast Association for the Employment of the Industrious Blind D 3563
   PRONI*
*Belfast Chamber of Commerce minute books D 1857/1/AA/1–3
   PRONI*
Belfast Charities files FIN 1 PRONI
Belfast Charitable Society minute book
Coey Sir E. letter book D 2926/1/2 PRONI
Cripples' Institute minute book
Diary of Visits to the Poor of Belfast D 1558/2/3 PRONI
General Assembly of the Presbyterian Church in Ireland minutes
House of Industry deeds of transfer D 1905/2/200 PRONI
Ladies' Industrial school D 1769 PRONI
Midnight Mission D 2072/1–2 PRONI
Mission to the Adult Deaf and Dumb minute book
Olivet National school Inspectors' reports ED2/836 PRONI
Prison-gate Mission for Men FIN 1/2/5 PRONI
Prison-gate Mission for Women D 1905/2/179B PRONI
Sinclair family D 3480/21/2 PRONI
Sinclair T, case over death, Grainger collection A 1 BCL
*Society for Promoting the Education of the Deaf and Dumb and the Blind
   minute book*
Society for the Relief of the Destitute Sick FIN 1 PRONI
Telford Barney reminiscences T 515 PRONI
Tennent R.J. papers D 1905/2/205A PRONI

British Parliamentary Papers (P P):

*Report of the select committee on the employment of the labouring poor in
   Ireland*, p. 1, H.C. 1823 (561), vi, 331.
Report of the select committee on the state of the poor in Ireland, p. 1, H.C.
   1830 (637), vii, 150.
*First report from his majesty's commissioners for inquiring into the condition
   of the poorer classes in Ireland*, p. 1, H.C. 1835 (12), xxxii, 1.
*Third report of the commissioners for inquiring into the condition of the poorer
   classes in Ireland*, p. 1, H.C. 1836 (43), xxxiv, 1.
*Report of Geo. Nicholls, esquire, to his majesty's principal secretary of state for
   the Home Department on poor laws in Ireland*, p. 1, H.C. 1837 (69),
   li, 201.

Bibliography

Report of the commissioners of inquiry into the origin and character of the riots
in Belfast in July and September 1857, p. 1 [Cd 2309], H.C. 1857–8,
xxvi, 1.
Report of the vice-regal commission on poor law reform in Ireland, ii, 1 [Cd
3203], H.C. 1906, li, 441.
Census of Ireland 1841–1901
Annual reports of Commissioners for the Relief of the Poor in
Ireland 1848–1872
Annual reports of the Local Government Board (Ireland) 1873–
1910
Judicial Statistics 1868–9
Judicial Statistics 1902

Theses:

Cleary G.C. 'Spatial expansion and urban ecological change in
Belfast with special reference to the role of local transportation
1861–1917' (Ph.D., Q.U.B., 1980)
Grant J. 'The Great Famine in the province of Ulster 1845–49: the
mechanisms of relief' (Ph.D., Q.U.B., 1986)
McClelland J.G. 'The development of educational facilities for handi-
capped children in Ireland with special reference to the deaf in
Ulster' (M.A., Q.U.B., 1965)
Wilkinson R.J. 'The Catholic elite in Belfast 1900–25' (M.Phil., N.U.U., 1983)

Printed works:

Allen Robert, Soul of a silent mission (Belfast, 1943)
Armstrong D.L., 'Social and economic conditions in the Belfast linen
industry 1850–1900' in I.H.S vii (1951)
Baines Edward jnr, The social, educational and religious state of the
manufacturing districts (London, 1843)
Baker Sybil, 'Orange and green' in Dyos H.J. and Wolff M. (eds.), The
Victorian city: image and reality (London, 1973)
Bardon Jonathan, Belfast: an illustrated history (Belfast, 1982)
Barkley J.M., The Presbyterian Orphan Society (Belfast, 1966)
Beckett J.C. and Glasscock R.E. (eds.), Belfast: the origin and growth of
an industrial city (B.B.C., 1967)
et al. (eds.), Belfast: the making of the city (Belfast, 1983)

Birch R.C., *The shaping of the welfare state* (London, 1974)

Boyd Nancy, *Josephine Butler, Octavia Hill and Florence Nightingale: three Victorian women who changed their world* (London, 1982)

Boyle Emily, 'Linenopolis: the rise of the textile industry' in Beckett J.C. et al. (eds.), *Belfast: the making of the city* (Belfast, 1983)

Brett C.E.B., 'The Edwardian city: Belfast about 1900' in Beckett J.C. and Glasscock R.E. (eds.), *The origin and growth of an industrial city* (B.B.C., 1967)

Buildings of Belfast (London, 1967)

Briggs Asa, *Victorian cities* (London, 1963)

Brooke Peter, 'Religion and secular thought' in Beckett J.C. et al. (eds.), *Belfast: the making of the city* (Belfast, 1983)
Ulster presbyterianism (Dublin, 1987)

Bruce Maurice, *The coming of the welfare state* (London, 1961)
(ed.), *The rise of the welfare state* (London, 1973)

Budge Ian and O'Leary Cornelius, *Belfast: approach to crisis* 1613–1970 (London, 1973)

Bullough V.L. and B., *Sin, sickness and sanity* (New American Library, 1977)

Burn W.L., *The age of equipoise* (London, 1964)

Calwell H.G., *The life and times of a voluntary hospital* (Belfast, 1973)
Andrew Malcolm: physician and historian (Belfast, 1977)

Caughey John, *Seize then the hour: the story of James P. Corry Ltd* (Belfast, 1974)

Chambers George, *Faces of change* (Belfast, 1983)

Checkland Olive, *Philanthropy in Victorian Scotland* (Edinburgh, 1980)

Clarkson L.A., 'Population change and urbanization 1821–1911' in Kennedy Liam and Ollerenshaw Philip (eds.), *An Economic History of Ulster* (Manchester, 1985)
'The city and the country' in Beckett J.C. et al. (eds.), *Belfast: the making of the city* (Belfast, 1983)

Cole G.D.H., *Short history of the British working class movement 1789–1949* (London, 1948)

Collins Brenda, 'The Edwardian city' in Beckett J.C. et al. (eds.), *Belfast: the making of the city* (Belfast, 1983)

Connolly S.J., 'Catholicism in Ulster 1800–50' in Roebuck Peter (ed.), *Plantation to partition* (Belfast, 1981)
'Religion, work discipline and economic attitudes: the case of Ireland' in Devine J.M. and Dickson David (eds.), *Ireland and Scotland 1600–1850: parallels and contrasts* (Edinburgh, 1983)

Convent of Our Lady of Mercy: St Paul's 1854–1954 centenary volume (Belfast, 1954)

Cooke Henry, *Sermon on behalf of the House of Industry* (Belfast, 1815)

Daly M.E., *Dublin, the deposed capital* (Cork, 1984)

Donajgradzki A.P., *Social control in nineteenth century Britain* (London, 1977)

Dyos H.J. and Wolff Michael, *The Victorian city: image and reality* (London, 1973)

Edgar Rev. John, *The penitent restored* (Belfast, 1841) Edgar, Rev. John, *Correspondence with Rev. J.S. Porter* (Belfast, 1844)

Edwards R.D. and Williams T.D. (eds.), *The great famine* (Dublin, 1956)

Evans Hilary, *The oldest profession* (Newtown Abbot, 1979)

Evans Neil, 'Urbanisation, elite attitudes and philanthropy, Cardiff 1880–1914' in *I.R.S.H.* xxvii (1982).

Farrell M.J., *The poor law and the workhouse in Belfast 1838–1948* (Belfast, 1978)

Garner M.A., *Robert Workman of Newtownbreda* (Belfast, 1969)

Garrard John, 'The middle class in nineteenth century national and local politics' in Garrard J., et al. (eds.), *The middle class in politics* (London, 1978)

Geary Francis, 'The rise and fall of the Belfast cotton industry: some problems' in *Irish Economic and Social History*, viii (1981)

Glass Ruth, 'Urban sociology in Great Britain' in *Current Sociology*, iv (1955)

Glasscock R.E., 'The growth of the port' in Beckett J.C. and Glasscock R.E. (eds.), *Belfast: the origin and growth of an industrial city* (B.B.C., 1967)

Green E.R.R., 'Early industrial Belfast' in Beckett J.C. and Glasscock R.E. (eds.), *Belfast: the origin and growth of an industrial city* (B.B.C., 1967)

Gregson Keith, 'The poor law and organised charity' in M.E. Rose (ed.), *The poor and the city: the English poor law in an urban context* (Leics., 1985)

Gwynn Stephen, *Famous cities of Ireland* (Dublin, 1915)

Hall Mr and Mrs S.C., *Ireland: its scenery, character etc.* (London, 1843)

Hamilton Margaret, 'Opposition to the contagious diseases acts', *Albion*, x (1979)

Harkness David and O'Dowd Mary (eds.), *The town in Ireland* (Belfast, 1981)

Harrison Brian, 'Victorian philanthropy' in *Victorian Studies* ix (1966) *Drink and the Victorians: the temperance question in England 1845–72* (London, 1971)

'State intervention and moral reform' in Hollis Patricia (ed.), *Pressure from without in early Victorian England* (London, 1974)

Hart Jenifer, 'Religion and social control in the mid nineteenth century' in Donajgradzki A.P. (ed.), *Social control in nineteenth century Britain* (London, 1977)

Hennock E.P., *Fit and proper persons* (London, 1973)
'Poverty and social theory in England: the experience of the 1880s' in *Social History* i (1976)

Hindle G.B., *Provision for the relief of the poor in Manchester 1754–1826* (Manchester, 1975)

Hodgson K.W., *The deaf and their problems* (London, 1953)

Hollis Patricia (ed.), *Pressure from without in early Victorian England* (London, 1979)

Horn Pamela, *The rise and fall of the Victorian servant* (Dublin, 1975)

Hulin J.P. and Coustilles Pierre, *Inquiry into destitution, prostitution and crime in Edinburgh* (Edinburgh, 1980)

Illustrated interviews: the story of the Cripples' Institute, People's Palace and Homes of Rest Belfast, Bangor and Ballygowan (Belfast, 1912)

Irwin Arthur, *Lights along the way* (Belfast, 1941)

Jamieson John, *The history of R.B.A.I. 1810–1960* (Belfast, 1959)

Jefferson H.L.S., *Viscount Pirrie of Belfast* (Belfast, 1947)

Jones Emrys, *Social geography of Belfast* (Oxford, 1960)
'Late Victorian Belfast' in Beckett J.C. and Glasscock R.E. (eds.), *Belfast: The origin and growth of an industrial city* (B.B.C., 1967)

Kennedy Liam and Ollerenshaw Philip (eds.), *An economic history of Ulster* (Manchester, 1985)

Kernohan J.W., *Rosemary St Presbyterian Church: a record of the last 200 years* (Belfast, 1923)

Kidd A.J. and Roberts K.W., (eds.), *City, class and culture* (Manchester, 1985)

Killen W.D., *Memoir of Rev. John Edgar* (Belfast, 1867)
Reminiscences of a long life (London, 1901)

Kinghan Rev. John, 'Historical sketch of the Ulster Institution for the Deaf and Dumb and the Blind' in *Quarterly Review of Deaf Mute Education* (Jan. and April 1891)

Kitson Clark G., *Churchmen and the condition of England* (London, 1973)

Leathem W.S., *The history of the Church of Ireland in St Mary Magdalene Parish Belfast* (Belfast, 1939)

McCord Norman, 'The poor law and philanthropy' in Fraser D. (ed.), *The new poor law in the nineteenth century* (London, 1976)

McDermott Rev. John, *Three great leaders* (Central Presbyterian Association, Belfast, 1899)

McDowell R.B., *Social life in Ireland* (Dublin, 1957)

    The Irish administration 1801–1914 (London, 1964)

McKenna L.J., 'Co-ordination of charity' in *Irish Monthly* xliv (1917)

    'An Irish Catholic Women's League', Ibid.

    'Relations of catholics to protestants in social work', Ibid.

MacLaren A.A., 'Class formation and class structure: the Aberdeen bourgeoisie 1830–1950' in Gordon G. and Dicks B. (eds.), *Scottish urban history* (Aberdeen, 1983)

McNeill M., *Mary Anne McCracken: a Belfast panorama* (Dublin, 1960)

    Vere Foster: an Irish benefactor (London, 1971)

Macaulay A., *Patrick Dorrian* (Dublin, 1987)

Maguire W.A., *Living like a lord* (Belfast, 1984)

Malcolm A.G., *A history of the General Hospital* (Belfast, 1851)

    The sanitary state of Belfast (Belfast, 1852)

Malcolmson P.E., 'Laundresses and the laundry trade in Victorian England' in *Victorian Studies* xxiv (1981)

Messinger G., *Manchester in the Victorian age* (Manchester, 1985)

Midwinter E.C., *Victorian social reform* (London, 1968)

Millin S. Shannon, *Sidelights on Belfast history* (Belfast, 1932)

Mokyr Joel, 'Industry and poverty in Ireland and the Netherlands' in *Journal of Interdisciplinary History* x (1980)

    Why Ireland starved (London, 1983)

Molloy John, *Belfast scenery in thirty views 1832* (Repr. Belfast, 1983)

Moore A.S., *Belfast today* (Belfast, 1907)

Moore F. Frankfort, *The truth about Ulster* (London, 1914)

Morgan Rev. James, *Recollections of my life and times* (Belfast, 1874)

Morris R.J., 'Samuel Smiles and self-help' in *Historical Journal* xxiv (1981)

    'Voluntary societies and British urban elites 1780–1850' in *Historical Journal* xxvi (1983)

Moss M. and Hume J.R., *Shipbuilders to the world* (Belfast, 1986)

Mowat C.L., *The Charity Organisation Society 1869–1913* (London, 1961)

Muir Ramsay, *History of Liverpool* (Liverpool, 1907)

National Association for the Education for the Deaf and Dumb Poor of Ireland deputation report 1856

Nicholls George, *A history of the Irish poor law* (London, 1856)

Norman E.R., *The Catholic Church in Ireland in the age of rebellion* (London, 1965)

O'Brien George, 'The new poor law in pre-famine Ireland: a case history' in *Irish Economic and Social History* xii (1985)

O'Hanlon William, *Walks among the poor of Belfast* (Belfast, 1853)

O'Leary Cornelius and Budge Ian, *Belfast: approach to crisis* (London, 1973)

'Belfast urban government in the age of reform' in Harkness David and O'Dowd Mary (eds.), *The town in Ireland* (Belfast, 1981)

Ollerenshaw Philip, 'Industry 1820–1914' in Kennedy Liam and Ollerenshaw Philip (eds.), *An economic history of Ulster* (Manchester, 1985)

O'Neill T.P., 'The Catholic Church and the relief of the poor 1815–45' in *Archivium Hibernicum* xxi (1973)

'Poverty in Ireland 1815–45' in *Folklife* xi (1973)

Owen David, *English philanthropy* (London, 1965)

Owen D.J., *History of Belfast* (Belfast, 1921)

Patton Rev. William, *New year's address to 3rd Ballynahinch Presbyterian Church Sabbath School Society* (Belfast, 1880)

Pelan R.E., *Malone Place Hospital 1860–1981* (Belfast, 1981)

Phillips P.T., *The sectarian spirit* (Toronto, 1982)

Pike W.T. (ed.), *Ulster contemporary biographies* (Brighton, 1910)

Pilson J.A., *History of the rise and progress of Belfast and annals of the county of Antrim* (Belfast, 1846)

Prenter S.L., *Life and times of Rev. W. Johnston* (London, 1895)

'Problems of a growing city' (PRONI, 1973)

Prochaska F.K., *Women and philanthropy in the nineteenth century* (Oxford, 1980)

Robins Joseph, *The lost children: a study of charity children* (Dublin, 1980)

Roome W.J.W., *A brighter Belfast* (Belfast, 1898)

For his sake (Belfast, 1903)

Rose M.E., (ed.), *The poor and the city: the English poor law in its urban context* (Leicester, 1985)

Sargaison E.M., *Growing old in common lodgings* (London, 1954)

Schupf, H.W., 'Single women and social reform in the mid nineteenth century: the case of Mary Carpenter' in *Victorian Studies* xvii (1974)

Scott John, *A moral mirror for the use of the mayor, his relief committee and the community* (Belfast, 1858)

Simey M.B., *Charitable effort in Liverpool in the nineteenth century* (Liverpool, 1951)

Sinclair Seamen's Presbyterian Church centenary volume (Glasgow, 1957)

St Vincent de Paul Society centenary volume (Belfast, 1951)

150th anniversary pamphlet (Belfast, 1983)

Stedman Jones G., *Outcast London* (London, 1971)

Strain R.W.M., *Belfast and its charitable society* (Oxford, 1961)

Sweetnam R., 'The development of the port' in Beckett J.C. et al. (eds.), *Belfast: the making of the city* (Belfast, 1983)

Thompson F.M.L., 'Social control in Victorian Britain' in *Economic History Review* xxxiv (1981)

Vaughan W.E. and Fitzpatrick A.J. (eds.), *Irish Historical Statistics* (Dublin, 1975)

Walkowitz Judith, *Prostitution and Victorian society* (Cambridge, 1980)

Walker B.M., *Faces of the past* (Belfast, 1974)
and Dixon Hugh, *In Belfast town* (Belfast, 1984)

Ward J.W., *'Belfastiensis' 1900–1910* (Collection of articles)

Webb J.J., *Municipal government in Ireland* (Dublin, 1918)

Winskill P.T., *The temperance movement and its workers* (London, 1892)

Withers J.H., *History of Fisherwick Presbyterian Church* (Belfast, 1973)

Workshops for the Blind centenary volume (Belfast, 1971)

Young G.M., *Portrait of an age* (London, 1936)

INDEX

Who cared?